NEW INDUSTRIAL URBANISM

Since the Industrial Revolution, cities and industry have grown together; towns and metropolitan regions have evolved around factories and expanding industries. *New Industrial Urbanism* explores the evolving and future relationships between cities and places of production, focusing on the spatial implications and physical design of integrating contemporary manufacturing into the city. The book examines recent developments that have led to dramatic shifts in the manufacturing sector – from large-scale mass production methods to small-scale distributed systems; from polluting and consumptive production methods to a cleaner and more sustainable process; from broad demand for unskilled labor to a growing need for a more educated and specialized workforce – to show how cities see new investment and increased employment opportunities. Looking ahead to the quest to make cities more competitive and resilient, *New Industrial Urbanism* provides lessons from cases around the world and suggests adopting *New Industrial Urbanism* as an action framework that reconnects what has been separated: people, places, and production. Moving the conversation beyond the reflexively-negative characterizations of industry, more than two centuries after the start of the Industrial Revolution, this book calls to re-consider the ways in which industry creates places, sustains jobs, and supports environmental sustainability in our cities.

Tali Hatuka, an architect and urban planner, is a Professor of Urban Planning and the head of the Laboratory of Contemporary Urban Design, at Tel Aviv University (lcud.tau.ac.il). Her work is focused primarily on two fields: urban society, and city design and development. Hatuka is the author and co-author of the books: *The Design of Protest, Violent Acts and Urban Space in Contemporary Tel Aviv, The Factory, State-Neighborhood, The Planners, City-Industry and Land-Gardens*. She also works as a city planner and urban designer advising municipalities and the public sector. Hatuka has received many awards, including a Fulbright Scholarship and a Marie Curie Scholarship at the Massachusetts Institute of Technology (MIT). She holds degrees from the Technion in Israel and Heriot-Watt University in the UK.

Eran Ben-Joseph is the Class of 1922 Professor of Landscape Architecture and Urban Planning and the former head of the Department of Urban Studies and Planning at the Massachusetts Institute of Technology (MIT). His research and teaching areas include urban and physical design, standards and regulations, sustainable site planning technologies and urban retrofitting. He authored and co-authored the books: *Streets and the Shaping of Towns and Cities, Regulating Place: Standards and the Shaping of Urban America, The Code of the City, RENEW Town and ReThinking a Lot*. Ben-Joseph worked as a city planner, urban designer, and landscape architect in Europe, Asia, the Middle East, and the United States. He holds academic degrees from the University of California at Berkeley and Chiba National University of Japan.

NEW INDUSTRIAL URBANISM

First published 2022
by Routledge
605 Third Avenue, New York, NY 10158

and by Routledge
2 Park Square, Milton Park, Abingdon, Oxon, OX14 4RN

Routledge is an imprint of the Taylor & Francis Group, an informa business

© 2022 Taylor & Francis

The right of Tali Hatuka and Eran Ben-Joseph to be identified as authors of this work has been asserted in accordance with sections 77 and 78 of the Copyright, Designs and Patents Act 1988.

Graphic Design and Cover by Rachel Freedman-Avital

Illustration Designer: Lee Ben Moshe

The Open Access version of this book, available at www.taylorfrancis.com, has been made available under a Creative Commons Attribution-Non Commercial-No Derivatives 4.0 license.

Trademark notice: Product or corporate names may be trademarks or registered trademarks, and are used only for identification and explanation without intent to infringe.

Library of Congress Cataloging-in-Publication Data
Names: Hatuka, Tali, author. | Ben-Joseph, Eran, author.

Title: New industrial urbanism : designing places for production / Tali Hatuka and Eran Ben-Joseph.

Description: New York, NY : Routledge, 2022. | Includes bibliographical references and index. |

Identifiers: LCCN 2021042324 (print) | LCCN 2021042325 (ebook) | ISBN 9780367427726 (hbk) | ISBN 9780367427719 (pbk) | ISBN 9780367855000 (ebk)

Subjects: LCSH: Urbanization. | City planning. | Technological innovations.

Classification: LCC HT371 .H36 2022 (print) | LCC HT371 (ebook) | DDC 307.76--dc23

LC record available at https://lccn.loc.gov/2021042324

LC ebook record available at https://lccn.loc.gov/2021042325

ISBN: 9780367427726 (hbk)
ISBN: 9780367427719 (pbk)
ISBN: 9780367855000 (ebk)

DOI: 10.4324/9780367855000

Typeset in Source Sans Pro
by Paul D. Hunt

Publisher's note
This book has been prepared from camera-ready copy provided by the authors.

NEW INDUSTRIAL URBANISM

DESIGNING PLACES FOR PRODUCTION

Tali Hatuka and Eran Ben-Joseph

CONTENTS

Preface 8

   Organization of the Book 9

   Acknowledgments 10

PART I

FOR PRODUCTION'S SAKE 14

---

1. People, Factories, and Making 21

   Factories, Architects, and the Design of Work Spaces 24

   Work Spaces: Building Types and Programs 35

2. Between Production and City Development 39

   Industrial Landscapes and Urban Life Dynamics 44

   Designing City-Industry Dynamic for the 21st Century 56

3. The Way Forward: New Industrial Urbanism 59

   From Overarching Concepts to Policy Initiatives 66

   The Future of Industry: From Parallel Initiatives to an Integrated Framework 69

   References 72

PART II

PLACES OF MAKING 76

---

4. Clustering New Industries 81

   Features of Clustering Industries 83

   Wageningen Food Valley, the Netherlands 94
   Kista Science City, Sweden 96
   Hsinchu Science Park, Taiwan 98
   Kendall Square, Cambridge, Massachusetts, USA 100

   The Industry–Place Nexus in Developing Clusters 104

5. Reinventing Industrial Areas 107

   Features of Reinventing Industrial Areas 109

   Jurong, Singapore 120
   HafenCity District, Hamburg, Germany 122
   Brooklyn Navy Yard, New York City, USA 124
   Fashion District, Los Angeles, USA 126

   Industry–Place Nexus in Reinventing Areas 130

6. Forming Hybrid Districts 133

   Features in Generating Hybrid Districts 135

   22@ District, Barcelona, Spain 146
   Innovation District, Medellín, Colombia 148
   Central Eastside, Portland, Oregon, USA 150
   Huaqiangbei, Shenzhen, China 152

   Industry–Place Nexus in Forming Hybrid Districts 156

7. Industry and Place 158

   References 166

PART III
OPEN MANUFACTURING 172

8. Advancing Regions 177

Regional Industrial Coordination 179

Research Triangle Regional Partnership (RTRP), Durham, North Carolina, USA 179

The Association of Bay Area Governments (ABAG), San Francisco, California, USA 182

The Regionalverband Ruhr, Ruhrgebiet, Germany 182

Plattelandscentrum Meetjesland, Regional Network, Meetjesland, Belgium 183

Towards Developing a Regional Ecosystem: The Case of Kiryat Shmona 186

Summary: Regional Socio-Economic Visioning 191

9. Integrating Urban-Industrial Systems 193

Regulating Variability: From Separation to Consolidation 195

22@District, Barcelona, Spain 202

Innovation District, Medellín, Colombia 203

Central Eastside, Portland, Oregon, USA 204

Shenzhen, Guangdong, China 205

Towards an Integrated System: Eastern Market Neighborhood, Detroit 206

Summary: Recoding the Industrial–Residential Nexus 210

10. Working, Living, and Innovating 215

The Variety of Synchronic Architectural Typologies 218

Strathcona Village, Vancouver, Canada 224

Iceland Wharf, and Fish Island, London, UK 226

415 Wick Lane, Fish Island, Hackney Wick, London, UK 228

Westferry Studios, London, UK 230

Summary: Locating Synchronic Architectural Typologies in the City 234

11. New Industrial Urbanism 237

New Industrial Urbanism: Key Planning Concepts 240

Scalar Strategies 241

Integrative Approaches 242

Coding Complexity 243

Synchronic Architectural Typologies 244

Experimenting and Developing a New Industrial Urbanism 246

References 250

Index 253

PREFACE

We possess the skills, resources, and innovative capacity to create many possible futures. Just as the majority of today's jobs had yet to be invented a century ago, much of the work of the 21st century has yet to be invented today. The challenge and the opportunity of the present is to build the work of the future.

Autor et al., 2020

Technological innovation is changing rapidly, and with it our life. Technological innovation is also expected to further change our labor markets, institutions, and production of goods. There are two acute core issues here. First, how to invest in workers and their skills, bringing to bear the full weight of modern teaching methods and training technology, as well as new institutions, to help them drive the jobs of the future (Autor et al., 2020) and second, how these specialized changes will be supported by the spatial and physical development of our cities and regions. Today's policy discourse focuses on the importance of manufacturing for economies as well as for the resilience of society. Scholars argue that manufacturing remains vital to local, regional, and national economic growth and comprises "the 'flywheel of growth' because the rate of growth of manufacturing output tends to drive the rate of productivity growth in manufacturing and in services" (Pike, 2009: 59). This approach is gaining recognition, particularly with the development of technology, which requires specialized, skilled labor (Pisano and Shih, 2012; Plant, 2014). But while the economic arguments for urban manufacturing and the policies that support it are maturing, the social and spatial strategies for supporting manufacturing in cities are still embryonic. Indeed, economic strategies are vital to the development of manufacturing; yet if these are not correlated with social and spatial policies, their chances of maturing are low.

That is the departure point of this book, which is based on two linked assumptions: (1) the importance of advanced manufacturing for cities' growth; (2) the need for cultivating varied socio-spatial strategies that can support manufacturing and would benefit diverse social groups in the city. This link between manufacturing, society, and space might help tackle the increasing global competition for resources, investments, and projects; unemployment as a side effect of globalization and as an effect of the transfer of production to developing countries; and the cost of energy for the transportation of goods. Although economic development cannot be considered separately from social or spatial development, most studies on manufacturing focus on economic strategies and/or environmental strategies. This book flips the coin, proposing to focus on social and spatial issues related to manufacturing in cities as a means to further examine and develop future economic strategies. In prioritizing people and space, this book responds to the "Fourth Industrial Revolution" by developing a socio-spatial framework that relates to advanced manufacturing, rather than seeing such manufacturing as a goal in itself.

The development of a socio-spatial framework that supports advanced manufacturing requires a paradigm shift in the conceptualization of the city-industry relationships. We suggest adapting "New Industrial Urbanism" as a new conceptual framework that reconnects what has been separated: people, places, and production. Accommodating technological changes and market innovation is both an opportunity and a challenge, which requires adopting collaborative frameworks, creating complex networks of action, and a different approach to city design. New Industrial Urbanism is neither a model nor a static concept but a flexible framework, a set of ideas that requires reflexive thinking about place. Indeed, production processes differ from one place to another, and lessons that might be suitable for one city might be inappropriate for another. Each city has its particular advantages, and city leaders and urban planners would do well to understand the opportunities that exist in their region or city and leverage them for the benefit of residents. The key question is how planners and city designers can guide the adaptation to the Fourth Industrial Revolution in a way that supports societal and spatial resiliency.

Developing the framework of New Industrial Urbanism started prior to the COVID-19 pandemic. However, this period of global crisis has not diminished the value of this framework but rather amplified its significance. During the COVID-19 pandemic practices of globalization, such as travel, shopping, and knowledge transfer, have either stopped or been significantly altered. An obvious practice, like placing an order on the web for a product and getting it a few days later, could no longer be taken for granted. The desperate need to provide missing supplies enhanced our awareness of the process by which products are invented, manufactured, transported, and ultimately find their way to store shelves or our doors. Shortages of critical products and goods exposed the vulnerabilities of the global supply chain and made clear that gaining a strategic advantage requires that countries and regions readdress policies that target the manufacturing sector and supply chain deficiencies. The roles of local power and production have never been more central.

Organization of the Book

The three parts of this book are devoted to the exploration of these ideas. Part I introduces contemporary ideas in the development of industry and urbanism in three sections. Section 1, "People, Factories, and Making," looks back at the early 20th century, and focuses on the worker in the production environment. The section briefly maps the contemporary typologies of work space as well as the evolving relationships between people and production, through the architectural and programmatic development of manufacturing places. Section 2, "Between Production and City Development," examines the diachronic development of spatial relationships between cities and industrial environments, and maps industrial development types. Section 3, "The Way Forward: New Industrial Urbanism," projects into the future, and presents key trends in the manufacturing sector that are influencing policy initiatives and the development of urban areas in relation to industry.

Part II offers an overview of physical planning and design strategies for the development of industrial areas in cities and regions today. More specifically, section 4, "Clustering New Industries," presents current trends in agglomeration. These trends evolve around industries such as food tech, biotechnology, and cyber technology that depend on knowledge-sharing and often benefit from the physical proximity to their main players, including academic institutions. Section 5, "Reinventing Industrial Areas," focuses on existing industrial sites and strategies of regeneration, reuse, and adaptation. Section 6, "Forming Hybrid Districts," is based on the premise that integration and mixing diverse uses is a primary policy for preserving and promoting industrial districts in cities. Hybrid industrial districts support a process of densification, the introduction of new building typologies, variety of land uses, and greater connectivity. Finally, Section 7, "Industry and Place," offers a reflection on these three approaches, summarizes their shared premises and strategies and the possible ways they might influence future planning.

Part III offers thoughts on the future of industry in cities and ideas for harnessing the potential of today's innovations in manufacturing to develop centers of urban industry. It argues that city and regional governments, private developers, and planners should encourage the convergence of users and activities to create vibrant manufacturing and mixed-use economic clusters. Embracing this approach will help support the next phase in the city-industry-region evolution. This part offers lessons and strategies in various scales: region, city, and building. Section 8, "Advancing Regions," summarizes key regional strategies and concepts designed and implemented to develop industrial ecosystems. Section 9, "Integrating Urban-Industrial Systems," focuses on the city scale, and discusses the processes of coding and regulating piloted in cities that have reinvented their industrial areas. Section 10, "Working, Living, and Innovating," presents new building typologies that integrate industry and manufacturing with other uses – especially housing and public amenities. Finally, the part ends with Section 11 which offers a vision for "New Industrial Urbanism," a socio-spatial concept in which manufacturing is integrated into the fabric of cities and regions. This framework serves as an opportunity to shape a future that works for all by prioritizing quality of life, diversifying our built environment and allowing choice.

More than two centuries after the start of the Industrial Revolution, we have a chance to re-consider the ways in which industry creates places, sustains jobs, and supports environmental sustainability. We believe that the future of manufacturing and this new type of Industrial Urbanism is the future of our cities.

Acknowledgments

Any product of a long journey owes a great deal to others. In working on this book, we have been extremely fortunate in being able to cooperate with friends and colleagues, students and professionals of great intelligence, questioning minds and profound passion for improving the built environment. We are most thankful to Lee Ben Moshe for her work on producing the illustrations in this book. The illustrations should be viewed as an integral part of the written text and are a significant part of the book. Among our many colleagues, we wish to express particular appreciation and gratitude to Amy Glasmeier, Dennis Frenchman, Tim Love, Elisabeth Reynolds, Matteo Robiglio, and Larry Vale, for sharing a path of inquiry and reflection while providing us with indispensable insights. To Patricia Baudoin, we wish to express particular thanks for her editorial assistance and thoughtful suggestions. We thank Shoshana Michael-Zucker for copyediting and Rachel Freedman for her layouts and design ideas. Our gratitude and thanks also go to the editors at Routledge, Kathryn Schell, Sean Speers, Christine Bondira, and Tom Bedford for their helpful comments, receptiveness, and interest.

We must acknowledge the vital role of former and current students at Tel Aviv University and the Massachusetts Institute of Technology (MIT), particularly Roni Bar, Anne Hudson, Minjee Kim, Sunny Menozzi Peterson, David Kambo Maina, Hen Roznek, and Dorothy Tang who were an integral part of this project and deserve much recognition. We also thank the many other former students who participated in varied projects associated with this undertaking: Ayelet Bar Ilan, Merav Battat, Neha Bazaj, Ran Benyamin, Efrath Bramli, Max Budovitch, Carlos

Caccia, Jonathan Crisman, Rebecca Disbrow, Yulia Furshik, Coral Hamo Goren, Carmel Hanany, Shelly Hefetz, Gili Inbar, Michael Jacobson, Karen Johnson, Michael Kaplan, Stephen Kennedy, Noah Koretz, Elizabeth Kuwada, Louis Liss, Hila Lothan, Nina Mascarehas, Max Moinian, Zoe Mueller, Kfir Noy, Einat Pragier, Jared Press, Nofar Ramer, Christopher Rhie, Yael Saga, Alice Shay, Naomi Stein, Tianyu Su, Merran Swartwood, Gary Tran, Alexis Wheeler, Zixiao Yin, and Yoav Zilberdik.

We are also grateful for research grants and other assistance from Tel Aviv University and MIT.

Portions of this book are related to research published as articles and working papers in various journals, conference proceedings, and professional reports.

Finally, we should acknowledge that all errors, misquotes, and mistakes are our responsibility.

Tali Hatuka and Eran Ben-Joseph, 2021

NEW
INDUSTRIAL
URBANISM

Seagate Plant, Wuxi, China. Photo by Robert Scoble, Flickr (CC BY 4.0).

PART I

FOR PRODUCTION'S SAKE

Right: Sofia, Bulgaria. Photo by Yaroslav Boshnakov on Unsplash (CC)

Below: Volga Automotive Plant, Tolyatti, Russia. Photo by minsvyaz.ru (CC BY 3.0)

PART I

For Production's Sake

Since the Industrial Revolution, cities and industry have grown together; towns and metropolitan regions have evolved around factories and expanding industries. Despite this shared past, popular notions of manufacturing and industry tend to highlight their negative aspects. Active industrial sites are associated with pollution, environmental degradation, and the exploitation of labor. Blight and abandoned industrial sites signify the decline of manufacturing in cities and countries with advanced economies. These popular notions are based on reality. Undeniably, foggy sky and polluted air over industrial cities are still common conditions in different parts of the world. Yet, dramatic technological advances are now occurring that mark a sea change not only in industry but also in the design and development of cities. The manufacturing sector has seen a shift from large, industrial-scale production and design to small-scale, distributed systems; polluting and consumptive processes are cleaner and more sustainable; the need for a more educated and specialized workforce has supplanted the demand for unskilled labor. Digital technologies and flexible borders that foster the flow of ideas, goods, and services are reshaping industry and commerce; reducing barriers to international partnerships; and streamlining the application of innovations in production and trade (Berger and Sharp, 2013).

One of the major changes is that technological change is simultaneously replacing existing work and creating new work. But rising labor productivity has not translated into broad increases in incomes because labor market institutions and policies have fallen into disrepair (Autor et al., 2020). It has been argued that improving the quality of jobs requires innovation in labor market institutions (ibid.), but it also requires innovation in the development and planning of cities.

With these technological developments and social challenges grew the recognition among politicians, stakeholders, and policymakers of the need to re-examine the relationships between manufacturing and cities (Berger and Sharp, 2013; Davis, 2020; Helper et al., 2012; Lane and Rappaport, 2020; Leigh and Hoelzel, 2012). Supporters of such a re-examination warn of severe negative consequences in countries that promote post-industrial policy with little attention to production. They argue, for example, that relocating plants to countries where labor is less expensive, as a means of reducing production costs, is not a viable strategy for the long term, and severing the connection between production and development impairs the ability to innovate in source countries (De Backer et al., 2015; Manyika et al., 2012; Pisano and Shih, 2012).

The approach towards re-examining the relationships between manufacturing and cities is thus gaining more attention, and influencing the design and development of cities and regions, in what this book conceptualizes as "New Industrial Urbanism." New Industrial Urbanism is a socio-spatial concept which calls for reassessing and re-shaping the relationships between cities, people, and industry. It suggests shaping cities with a renewed understanding that an urban location and setting give industry a competitive advantage thanks to the access to skilled labor, educational institutions (centers of research and experimentation), and customers. This concept calls for a socio-spatial paradigm shift in the way we understand and address production in cities and regions.

As a first step towards outlining this vision, Part I, "For Production's Sake," introduces key historical and contemporary concepts, typologies, and approaches associated with the city-industry dynamic. Focusing on planning, design, and architecture, this part looks at how industry and cities have been interlinked, and how they shaped one another from the 20th century to date. It ends with the more recent changes in industry that are affecting spatial approaches to urbanism and design development. This use of a spatial lens for understanding and developing industry in cities complements the economists' and sociologists' perspectives (which tend to classify industry by ownership, scale, number and dynamic of employees, and/or products) – and suggests that industry is an essential tool for cities aiming for economic development and revitalization.

In addressing this premise, Part I introduces contemporary ideas in the development of industry and urbanism in three sections. Section 1, "People, Factories, and Making," looks back at the early 20th century, and focuses on the worker in the production environment. The section briefly maps the contemporary typologies of work space as well as the evolving relationships between people and production, through the architectural and programmatic development of manufacturing spaces. Section 2, "Between Production and City Development," examines the diachronic development of spatial relationships between cities

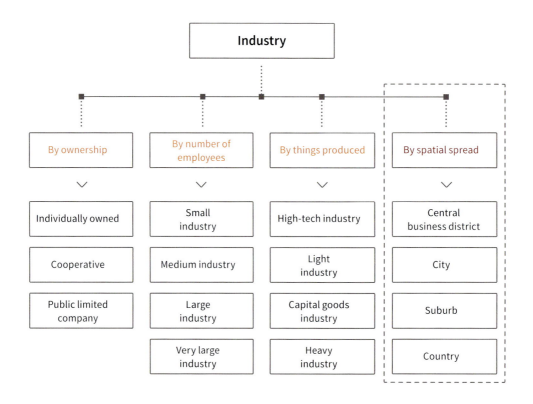

■ Common Industrial Classification

and industrial environments, and maps industrial development types. Section 3, "The Way Forward: New Industrial Urbanism," projects into the future, and presents key trends in the manufacturing sector that are influencing policy initiatives and the development of urban areas in relation to industry.

These key ideas and trends are the point of departure for reflecting on contemporary cities' industrial development and for addressing the key question of this book: How, and through what means, will industry shape our city of tomorrow?

Right: Working on a VW Beetle. 1957. Photo by Unknown. Austrian National Library on Unsplash (CC).

Below: Robotic manufacturing. Photo by Lenny Kuhne on Unsplash (CC).

1

People, Factories, and Making

People, Machines, and Making

American Writing Paper Co., Mt. Holyoke, MA, USA 1936. Photo by Lewis Hine, U.S. Library of Congress.

Glass works, Midnight, Indiana, USA 1908. Photo by Lewis Hine, U.S. Library of Congress.

Hamilton Watch Co., Lancaster, PA, USA 1936. Photo by Lewis Hine, U.S. Library of Congress.

Machine gun production, Flint, Michigan, USA 1942. Photo by Ann Rosener, U.S. Library of Congress.

Virginia-Pocahontas Coal Company, Richlands, VA, USA 1974. Photo by Jack Corn, U.S. National Archives.

1908 **1936** **1942** **1974**

1917 **1940** **1962**

Hawthorn Farm, Hazardville, CT, USA 1917. Photo by Lewis Hine, U.S. Library of Congress.

Frankford Arsenal, Philadelphia, PA, USA 1940. Photo by Unknown, U.S. National Archives.

Kumsung Radio Factory, South Korea 1962. Photo by Unknown, Korean National Archives.

Optoelectronic devices Assembly Line, 2006. Photo by Steve Jurvetson (CC BY 2.0).

Quill-winding operation, Jacquard-Weaving Mill, Paterson, NJ, USA 1994. Photo by Cooper, Martha, U.S. Library of Congress.

Sewing Factory, 2006. Photo by Maruf Rahman (CC).

Clean room at NASA's Goddard Space Flight Center, 2015. Photo by Chris Gunn, NASA.

1994   **2006**   **2015**

1985   **2010**   **2019**

Machinery Production, Wittenberg, Germany 1985. Photo by Wolfried Paetzold, German Federal Archive.

Food Factory, Brazil, 2010. Photo courtesy of Nestlé (CC BY 2.0).

Human-Robot Collaboration, 2019. Photo courtesy of Universal Robots A/S.

1

People, Factories, and Making

All production requires producers. All work involves workers. And, although we tend to discuss work and the industry as a means of achieving particular goals, for most of us work also contributes to our identity – who we are, our way of life, and what we are able to achieve in our lifetimes. Physical working environments, arenas where employees sell their labor power and accumulate their personal fortune, are significant places in every person's life. Work environments embody dynamic relationships between employers, their employees, and their products, which are each influenced by various elements including the physical design of the place, the technology of production processes, the terms of employment, and global competition. As such, work environments are complex arenas that always leave a mark not only on the people who work in them, but also on the landscapes of cities.

There are different approaches to understanding work environments or production units. The *institutional approach* sees a work space as an economic unit, an evolving framework of accumulated skills and knowledge that allows for dealing with speculation and the uncertainty of the market. Another approach, the *cultural approach*, sees the work space as an array based on the assimilation of cultural, social, and cognitive codes among the employees, who contribute to the development of sophisticated knowledge and production processes. A third approach, the *instrumental approach*, sees society as a kind of temporary coalition that seeks to achieve goals at a certain point in time in a way that works well for all members of the organization. Each of these approaches attempts to challenge the perception that focuses on the work environment from an economic-rational perspective of profit and efficiency (Taylor and Oinas, 2006). This is where the following discussion begins as it seeks to expand the economic-rational conception and focus on the dependent connection between the economic arena and the human one (Barnes, 2001; Biggs, 1996), as well as between the production process, the physical place, and location. More specifically, the discussion focuses on the role architecture plays in production processes, and the way social theories influence the architectural design of these spaces. This section presents a variety of typologies for factories and workshops, illustrates them with various examples, and then discusses the programmatic evolution of work space and its impact on the built space.

Factories, Architects, and the Design of Work Spaces

The spatial evolution of industry started from the object, from the work station, the factory. The word "factory" is a universal term that refers to a building or range of buildings for the processing of substances or materials. It is an abbreviation of an earlier term, a "manufactory," which refers to a place where a product is manufactured; especially one where articles are handmade (Oxford English Dictionary, 2020). Unlike manufacturing workshops, factories are places where manual tasks are performed with partial use of machinery (Bradley, 1999: 6–7), characterized by a central, controlling force. In Europe and North America, the term "factory" has been used extensively since the beginning of the 20th century, and is often perceived as a capitalist venture that requires its owners' knowledge of accounting, awareness of market dynamics, ongoing supply of the product, and examination of all aspects affecting the status and functioning of the employee. Sociologists and economists have viewed factories of the early 20th century as central to modern life, and debated the role and place of the worker in the plant. Max Weber, for example, argued that the factory's most distinctive feature, especially since the 18th century, is the status and role of the entrepreneur as the super-coordinator of the means of work, production, and raw materials (Weber, 1968). The concentration of work in one space and the practices used to discipline workers set the conditions for the massive use of mechanization. Moreover, not only did the development of technology affect the character of the factory and help to expand production, freeing it from human or animal labor constraints, but the factory also accelerated technological inventions aimed at lowering production costs and product prices, while also inventing new goods (Weber, [1927] 1981: 305–306).

The first industrial buildings of the 19th century were relatively small buildings that rose to a height of four or five stories, usually close to a water source used to power energy (Ackermann and Spong, 1991). Factories of this type were built by factory owners in collaboration with engineers. Surprisingly, despite the visibility of industrial factories in Europe during the 19th century, architects only began to show interest in the design of industrial buildings at the beginning of the 20th century. This sea change in the involvement of architects in factory design resulted in part from the architects' own recognition of the importance and impact of modern industrialization (Le Corbusier, [1923] 1970). The major reason, however, for greater architectural involvement in industry relates to owners and developers recognizing that the quality of the product improves as the health and comfort of the workers increases (Bradley, 1999: 24). This attitude was born out of the need for a skilled, satisfied workforce, and the belief of many factory owners that aesthetic and comfortable work environments would help them manage the workforce (Biggs, 1996: 3). Attending to the health and safety of workers was manifest in the design of light, ventilation, and building materials. The desire to address worker welfare influenced factories' plans, which would now include amenities such as employee services, bathrooms, dining rooms, clinics, and the like. In addition to paying attention to the factory' inner space, care was given to the image of the factory as an icon. This often included the design of a special facade and entrance, as well as areas for visitors, and areas from which the production process could be viewed. Open areas near the factory, also of great importance, were often designed in contrast to the structure of the factory itself (ibid.: 25–54).

Thus, since the beginning of the 20th century, with the use of iron and concrete in construction and the emergence of new social concepts in workforce organization, architects were given the lead in designing industrial buildings. The central ideal that guided the development of the factory's architectural design was the engineers' and architects' efforts to build a *rational factory*, one that could work like a giant machine, and also provide an aesthetically pleasing environment. This conception of the factory as a rational production system emerges from the Enlightenment period, which saw rationalism and progress as fundamental to the development of society. The introduction of design as a rational approach to planning factories closely tied production processes to (re)organizing factory structures. Engineers and architects entrusted with the planning and design of factories tended to see the factory as a controllable system that could be organized in a systematic and regular manner, which would save time for workers, circumvent existing production problems, and adapt to advanced production systems. This approach to factory design addressed human factors as one among the many variables in optimizing the process of production.

The involvement of architects and their connection to changes in the industrial world contributed to the construction of iconic, distinctive factories. One distinct example of a factory as a representation and as an image of corporate power is the AEG turbine plant. This factory was designed by architect Peter Behrens (1868–1940) in collaboration with engineer Karl Bernhard (1859–1937), inside an existing building complex of the corporation in Berlin. The factory, opened in 1910, necessitated the construction of a new space to suit its production needs. The demands placed on Behrens included: building a large central production hall, positioning large cranes that could carry heavy machinery above the work level, additional cranes at points around the hall, and maximum light input. Behrens designed the plant in the form of a long box whose upper part is a three-jointed arch made of glass, iron, and concrete (materials representing industrialization). The building's main hall is about 207 meters long. One facade of the main building faces the street, and the other, the one facing the compound, is a two-story secondary wing. The combination of new materials is not intended to create a sense of transparency or lightness, which could characterize the use of iron and glass, but rather to emphasize heavy materiality. In other words, Behrens sought to establish a "classical-new" unity through the building materials. The plant's design can be seen as a physical and corporate expression of ARG's desire to create a monument of a "new nature" for a culture based on industrial power (Anderson, 2000: 129–145).

Another iconic factory of the time is the Fagus shoe factory in the German city of Alfeld. The factory, one of the first works of Walter Gropius (1883–1969), later known as the founder of the Bauhaus school, was designed jointly with Adolf Meyer (1881–1929). As evident in the way Siegfried Giedion describes it, the factory

became known as Gropius' first work in which the new engineering construction technique using steel and glass was central in a "truly" architectural design (Giedion, 1992: 23–24). Gropius' and Meyer's collaboration began in 1911 with a request to focus on designing the facades so that they would faithfully represent its spirit as a modern plant, operating on the principle of maximum efficiency (Jaeggi, 2000: 6, 21–22). In the first phase, Gropius and Mayer focused on the facades as well as the factory's main production hall; the design intention that guided them was reducing the presence of material mass, limit form, material, and color, and maintaining uniformity in all parts of the factory. Thus, all the buildings stand on a 40 centimeter high base of black bricks, above which rise, as if floating, light-yellow rectangular walls. Their orthogonal shape emphasized both the external contours and the clear division into floors and sections of the large, square glass windows through which natural light entered (ibid.: 25–31). The best-known feature of the plant is the column-free corner, where two glass walls meet without any visible support – the first example using new engineering means to favor a design that replaces mass with weightless transparency.

The most prominent factory of the period, clearly demonstrating the aesthetic victory of engineering and perceived as a symbol of modern Europe, is the Fiat Lingotto factory. The engineer Giacomo Mattè Trucco designed the plant, which Corbusier crowned as the "Temple of Progress and Speed." It was built from 1914 to 1926 in Turin, Italy (Darley, 2003: 153). The designer's reference model was the Ford factory in Detroit, designed by the architect Albert Kahn (1869–1942), which was identified with the innovative production line. At the Ford plant, the production process takes place in accordance with gravity, and the complete car rolls out of the plant at ground level. Angeli and Trucco designed a rectangular structure of concrete, containing two parallel blocks about 500 meters long, connected by three intermediate structures, and they reversed the Ford plant model: they placed the end of the production process on the roof of the factory. Such a reversal of the order of the production line meant placing the test track for cars on the roof of the building, which became its prominent symbol. This reversal also connected the production process on the production line with weightlessness and turned the plant itself into a stage that showcased its products (Costa, 1997: 91–94).

These examples offer a partial illustration of the iconic factories constructed in the early 20th century. Using principles of scientific rationalism, they translated the symbiosis between methods of work, factory structures, and industrial city systems into a physical reality that reorganized the work space and living environment. Most of all, these factories reflected Frederick Winslow Taylor's idea of "scientific management" (Flink, 1988; Raushenbush, 1937).

Taylorism understands industrial workers as "economic animals," and argues that they should be encouraged to sell their labor power and allow managers to think in their stead. According to Taylor, this approach promises to achieve maximum results for employees and employers as well as neutralizing conflicts among them (Taylor, 1967). Scientific management includes systematically analyzing and optimizing plant tasks; having managers organize work, separate planning from execution, as well as preparation and production tasks; using schedules and control systems as tools to coordinate all elements of work; and economic incentives to stabilize effort. The relationships between employees and supervisors were hierarchically defined. Furthermore, Taylor's study assumed that employees are driven by rewards, and thus he set standards for the amount of time allotted for each task and the physical routines each task should include. The key idea is that rewards are given in relation to efficiency and professional ethics. Based on this rationale, Taylor suggests breaks for employees and managers, viewing this as a means of increasing production. In general, management focuses on the work of thinking, assigning responsibilities, designing products, scheduling, and examining execution. These activities usually took place in rooms located above the production area in transparent spaces. As a result, the organization of production was compacted; product design and production were separated from each other, and the control process became central. Work became a set of specific, repeated tasks. This model, distributed throughout the United States and Europe, emphasizes quantity over quality and invention.

Yet this rationalist conception, which spread all over the world, began to crack in the 1960s, especially in Europe and the United States. New approaches began to emphasize the significance of social systems at play in factories and the involvement of workers in production processes, as well as the connection among workers (Herzberg, 1996). These newer approaches replaced managerial notions by Taylor and others with an approach that saw the industrial organization as a social system, a living organism engaged in a constant search for stability. This psychological humanism supports the involvement of workers in thinking through processes, planning work, and working in groups.

This approach also influenced the design of the work environment. For example, the Inmos Microprocessor Factory, designed by architect Richard Rogers, was conceived at the time of its establishment as part of the new electronics industry boom accompanying the weakening of traditional industries (Powell, 2008: 229). The plant's construction in 1982 in South Wales used prefabricated construction techniques and was completed rapidly, in about 14 months. Unlike the international-style approach, which carried the banner of functionality but ultimately relied on rigid rules and structures, here Rogers was required to focus on a flexible and scalable program (Rogers and Burdett, 1996: 78–83) that could address the ever-changing needs of new technologies. The need for flexibility meant some uncertainty regarding the location of the plant, and its early design model was not adapted to a specific site. In this case, as with factories of the early 20th century, the client asked the architect to design a factory that, in addition to meeting the unique functional needs of the new industry, would have an iconic structure (ibid.: 233). The plant plan is based on an elongated rectangular shape, divided in the center by

Fagus Factory: Design and Use

Fagus factory

1911–1925
Walter Gropius
and Adolf Meyer,
Saxony, Germany.

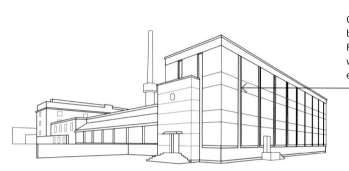

Concrete columns inside the building to free the facade. Fully glazed exterior corners, which are free of structural elements.

Emphasis on the social aspect of architectural design, suggesting that improving working conditions through increased daylight, fresh air, and hygiene would lead to a greater worker satisfaction, and therefore, increase overall production.

Production
Office
Public amenities
Power center
Dormitory
Green/open space

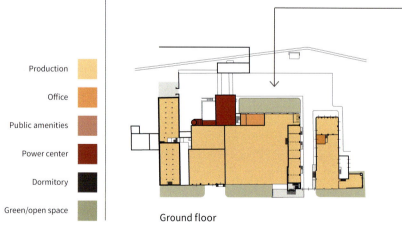

Ground floor

Program relations

1 | PEOPLE, FACTORIES, AND MAKING

Inmos Microprocessor Factory: Design and Use

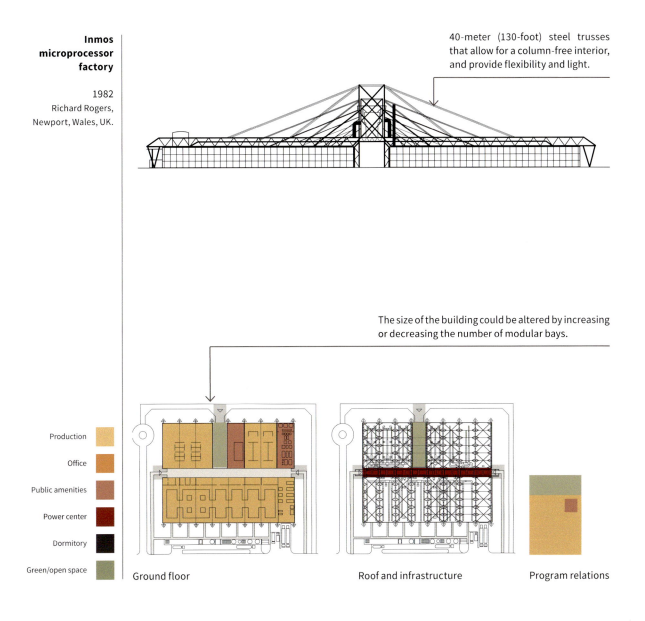

PART I | FOR PRODUCTION'S SAKE

Apple Park: Design and Use

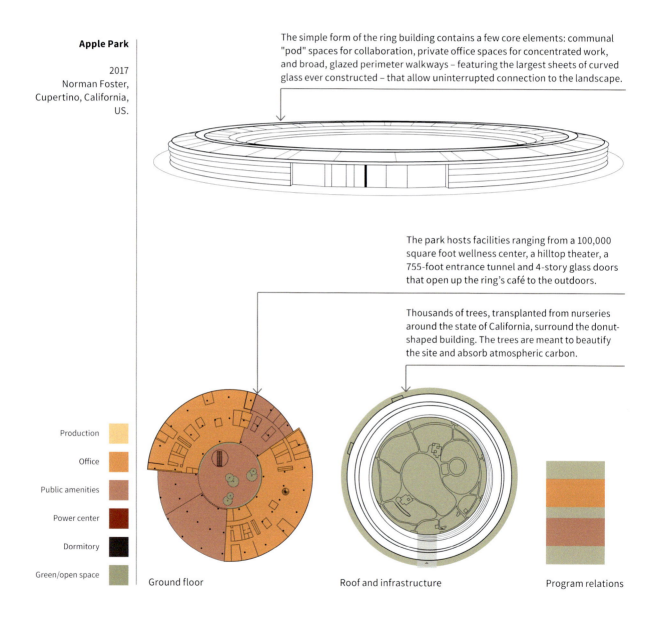

1 | PEOPLE, FACTORIES, AND MAKING

■ Chengdu Chipscreen Medicine Industry Production: Design and Use

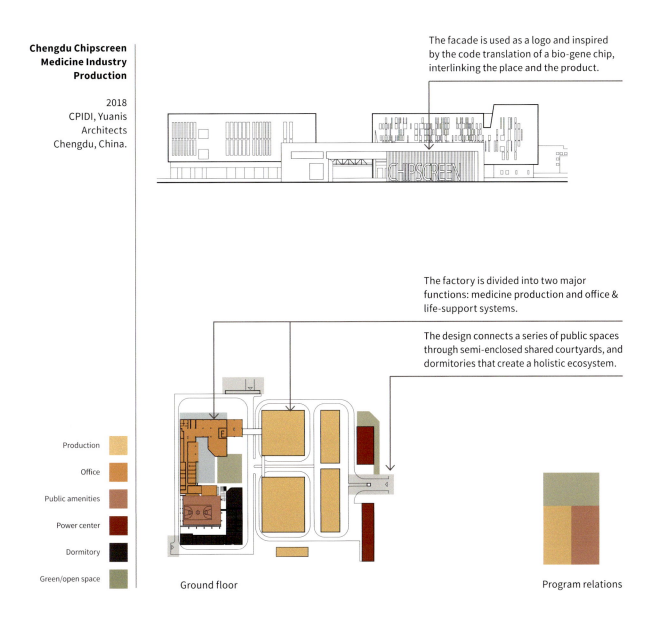

PART I | FOR PRODUCTION'S SAKE

■ Factories' Design and Use: A Diachronic Perspective

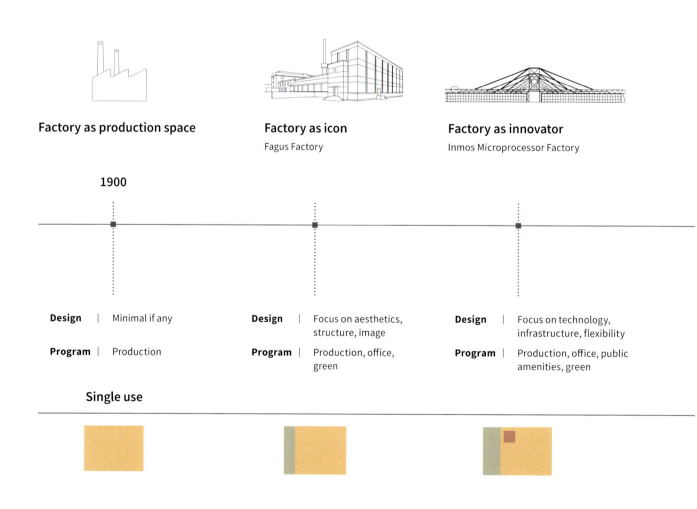

1 | PEOPLE, FACTORIES, AND MAKING

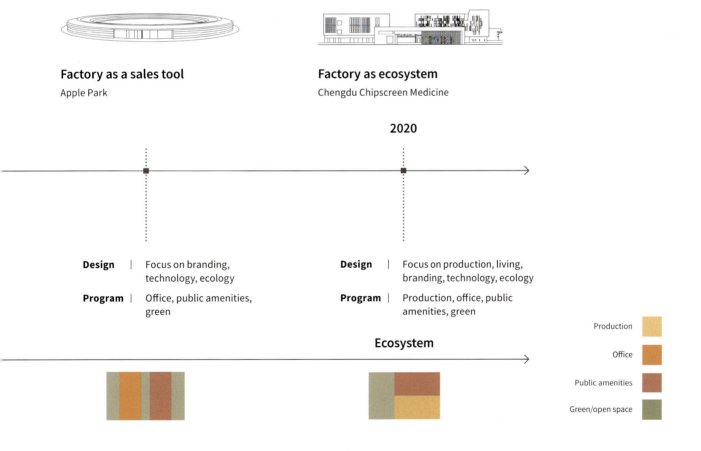

33

a central corridor, with a production wing on one side and an office and cafeteria wing on the other. Structurally, the plant uses trusses. Its center is an extensible spine, about 106 meters long, from which a system of taut rods emerges to support internal columns within the structure that can be extended for increased flexibility. The blue bars that surround it are visible from a distance and the wall cladding includes opaque, semi-transparent, and transparent parts. Along with the maximal cleanliness and efficiency that characterize the factory, it recognizes and emphasizes the importance of social spaces in the work environment. For example, Rogers designed a "central street" that serves as an active social space in the factory. This concept of social space as important to the production process and the thinking that goes on in the work environment has enhanced the use of urban terminology such as "street" or "square." These ideas were adopted in the design of varied work spaces and factories, and are still influential today.

Two other contemporary examples further illustrate the development of the program, design, and scale of work environments. The first is Apple's planned project in the city of Cupertino, California, located on the edge of the city and part of the Silicon Valley suburban continuum. The building, designed by Fosters + Partners, is a four-story ring covering 24,155 square meters and planned to accommodate about 12,000 workers. The underground car park for 2,400 vehicles and gym are built on an area of 10,000 square meters. The building includes multiple cafeterias and a dining room that can serve 3,000 people. The scale of the structure and the services offered in the building create an autarkic world, which is further supported by the scenic development and thousands of fruit trees, such as peach, persimmon, and apple, which are planted in the complex as a gesture toward California's agricultural and marketing heritage. The ring structure and the development of the scenery emphasize the unattached structure and its function as a self-contained system with maximum control capability. This perception of the factory as a world that offers all services to its workers is also apparent at the Shen-

zhen Chipscreen Biosciences Co. factory, established in 2001. This 40,000 square meter complex is located in the West of Chengdu High-Tech Zone, Sichuan. Its design breaks with traditional single-functional layouts of factory buildings and connects a series of amenities including public spaces for meetings, training, exhibitions, sports, canteens, and leisure bars, with office and living areas through semi-enclosed, shared courtyards. The complex uses design elements such as waterscape, landscaped steps, overhead corridors, activity platforms, and leisure terraces, which are all spaces for community activities. The facade of the office building is designed in the spirit of enterprise, using the "Gene chip expression spectrum" as its theme and logo.

What can be learned from this non-comprehensive set of examples? First, factories are concrete structures that represent social conceptions. The architect designs elements with an aim of building an identity that could strengthen the connection between the worker and the organization, by creating a sense of belonging and commitment; and between the organization and the wider environment, for branding. Second, developers and architects alike have dramatically evolved in their conceptualization of work spaces. Two major changes have occurred in the design of factories: (1) expanding the program, from a production space to a structure that includes varied leisure and recreation amenities providing for all of the workers' needs. This expansion serves as a means for enhancing innovation and production; (2) increasing the symbolic role of the building to support a variety of features including innovation, technology, ecology, aesthetics, and branding.

The design of the factories continues to evolve. It is expected to be highly influenced by future technologically based factories. Large manufacturing firms are planning future factories, and in some cases they are "already setting up early models and pilot programs" (Helper et al., 2021: 8). This is a speculative process in an uncertain future. Models of future factories are not unified and firms anticipate adopting different models depending on their market niche. "Increased technological sophistication at some firms allows for more flexibility, responsiveness, and customization in the production process rather than simply higher output. Other firms anticipate moving in quite the opposite direction, looking to automate the few remaining tasks performed by workers" (ibid.: 8). These varied approaches to future factories development, "with some quite labor-intensive and flexible, and others closer to an even more technologically intensive form of mass production" (ibid.), are also expected to influence the design of factories, their location, and program. The labor-intensive factories are likely to locate near or in the city, providing varied amenities within the building, and the more technologically intensive, mass-production factory, with minimal amenities, to locate distant from the city.

Work Spaces: Building Types and Programs

The complex and dynamic relationships between spaces of production, social ideas, and city development, as it evolved over the last 100 years, have influenced the design, scale, and location of work spaces. This evolutionary development resulted in a set of five primary building types: the *street*, the *complex*, the *campus*, the *box*, and the *tower* (Hatuka et al., 2014). Each of these building types offers a different relationship with the built environment, and a different day-to-day experience for employees, city residents, and passers-by.

The *street* is a traditional feature of the pre-industrial workshops. It is a sequence of adjacent units, single-story or two-stories high, developed as part of the existing urban fabric. Streets are a solution for providing services and small-scale production. At the urban level, the most prominent feature of the street is the way in which its space can be appropriated for different needs (display, work, etc.). Despite the tendency to mourn the street (in many cities and industrial areas built in the second half of the 20th century, the street was converted into high-rise towers), it seems

that with increasing awareness of the environmental, social, and economic price of long-distance transportation, the industrial street is experiencing a revival.

Another prominent feature, present as early as the beginning of the 20th century, is the *complex*: a flexible space suitable for a variety of purposes (production, development, research, training, services) that rises to a height of two to five floors. At the beginning of the 20th century, most of the planned industrial buildings (e.g. AEG and Fagus) were based on a building type that contributed to the construction of iconic factories, with distinct images, which tried to reinvent the production process. Consisting of a number of building units that share a common and continuous space, the complex was often based on a separation between production processes, that were regarded as dirty and noisy; and factory management was viewed as supporting and promoting the image of the company.

The industrial landscape of the 1950s and 1960s, dominated by the street and complex as building types suitable for production, changed in the 1970s. During these years, much of the heavy industry in Western Europe, the United States, and Canada moved to other places, such as Africa, South America, and Asia. Countries with advanced economies sought ways to further reduce production methods and circumvent environmental constraints and labor laws – which resulted in moving from a manufacturing economy to a services economy. Thus, from the 1970s on, the division of labor changed and was manifest in a strict separation among production, development, and services, which contributed to the development of new architecture building types: the campus, the box, and the tower.

The *campus*, an extension of the complex, developed in response to the growth of large factories and the need to separate production, research, and service areas. This need contributed to the formation of bounded spaces in which a series of autonomous but centrally managed structures support varied purposes. This preferred centralized management model suited corporate firms and enabled both flexibility and control over many other variables such as traffic, resource development, and management. The decentralized factory, manifested as a campus, has gained presence in recent decades with the dynamic relations between economy, consumption, and the flow of knowledge; the latter have at the same time lessened the importance of place and location.

This approach also enhanced the development of the *box*, perceived as a temporary space for transporting goods, as a storage space that does not require the development of a connection with the physical and human environment. The box is an autonomous structure detached from its surroundings. It is usually divided into several halls, the main one of which occupies most of the building's volume and has an array of shelves for storing goods. Climatically, boxes are controlled as required by the type of goods they store, and for the most part the shelving work is done by advanced robotic technologies and computing – with limited human activity. The decentralization of the production process, as evident in the presence of campuses and boxes in the suburban-industrial environment, also boosted the presence of high-rise towers in cities. *Towers*, a profitable use of land resources, rise to great heights and architecturally offer a shell, which allows companies flexibility: they can rent or purchase a space of the size they desire and design the interior environment according to their needs. The towers are a sort of container in which content is molded to the characteristics of the company and the changing fashions of an organizational culture. In order to suit as many companies as possible, these structures are generic in their design and offer companies the option of placing their logo on the facade. The tower often provides commercial and catering areas and, on the subterranean levels, storage, service, and parking areas to meet the needs of the employees. As a rule, buildings have sophisticated mechanized systems that include traffic and climate control and allow for strict enforcement and supervision.

These changes in the development of both programs and building types over the last century have a crucial impact not only on the way people work but also on the location of their work spaces. Thus, for example, we are witnessing the strengthening of certain building types over others in different geographical areas (the tower and the street in city centers as opposed to the campus, the complex, and the box in industrial parks). The geographical segmentation of the building types represents the programmatic separation between development (often located in cities), production (tends to be located in the periphery), storage, and service array. This programmatic segregation also shapes the global production map, while pushing physical production to the periphery and reinforcing unequal class division (Massey and Wield, 2004).

Yet, over the last decade, new models are challenging this process of programmatic segregation, with the emergence of a new building type, the synchronic complex (see section 10). This type of complex is characterized by integrating residential and industrial uses (Hatuka et al., 2020). Synchronization, unlike mixed-use, supports different operations existing and functioning in parallel, in the same built space, without interfering with each other while optimally sharing resources. Synchronicity, as a conceptual approach, was further enhanced in response to the global crisis of COVID-19 pandemic, which forced firms to think anew on the work management models and work spaces. One of the prominent related concepts that shapes this new approach to work is hybridity, which "promises organizations the benefits of remote working (increased flexibility, reduced carbon footprint, labor-cost optimization, and increased employee satisfaction) alongside the critical strengths of traditional, co-located work (smoother coordination, informal networking, stronger cultural socialization, greater creativity, and face-to-face collaboration)" (Mortensen and Haas, 2021). Although this hybrid management model and synchronic building type are still in embryotic stages, they signal the development of new working spaces. It is anticipated that in the next two decades, with robotics and automation playing an increasingly crucial role, and with adoption of the hybrid working model, synchronic complexes will be more present in cities. No compelling historical or contemporary evidence suggests that this approach will totally change the landscape of industry; on the contrary, history teaches us that it will be added to the existing set of building types.

This new building type, along with familiar building types and their spread in space, will shape the relationships between cities and industries.

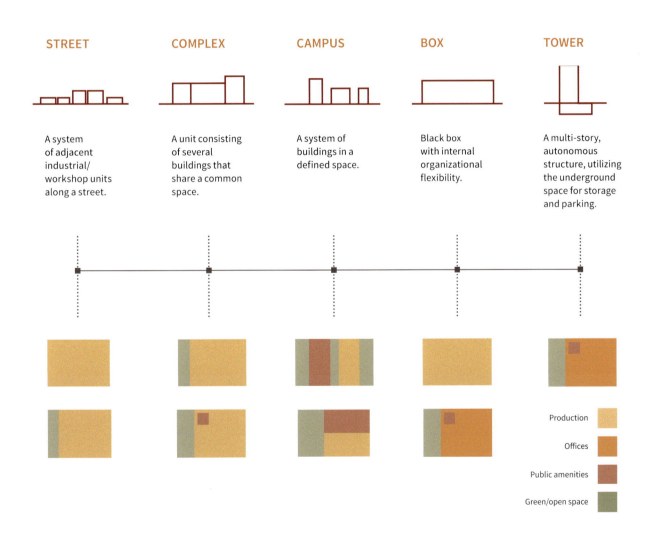

■ Contemporary Programs and Building Types

2 Between Production and City Development

2

Between Production and City Development

The relationships of cities with industry are processual. Historically, the primary mode of production up until the 18th century was artisanal manufacturing in individual households; therefore, manufacturing activities were closely integrated with other parts of everyday life, specifically residential and commercial activities. The merchants' town that grew from trading goods and wholesale products became one of the most rapidly emerging patterns of urbanization in Western cultures. However, the industrial revolution spurred large-scale urbanization as new technologies enabled the adoption of water wheels, coal-fired steam power, and intercity railways, dramatically changing the urban landscape.

From the 1750s on, four phases in the evolving spatial dynamic between city and industry have been identified (Hatuka and Ben-Joseph, 2014, 2017; Kim and Ben-Joseph, 2013).

The first phase is associated with the *emergence of the industrial city* (1750–1880). The evolution of textile manufacturing and steam engine technologies revolutionized production processes. Cities were the logical centers of production, and industrial cities quickly outgrew their older counterparts (Hoselitz, 1955). Industry also benefited from cities' labor pools, transportation hubs, and entrepreneurs (Rappaport, 2011). Consequently, cities experienced unprecedented population growth, with manufacturing driving urbanization and economic development. Yet the basic necessities of shelter, water, and waste disposal were not being met, and additional exacerbating factors, such as pollution from coal, gave rise to the need to reassess the relations of industry with its adjacent surroundings. This reassessment resulted in numerous plans and models aimed at creating a balance between living and producing in cities.

The second phase can be viewed as *a search for an ideal industrial city* (1880–1970), that is, a planned city that might be able to absorb the needs of industrialists while providing livable conditions. Towards the end of the 19th century, planning models included mill towns and new sets of zoning regulations to handle the problem of factories' nuisance activities. The attempt to provide healthier living conditions for factory workers materialized in the form of a garden city promoted by Ebenezer Howard (1898). These ideas served as a model for many towns built after the end of World War I. Howard, who developed the idea of the garden city, perceived industry as a necessary part of the garden city economy. Industry was to be located within city limits, maximizing the use of urban transportation systems, particularly rail transport. Countries such as Israel (Hatuka, 2011), Iran, Sweden, and Japan also implemented these principles in the construction of new towns, designating industrial lands as part of newly planned cities. These industrial spaces were typically situated so as to have the smallest possible effect on residential areas. Architect Tony Garnier (1869–1948) developed another model as a utopian form of living located between a mountain and a river to facilitate access to hydroelectric power (Garnier, 1917). The core idea of functional separation was later adopted by the members of *Congrès International d'Architecture Moderne* (CIAM) and ultimately influenced the design of cities with industry.

Another prominent model for reassessing the relations between city and industry was the company town, which integrated industry and housing. Built by or around a single employer, company towns have enjoyed differing levels of success, depending on the character of the founding firm (Porteous, 1970). The first company towns emerged in the 18th century as a way to house new factory workers in rapidly expanding industries. Often commissioned by a single employer, towns such as Lowell, New Hampshire (textiles), Pullman, Illinois (railroad cars), Essen, Germany (iron works), and Saltaire, England (woolen textiles) are prominent examples of company towns.

World War II, and the resulting importance of the location of industrial production, had a tremendous impact on the spread of these models; a rapid increase in industrial demand led to the development of production facilities that could no longer be located within existing urban fabrics. Environmental degradation and increased pollution led to a desire to separate industry and manufacturing from housing and the establishment of stricter environmental laws and regulations.

The third phase is linked to the process of *deindustrialization*, which began in the 1970s. During this time, many countries with advanced economies, especially in Western Europe and North America, reduced their industrial capacities or activities and developed planning tools to segregate industry from other land uses (Lever, 1991). There are several reasons for this process. It emphasizes the natural development of the economy and a gradual transition from agriculture and mining to mass production, services, and,

increasingly, knowledge-based industries. Another reason stems from trade specialization, which offers comparative advantages to places that specialize in a particular economic activity, explaining in large part that wage and labor-intensive activities have moved from West to East.

The process by which industrialization dampens competitiveness is also an outcome of the failure and lack of investment by international companies that relocate geographically to take advantage of differences in production costs (Pike, 2009). Deindustrialization has been experienced unevenly in different countries, regions, and localities and also by different industries, firms, social groups, and individuals (Massey and Wield, 2004; Pike, 2009). In many cities, the trend that disfavors manufacturing, coupled with regulatory zoning practices that essentially provide advantages to commercial and, above all, residential uses of real estate, results in a loss of industrial land. There are other ways in which deindustrialization has reshaped the geography of industry: storage and distribution facilities were often located in the hinterlands, where land values are the lowest, whereas industrial parks tended to be located in the suburbs or on the periphery of the city (Harrington and Warf, 1995). What is left in the city are office parks (i.e. the service industry), which are less land-intensive. The urban factories remaining in cities are a reminder of a forgotten era when the city functioned as a place of production.

The contemporary and fourth iteration emerges from the *Fourth Industrial Revolution* (Schwab, 2015) and calls for "hybridity," an idea that addresses the limits of zoning and the separation of the residential environment from manufacturing in cities. The idea of hybridity supports a process of densification that results in hybrid buildings that may improve the walkability of industrial areas, thus promoting alternative transportation modes and neighborhood retail (Love, 2017). This approach suggests that factories could now be built as hybrid buildings in mixed-use neighborhoods because industry is smaller, cleaner, and quieter (Rappaport, 2015).

PART I | FOR PRODUCTION'S SAKE

■ Industrial Revolutions and Development Patterns

| 1750–1870 | 1870–1950 |

The Industrial Revolution

Innovation | Water, steam power, and mechanization

Planning | Unplanned industrial development

Model | The integrated city conflict between living and production

- Industry
- City
- Green/open space

2nd Industrial Revolution

Innovation | Electrical energy and mass production

Planning | Emergence of zoning, garden city, company towns, continuation of integrated city

Model | Garden cities, zoned cities a search for the ideal city

2 | BETWEEN PRODUCTION AND CITY DEVELOPMENT

1950–2000

3rd Industrial Revolution

Innovation | Automation, computerization

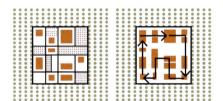

Planning | Construction of suburban and ex-urban industrial parks, abandonment of industrial sites, adaptive reuse

Model | Industrial + eco-industrial parks workplaces on periphery and deindustrialization

2000 …

4th Industrial Revolution

Innovation | Digitization, IOT, cyber systems

Planning | Industrial urbanism, planned, integrated development hybridization of industrial and non-industrial uses

Model | Back to the city a refined "integrated city"

This evolving dynamic between city and industry has left spatial and geographical footprints. These footprints influence the daily lives of workers around the world.

Industrial Landscapes and Urban Life Dynamics

One of the dramatic changes in the 20th century which irrevocably shaped urban life in general and production in particular is the reduced cost of automobile commuting and truck shipping. Add subsidized highway infrastructure and the effect – a horizontal sprawl of industrial areas – was fast and of great importance (Leigh and Hoelzel, 2012). The new industrial landscape was not unified, but varied, and could be viewed as an agglomeration of three spatial types of industrial areas: "integrated," "adjacent," and "autonomous" (Hatuka et al., 2014). Each type affects city life and economic needs differently, and some cities cultivate more than one type in their juridical boundaries. The adoption of one type or another is often a manifestation of historical, cultural, political, and economic factors.

The Integrated Industrial Space. The key feature of this type is the symbiosis between living and working. This symbiosis impacts the form and the fabric of the city. Integrated industrial zones are often enclaves within a city with the goal of better exploiting land resources, yielding higher profits, and increasing tax revenue. The last feature, which is administrative, concerns the responsibility of the city to meet the needs of both businesses and residents, and resolve tensions related to their geographical proximity. The integrated type may generate varied benefits to diverse agents: residents enjoy nearby employment; businesses in the industrial area enjoy proximity to services (such as catering or office supplies) and existing infrastructure (public transportation); and municipalities strengthen the urban economy. However, this kinship may also induce problems and tensions, especially with regard to environmental pollution, noise, smell, and transport systems congested with trucks and private cars. In many cases, the evolution of this type is not planned and sometimes creates intractable conflicts. The physical presence of an industrial area that is adjacent to residential environments may nonetheless serve as the main growth engine of the city.

One example of an integrated industrial space is Munich, Germany. Known for its electronics and advanced manufacturing, Munich is one of Germany's leading manufacturing regions, supporting a breadth of activities, ranging from small crafts to innovative service and high-tech assembly. One of the city's most notable manufacturing plants, BMW Werk München, originally opened in the 1920s to produce aircraft engines and power units. The site was rural land, and the surrounding area remained undeveloped until after World War II, when the city expanded; the plant gradually became delimited by housing and commercial developments. This pattern changed after 1972 when the Munich Olympic Park opened to the west of the factory, forming the final boundary of the site. Since then, the plant has expanded vertically rather than horizontally. Over the course of four decades, residential and commercial areas have gradually grown around the factory. Today, the campus is located south of a major train station and within a 15-minute drive of downtown Munich. Smaller manufacturing and related facilities surround the BMW plant. Their uses vary from automotive to service-related firms.

Another example is the spatial spread of industry in the city of Chicago. Chicago is home to 2.7 million residents, making it the third most populous city in the United States and part of the third-largest metropolitan area, after New York City and Los Angeles. Owing to its location, the city became a major transportation hub and, consequently, a major center for manufacturing, retail, and finance in the late 19th century. The city's layout features a gridded street network with major diagonal arterial roads and railways radiating from the downtown center. In the 1980s, the city lost industrial jobs, partially due to increased foreign competition along with residential and commercial development pressures. In 1988, the city created its first Planned Manufacturing District (PMD) to retain industrially zoned land and prevent further job losses. As a result of Chicago's effort to protect manufacturing, there are now 24 industrial corridors. Most of the land with a manufacturing zoning designation is located within or adjacent to one of these industrial corridors (Chicago Department of Housing and Economic Planning, 2011). The industrial corridors are tightly knit with residential and commercial land uses, and are an important part of Chicago's urban landscape. PMDs are considered to have been effective in fostering manufacturing activities within Chicago, as they ensured long-term stability for industrial businesses looking to invest and expand within the city's districts. The PMDs are concentrated along major transportation networks, such as arterial roads, railroads, and rivers, resulting in a concentric, finger-shaped pattern that converges towards Lake Michigan and the downtown area. Such development patterns are consistent throughout Chicago's development history, which is also clearly illustrated in Chicago's 1904 Industry and Railroad Map and its 1965 comprehensive plan (Chicago: Department of City Planning, 1965; Talbot, 1904). The infrastructure network supports the PMDs. An extensive railroad system and a network of roads connect them to the larger transport system. The dense grid network of the local roads demonstrates the typical relationship between PMDs and Chicago's built areas. The PMDs are tightly integrated with the rest of the city's fabric, yielding an urban pattern that accommodates industrial uses within a city.

The integrated type implies a fusion or close proximity between residential and industrial uses. Often an outcome of (unplanned) urban growth, this type makes manufacturing an integral part of the city's structure and grid, although its parceling may vary and create larger lots and blocks for industrial uses. Aside from the recurring presence of walls and barriers surrounding the factories themselves, these areas usually do not have distinct borders and tend to dissolve into the urban environment. In some cities, small-scale manufacturing remains in residential neighborhoods, pre-serving family-based ownership models and proximity between home and the workplace.

The Adjacent Industrial Space. The organizational outline of adjacent industrial spaces is based on zoning and the separation between living and working. Inter-urban roads, railway lines, and open spaces often enhance the division between the city and the industrial area. This type is associated with the implementation of the new urban models of the early 20th century that sought to address the nuisances of industrialization by providing an ideal model of the industrial city. Its key feature is geographical and administrative duality, with the industrial area located close to the city or linked to it. Even though the employment relationship between the residents and industry is not exclusive and some employees come to work from elsewhere, geographical proximity plays a crucial role in the local employment market.

Architecturally, the adjacent industrial type is characterized by a large tract of land and uneven, often low, structures, especially since many peripheral areas have a larger inventory of land. In terms of management, although industry is relatively autonomous, it operates under municipal laws and regulations. Despite the geographical proximity, this model most often produces a physical separation between the two and contributes to cognitive distance between the city's industrial area and the rest of life.

One example of the adjacent type is Kiryat Gat, Israel. Located 50 kilometers south of Tel Aviv and 40 kilometers north of Be'er Sheva, Kiryat Gat is surrounded by open, arid land devoted to agricultural production and wildlife preserves. This small city is home to one of the largest manufacturing plants for Intel that, together with other high-tech firms, is fueling an industrial revival in the city. Production has played a vital role in the economy of this city since its beginnings as a new Israeli town in the 1950s. The threat of economic decline in the 1980s prompted government incentives to encourage foreign investment, shifting Kiryat Gat's manufacturing portfolio from sugar and textiles to advanced production, including companies such as

Hitachi, Zenith Solar, and HP-Indigo, in addition to Intel. Due to this incentive, Kiryat Gat's industrial area consists of several types of manufacturing, including traditional manufacturers, large plants, and enclosed high-tech campuses. Despite its influence on the overall economy, industrial manufacturing remains spatially removed from the rest of the city. A pattern of single-purpose zoning reflects a distinct separation between residential neighborhoods to the west and industrial development to the east. Kiryat Gat's development pattern is bifurcated, with relatively dense, mostly residential neighborhoods juxtaposed with a distinctly industrial zone. This divide is also reflected in the city's socioeconomic landscape. The city is a home to diverse communities from a broad range of socioeconomic conditions, but these communities have benefited little from the economic benefits of residing in proximity to the industrial zone. In the eastern half of the city, industrial employees lack a connection to Kiryat Gat's city center, and companies have relied on enclosed campuses for employee services. The majority of these workers live outside of Kiryat Gat and commute to the city by car.

A very different example is Pohang in South Korea. It was originally incorporated in 1949 as a maritime city, although it traces its origins to settlements dating back two millennia. Until the late 1950s, Pohang was primarily a fishing port, with seafood processing and marine products as its main industries. The city underwent a major growth period following the 1960s when the Pohang Steel Company (POSCO) built Korea's first integrated steel mill, established with the help of a public subsidy and support from the Korean government. The largest steel manufacturing company, POSCO, occupies most of the territory within Pohang's industrial zone at the claw-shaped tip of the landmass. The smaller steel companies are all located to the south of POSCO. Aside from the Hyundai Steel Company, which is the second-largest factory in the area, the smaller companies largely depend on POSCO's production processes, using scrap metals and other leftover resources.

Given Pohang's long history of development and mountainous topography, its street network does not reflect an orderly pattern. Nevertheless, two distinctive areas have emerged in the inner city: a historic city center to the north of the Hyeongsan River and an industrial area to its south. The river physically separates Pohang's southeastern industrial areas from the older residential and commercial parts of the city, partially mitigating the environmental impact of manufacturing activities. An arterial road and a railroad line cross the river. Newer residential enclaves that grew in the 1980s and 1990s are spread around the southeastern periphery of the industrial zone. Surrounded by forest to the east and the East Sea to the west, the city's port access facilitates shipping to and from Pohang, making the location appealing to manufacturers.

The adjacent type implies planned segregation between the industrial and residential areas of the city through zoning (often via a physical barrier or natural elements) that aims to isolate incompatible land uses and prevent environmental hazards. Today, this type is in the process of changing, affected as it is by the dynamics of the market and competition. Factories and companies are leaving for areas that provide services and the better infrastructure conditions in industrial parks.

The Autonomous Industrial Space. This type of industrial space is characterized by large-scale areas of industrial buildings, defined by distinct physical boundaries. These industrial areas (also known as "industrial parks") are typically located on sites with high access to transportation infrastructure to allow easy access to airports and seaports. Their separation from the urban fabric often makes it difficult to establish an efficient mass transit system for the workers, and employees rely on their private vehicles or buses operated by their employer. Although often located at the periphery, near natural or agricultural land, these features are not integrated into the industrial space. The streets are used primarily for vehicular traffic, and their width is determined by the trucks. Plots are relatively large so as to attract companies with high capital turnover, often including international companies that employ hundreds of workers. Although autonomous industrial areas often contribute to regional development in terms of infrastructure, such as the construction of roads, railway stations, and waste disposal systems, they also compete with old industrial zones within nearby cities and sometimes weaken their economy.

Lordstown is a village in northeastern Ohio, USA located between Cleveland and Pittsburgh, Pennsylvania. The village is best known for the Lordstown Assembly, a General Motors plant that started production in 1966. Most of Lordstown's residents work at the plant. Despite the village's small size, it supports more industrial jobs than any other municipality in the Youngstown-Warren-Boardman metropolitan statistical area. The presence of the assembly plant and the adjacent rail yard dominates Lordstown's layout. Most of the land area is made up of sparsely populated residential zones with only a small downtown commercial zone. Lordstown Assembly and the rail lines occupy approximately one-quarter of the total land area. The village can be characterized as dependent on the plant. Located in the middle of an agricultural area, the General Motors Lordstown complex essentially occupies all of the town's industrial area. The plant is physically separated from the community, although many of the plant's employees live in Lordstown and use its services and amenities. Company housing exists across from the complex, with approximately 200 single-family homes housing the plant's employees. While multiple rail lines connect the plant to the rest of the country, the automobile is the primary mode of transportation for employees living in and commuting to the complex from other areas. The Lordstown site exists in physical isolation from surrounding land uses and is served by its own infrastructure. The site includes a large parking lot, which is connected to Interstates 80 and 680. The highways cut through the surrounding farmland, linking the site to the greater Youngstown region.

Another example of an autonomous industrial type of layout can be seen in the industrial districts around Hartsfield-Jackson Atlanta International Airport in Georgia, USA. These industrial sites are spread across three different municipalities: the city of Atlanta to the northeast of the airport, the city of Forest Park to the southeast, and the city of College Park to the west. Each municipality has a zoned cluster of industrial land and suburban subdivisions surround these clusters. The industrial sites have excellent highway access and are also served by a large rail yard, which is located in Forest Park. The industrial land is adjacent to Atlanta International Airport and is surrounded by suburban developments. These industrial facilities range from food to car manufacturing. One of the industrial area's planned manufacturing districts, Southside Industrial Park, was developed on a brownfield site. In general, smaller parcels define the Southside Industrial District (SID), with an overall layout that reflects a separation of uses by level of intensity. The heavy industrial companies and highest traffic-generating uses can be found along the Browns Mill Road and Empire Boulevard. The Zip/Browns Mill/Empire area is less uniform, with smaller lots and irregular spacing between buildings. The new Southside Industrial Park contains newer and uniformly larger light-industrial lots, while Zip Industrial Boulevard is lined with a mixture of offices and other smaller-scale businesses (Driemeier et al., 2009: 12). Atlanta sits to the north of SID and is connected by heavily used highways, Interstates 75 and 258, as well as by rail and minor roads.

The autonomous industrial type refers to standalone industrial/business parks or large factories working autonomously from both the spatial and managerial perspectives. Often functioning as independent campuses, these areas are frequently surrounded by open spaces and located in close proximity to major infrastructure such as railways, highways, and airports. This allows workers to commute to and from work, and facilitates the shipment of products and goods. To date, the industrial park typology is the preferred model for many countries and manufacturers that aspire to create a setting that fosters a global image. This

PART I | FOR PRODUCTION'S SAKE

▬ Integrated Industrial Space

Type |
Integrated

Symbiosis between living and working.

Structure |
Layered

Land Use |
Mixed

Munich, Germany

Location

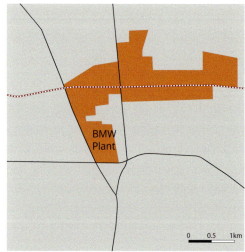

Relationships

Chicago, USA

Location

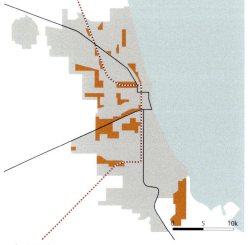

Relationships

■ Industrial fabric   ■ Residential fabric   ■ Puplic/commercial   ■ Green/open space

48

▬ Munich, Germany
BMW Headquarters and Assembly Plant, Munich, Germany. Photo by Diego Delso (CC BY-SA 4.0).

PART I | FOR PRODUCTION'S SAKE

▬ Adjacent Industrial Space

Type |
Adjacent

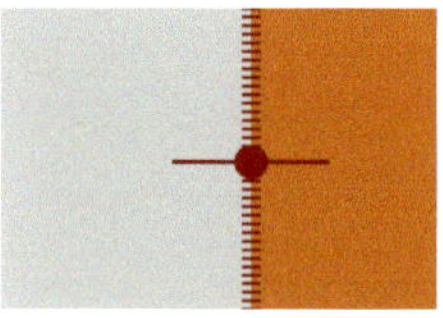

Zoning and separation between living and working.

Structure |
Parallel

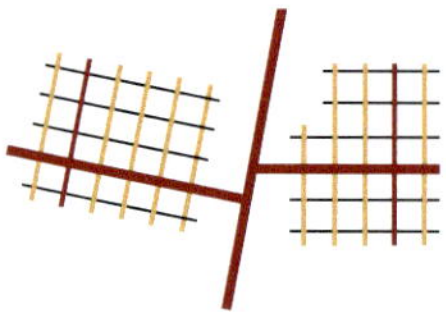

Land Use |
Partial zoning

Pohang, South Korea

Location

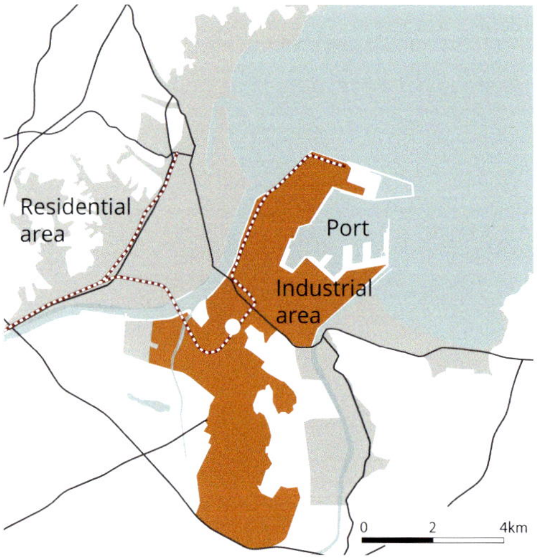

Relationships

Kiryat Gat, Israel

Location

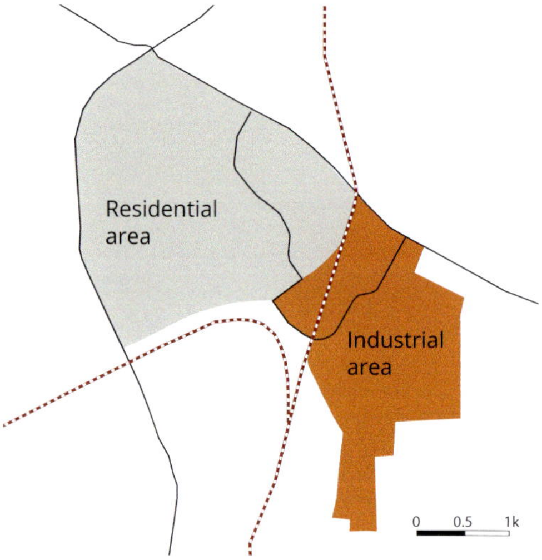

Relationships

🟧 Industrial fabric		⬜ Residential fabric	⬛ Puplic/commercial	🟩 Green/open space

50

2 | BETWEEN PRODUCTION AND CITY DEVELOPMENT

■ **Kiryat Gat, Israel**
Industrial zone, Kiryat Gat, Israel. Photo courtesy Kiryat Gat Municipality.

PART I | FOR PRODUCTION'S SAKE

▬ Autonomus Industrial Space

Type |
Autonomous

Large-scale zones occupied by uniform industrial buildings and surrounded by various physical boundaries.

Structure |
Unified

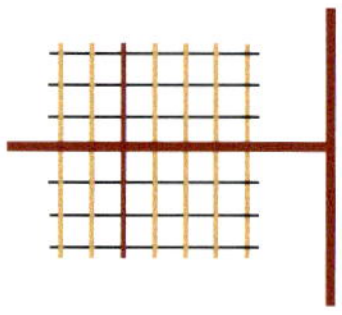

Land Use |
Zoning

Lordstown, USA

Warren

Lordstown

Youngstown

Location

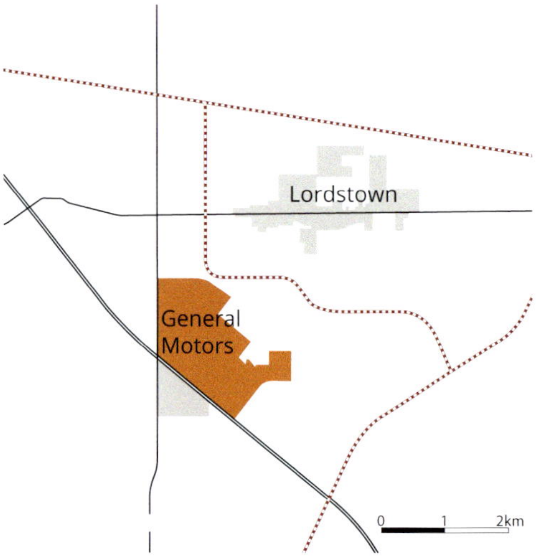

Lordstown

General Motors

Relationships

Atlanta, USA

Atlanta

Airport

Location

Airport

Industrial Area

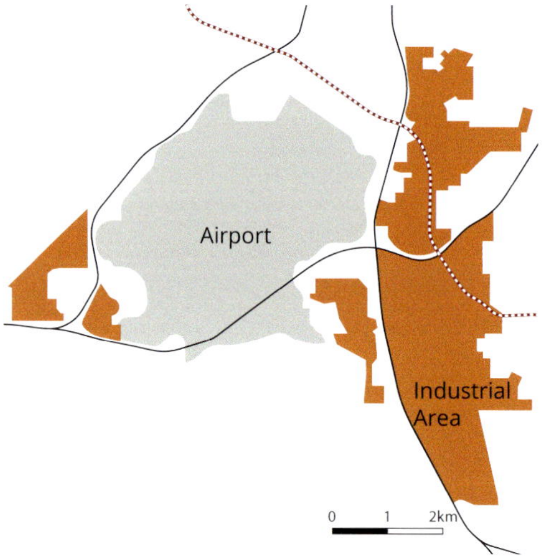

Relationships

■ Industrial fabric   Residential fabric   Puplic/commercial   Green/open space

52

2 | BETWEEN PRODUCTION AND CITY DEVELOPMENT

■ **Atlanta, USA**
Logistics and industrial areas adjacent to Hartsfield–Jackson Atlanta International Airport, GA, USA. Photo by Google Maps

PART I | FOR PRODUCTION'S SAKE

sprawl of industry to the suburbs and rural areas has further contributed to the lack of consideration given to manufacturing in city planning. The city was perceived as a place of living, consumption, and leisure and the periphery as the space of production.

These three types – integrated, adjacent, and autonomous – demonstrate the increasing separation of manufacturing from the city, the strengthening of the central management of industrial zones, and the growing influence of international companies on local economies and physical spaces. Programmatic and geographic changes in the urban region accompany this split between cities. As a whole, these three spatial types manifest economic development, and the political and spatial relationship between city and industry highlighting three main trends (Hatuka et al., 2014). The most notable trend is a *shift of industry away from the city*. This process began with the concept of strengthening the region at the beginning of the 20th

Common Industrial Type: Patterns, Order and Geography

Type		Structure	Land Use
Autonomous	This type is characterized by large-scale zones occupied by uniform industrial buildings and surrounded by various physical boundaries.	Unified	Zoning
Adjacent	The organizational outline of the adjacent type is based on zoning and the separation between living and working.	Parallel	Partial zoning
Integrated	The key feature of this type is symbiosis between living and working.	Layered	Mixed

century. Following the models of the Garden City, the Industrial City, and the Radiant City, this trend was reinforced by a strengthening global economy that favored the autonomous model, which was centralized and not dependent on location. A second trend is the bolstering of the *centralized management* model, particularly the growing power of international companies and their impact on local economies. These forces changed the types of industrial areas, enhancing the development of the centrally managed industrial park, with its academic-technological image. A third trend is prioritizing the development of *specialized industrial environments*, which are associated with the promotion of science and are considered "innovative" and "clean." They express the desire to create a place that is "out of place," a sterile environment, with neither context nor history, which could be located anywhere around the globe.

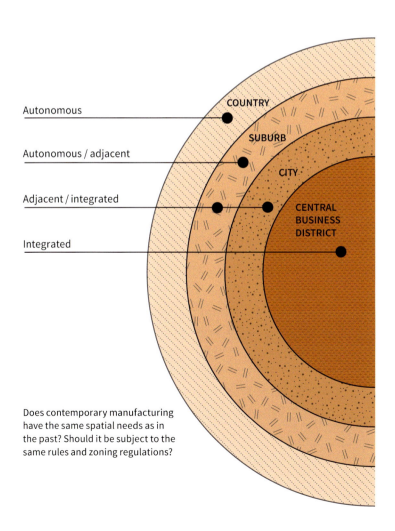

Does contemporary manufacturing have the same spatial needs as in the past? Should it be subject to the same rules and zoning regulations?

Designing a City-Industry Dynamic for the 21st Century

Manufacturing constitutes a significant share of the world's total economic activity, and industry occupies large areas of our built environment, yet we tend to think of industry in an economic or political context divorced from geographic, locational, or spatial considerations. The outcome is a rather unsophisticated relationship between industry and the city. However, as the global sustainability movement has taken root, all sectors of society have come under scrutiny for their potential to reduce human-driven climate change. Private actors in industry are reacting strongly, not only complying with environmental regulations but also seeking opportunities to strengthen their ethos of corporate responsibility while enhancing the bottom line. New thinking on supply chain management, especially with regard to local production, is beginning to take root, supplanting modernist concepts of separating the phases of production. Cities are recognizing the opportunities that industry can bring, especially in terms of job creation. Technology makes it possible to once again introduce urban manufacturing (The Economist, 2012). Indeed, no one can predict what future manufacturing will require, but cities are beginning to respond to manufacturers' needs by establishing the right conditions and embracing a new extant urban industry. In short, a major opportunity to redefine the role of industry in the city is emerging, making it as much a part of the urban fabric as housing and commerce are.

There are four central challenges to taking full advantage of this opportunity. First, a conceptual challenge: with the rapid growth of biotechnology, internet-related digital media, and digital fabrication, there is pervasive confusion regarding terminology. What exactly do we mean when we speak of "industry, "manufacturing," or "production?" (Cohen et al., 2007). The second challenge is public awareness. The public's lack of exposure to modern industry often results in outdated, negative perceptions about industrial activity that tend to linger. The third challenge is the lack of

progressive planning policies, including local and regional industrial policies that encourage the return of industry to urban sites, and tools for the retention and attraction of manufacturers in cities (Leigh and Hoelzel, 2012). The fourth difficulty is the spatial challenge caused by the limited and declining supply of centrally located urban land that is zoned for industry.

Three key reasons should not prevent us from dealing with these challenges and addressing manufacturing in our cities. The first reason is *production*. Fundamentally, urban manufacturing provides products and job creation in cities that lack economic opportunity. When manufacturers began to move their operations from the city to the suburbs to reduce costs, they separated the factories from the city's workforce, creating a "spatial mismatch" between class and income. The commuting costs of the working class increased, which negatively impacted access. Bringing manufacturing jobs back to the core city could mitigate the harmful effects of industrial sprawl (i.e. the densification of existing fabrics) and integrate a variety of people into the labor market.

The second reason is *growth*. Urban manufacturing offers a chance to locate living-wage jobs where people live, something that has been overlooked by smart growth advocates who have concentrated on employment in a post-industrial economy (Leigh and Hoelzel, 2012). Measurable environmental benefits are associated with shortening commutes and reducing delivery distances between firms. Proximity can bolster the strength of economic clusters thanks to the positive effects of knowledge spillover and a robust labor market. Manufacturing's multiplier far exceeds that of service jobs. For every job gained or lost, two to three supporting jobs are similarly affected. Promoting urban manufacturing is also good fiscal policy, as cities can generate additional revenue by allowing industrial land to be used efficiently.

The third reason is *livability*. There is a visceral quality to urban manufacturing that is essential to place-making and civic pride in cities with an industrial core. Livability is about connecting to the means of production and tapping into the city's creative and constructive spirit. By implementing recycling models between plants and promoting a multidimensional resource management model, cities built on industry celebrate their past, present, and future as centers of production. In addition, technology can help cities to face and tackle the many nuisances that factories do create.

3

The Way Forward:
New Industrial Urbanism

■ Planning the Way Forward

Strategies

What physical planning and design strategies should cities pursue to retain, attract, and increase manufacturing activity?

Regulations

Should contemporary manufacturing be subjected to the same rules and zoning regulations as it predecessors?

Design

What criteria should be considered when designing a flexible new industrial areas?

Aerial view of western HafenCity and Speicherstadt, Hamburg Germany. Photo by Thomas Fries (CC-BY-SA-3.0).

3

The Way Forward: New Industrial Urbanism

Cities need industry, argue Jessica Ferm and Edward Jones (2017), "to keep the city functioning, to provide goods and services to its business and residents, to deal with its waste, to provide materials for its construction, and so on" (ibid.: 6). Yet, although this sounds obvious, it is not a simple, local task. Industrial development does not take place in a void, but exists in the context of an increasingly interconnected, globalized world. As the profitability of traditional manufacturing diminishes, entry into the next phase of industrial modernization has become imperative for many countries around the world. Importing manufactured consumer goods and intermediate goods (e.g. steel) that were previously manufactured locally has become commonplace. This trend has led to job losses in the manufacturing sectors of many advanced economies; thus, the United States, for example, lost almost 41% of its manufacturing jobs between 1979 and 2010 (Helper et al., 2012: 3). Partially in response to regional problems of unemployment, and because the economic drivers of offshore manufacturing have lessened due to wage increases in developing economies (Helper et al., 2012), some advanced industrial nations have initiated policies to promote domestic production (De Backer et al., 2015: 29; Kotkin, 2012; Northam, 2014). The need to pay attention to the dynamic of manufacturing and its impact on employment is also supported by scholars who claim that manufacturing remains vital to local, regional, and national economic growth, and acts as "the 'flywheel of growth' because the rate of growth of manufacturing output tends to drive the rate of productivity growth in manufacturing and in services" (Pike, 2009: 59; see also Manyika et al., 2012). This perspective is gaining recognition, particularly with the development of novel technologies which require new specializations and skilled labor both for their production and their application (Pisano and Shih, 2012; Plant, 2013).

Seeking a competitive advantage through digitization, the incorporation of robotics, and the employment of fewer but more highly skilled workers, a number of countries are now trying to cultivate some of the conditions that make it advantageous for manufacturers to move their facilities back to urban areas. The idea is to view the current phase of industrial modernization, which relies on access to skilled workers, proximity to places of innovation (e.g. educational institutions), and government funding (often filtered through educational institutions), as an opportunity to regenerate urban areas and redefine the role of industry in the city.

In this process of redefinition, most strategies, policies, and even government-supported industrial developments focus on economic incentives (e.g. tax incentives, recruitment of firms or national research and development (R&D) assets) and rarely include consideration of physical planning and environmental design. Indeed, manufacturing, whether advanced or

New Key Concepts in Industrial Development

New Industrial Urbanism

Urban manufacturing
Cleaner, quieter industry with a small footprint
Live-work communities
Mixed-uses

Industry 4.0

Additive manufacturing
Digital fabrication
Automation
Artificial Intelligence

Industrial Ecosystem

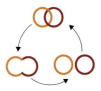

Cross sectoral collaboration
Scaling up and down the supply chain
Clustering

Industrial Ecology

Zero waste
By-product reuse
Sustainability

traditional, is much more than an economic challenge. It should be viewed as a complex sociopolitical project that includes four related dimensions; the *economy*: increasing global competition between cities and regions for investments and projects; *society*: unemployment as a side effect of globalization and the transfer of production to emerging markets and developing economies; *planning*: demographic growth along with a trend toward rapid urbanization; and the *environment*: changes in consumption and the cost of energy in the transportation of goods.

Accordingly, we suggest that economists' quantitative, abstract framework be extended into a concrete, comparative, multilevel analysis that includes the physical environment. This framework must focus on the future possible relationships between cities and industry, and between current urban planning practices and the places that are being dedicated to the production of goods. More specifically, it looks at the spatial implications and physical manifestation of contemporary manufacturing in the city: What physical planning and design strategies should cities pursue to retain, attract, and increase manufacturing activity? Should contemporary manufacturing be subjected to the same rules and zoning regulations as its predecessors? What criteria should be considered when designing flexible new industrial areas? These questions are both epistemological – i.e. they concern the way we conceptualize industry today – and methodological – namely, they will influence how we act and respond to these challenges. In addressing these questions, manufacturing, whether advanced or traditional, should be viewed as a complex sociopolitical project, as a "New Industrial Urbanism," to help develop future cities.

New Industrial Urbanism is a concept that focuses on cities. It refers to typologies in which industrial areas are integrated into the city, and offers an alternative to the autonomous industrial park, which contributes to extra-urban and suburban sprawl (Hatuka and Ben-Joseph, 2017). It is based on the premise that technological evolution is altering manufacturing's physical footprint, distribution processes and networks, access to transportation, and preferred geographical locations. It is shaping the city's physical form through the idea that an urban location confers a competitive advantage thanks to access to skilled labor, educational institutions (centers of research and experimentation), and customers (Hatuka and Ben-Joseph, 2017; Hatuka et al., 2017; Lane and Rappaport, 2020; Love, 2017; Rappaport, 2011). Embracing this concept might have a significant effect on the local economy, as demand for industrial land within cities, especially near academic institutions, becomes more valuable to manufacturers, including knowledge-intensive manufacturers. This concept also affects the local, social sphere; it "empower[s] small and medium-sized firms and individual entrepreneurs" (Markillie, 2012: n.p.), and it may make it increasingly possible to "buy local," thereby buttressing localism. One of the primary challenges this trend brings to light is the extent to which cities' zoning codes must be reformed in order to facilitate the mixing of land uses that include industrial and commercial properties. The New Industrial Urbanism is linked to three overarching concepts of contemporary industrial development, *Industry 4.0, industrial ecosystems,* and *industrial ecology.*

The term "Industry 4.0" refers to digitization in manufacturing processes and consumer goods. It includes technological innovations ranging from artificial intelligence and autonomous machines to biotechnology, among other things (Reynolds, 2017; Schwab, 2015). Industry 4.0 is viewed as a phase in industry that encourages and supports fusion, collaboration, and crossovers in learning and knowledge transfer between different types of manufacturers. This phenomenon encourages the development of new, intersectional technologies and products (Reynolds, 2017; Schwab, 2015). Furthermore, this type of technological development promises greater energy efficiency and cleaner, quieter industrial processes (Love, 2017). Unmitigated, Industry 4.0 may boost inequality because it may have the highest demand for highly educated workers and low-skilled workers (especially in the service sector), and far less for those between the

two: somewhat educated, moderately skilled workers (Schwab, 2015). These trends might put pressure on the middle class, often perceived as a stabilizing force within society. Thus, Industry 4.0 is viewed as both an opportunity and a challenge: cities will aim to maintain balance by courting advanced manufacturers and supporting traditional manufacturers.

Another concept that cultivates cooperation and exchanges is the "industrial ecosystem," which considers the manufacturing sector as an ecosystem (or several ecosystems) and encourages relationships and exchanges (Berger, 2013; Berger and Sharp, 2013; Cortright, 2006; Mills et al., 2008). This is done by developing "clusters" within a geographical area, which may be grouped by product, and include firms that participate in different points in the product's production (i.e. up and down the supply chain). This trend views the economy of a region and its manufacturers as a system and aims to encourage innovation and, in turn, growth through the collaboration of manufacturers, educational institutions (especially universities), and governmental agencies/organizations (Etzkowitz, 2012). In addition, it emphasizes the relationships between high-tech and low-tech manufacturers, and sees manufacturer diversity as an important, if not central, component of the system (Hansen and Winther, 2011). Social capital is especially important to this trend, and, within the social sphere, it encourages: (1) cross-sector relationships between academia and industry, government and academia, and government and industry; (2) cross-scale relationships between entrepreneurs and established firms, or small and medium firms and large firms; and (3) up- and downstream relationships between suppliers and producers. One of the key challenges in implementing this concept is leadership, often taken by a university. Major research universities (e.g. Massachusetts Institute of Technology and Harvard University in Cambridge, MA; Duke University, North Carolina State University, and the University of North Carolina at Chapel Hill in the Research Triangle region of North Carolina) have led successful efforts to collaborate across sectors in a number of cities that might be said to have an industrial ecosystem.

The last concept, "industrial ecology," is the development of industrial projects based on environmental considerations, especially with goals of sustainability, energy efficiency, and waste reduction (Deutz and Gibbs, 2008; Kalundborg Symbiosis, 1972; McManus and Gibbs, 2008). For the economy, industrial ecology means increasing efficiency (e.g. improving energy production and use, water production and use) and establishing more sustainable, closed systems that eliminate waste. These changes reduce costs and yield savings. In the social sphere, this idea may be used as a branding strategy to influence public perception and opinion. Industrial ecology also involves the practice of reducing industrial waste by establishing a loop in which one manufacturer uses the by-products of another, and so on (Gibbs and Deutz, 2007). Spatially, eco-industrial parks are typically autonomous industrial parks that are committed to this practice in principle and to other environmentally conscious practices (e.g. green building technology, solar power generation and use of solar power, greater energy efficiency). One of the main challenges, though, is the frequency with which top-down planning fails to lay the groundwork for the recycling loops that underpin industrial ecology. Loops work best when established through bilateral agreements between firms, in response to particular needs, which is to say, when they are driven by market requirements.

New Industrial Urbanism and the three related concepts, Industry 4.0, industrial ecosystems, and industrial ecology aim at impacting industrial development in similar ways. First, they tend to *value proximity in developing industrial areas*. According to these concepts, being near firms in the same or related industries is viewed as improving firms' access to "specialized workers, suppliers, and customers," as well as to institutions that support their work (e.g. academic institutions and research centers) (Helper et al., 2012: 2). It further presumes that relationships and intersections, or crossovers, create an ecosystem. The cate-

gorization of firms as either manufacturers or service providers reflects antiquated economic thinking and classifications, especially in OECD countries (De Backer et al., 2015: 29). This position is further supported by studies showing that: (1) strong manufacturing does not require low-wage labor; (2) dense ecosystems preserve jobs by dissuading companies from relocating or shifting jobs elsewhere; and (3) real innovation occurs in scaling up firms and rebuilding the capabilities of the industrial ecosystem (Berger, 2013). Second, these concepts point to *the increasing power of localism and community*. Technological change is viewed as empowering small and medium-sized firms and individual entrepreneurs (Markillie, 2012). This trend toward localism does not mean, however, that large multinational firms will relocate their operations to their countries of origin (Pisano and Shih, 2012). Rather, for large multinational firms, expanding markets (especially in emerging economies) will be more attractive than lower labor costs (De Backer et al., 2015: 13). Third, these concepts point to the need *for adaptive and resilient land use regulations* in the planning strategies of cities. A major factor in manufacturers' site selection is the speed of delivery to customers; manufacturers are increasingly choosing locations based not on land costs but rather on labor availability and access to transportation (which affects the speed of delivery). This shift suggests that manufacturers are willing to compete to purchase land in mixed-use zones that permit industrial uses. Nonetheless, land use, zoning regulations, and building codes continue to prevent manufacturers of various types of products (from pharmaceuticals to food products) from building factories in cities (Hatuka and Ben-Joseph, 2017; Love, 2017).

To conclude, these concepts are changing industrial development and are influencing economic geography, society, and planning.

3 | THE WAY FORWARD

■ Contemporary Manufacturing as Multifaceted Challenge

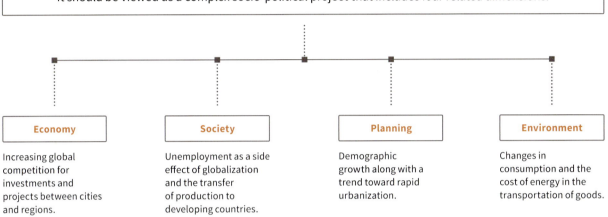

Manufacturing, whether advanced or traditional, is much more than an economic challenge. It should be viewed as a complex socio-political project that includes four related dimensions:

Economy
Increasing global competition for investments and projects between cities and regions.

Society
Unemployment as a side effect of globalization and the transfer of production to developing countries.

Planning
Demographic growth along with a trend toward rapid urbanization.

Environment
Changes in consumption and the cost of energy in the transportation of goods.

Bukit Merah, Singapore. Photo by chuttersnap on Unsplash (CC).

65

From Overarching Concepts to Policy Initiatives

Governments and cities are certainly not indifferent to key trends and changes in industry. They express their reactions in policies used to encourage industrial development, land allocations, and planning strategies for hosting and cultivating industries. So what are policymakers doing? Although it is impossible to map all policies, and policies are clearly embedded in local political and economic contexts, it is possible to categorize generic strategies using their underlying intentions and goals. When categorizing strategies according to their declared goals, one can identify four generic strategies and related policies: collaboration, specialization, balance, and conversion.

Collaboration. A strategy that focuses on collaboration addresses the region as a platform for innovation and development. Viewing a metropolitan area and its manufacturers as a system, this strategy aims to encourage innovation and, in turn, growth through the collaboration of manufacturers, educational institutions (especially academic institutions), and governmental agencies/organizations (Etzkowitz, 2012). This approach emphasizes the relationships between high-tech and low-tech manufacturers, and sees manufacturer diversity as an important, if not central, component of economic growth (Hansen and Winther, 2011). Policies associated with this strategy view universities, for example, as innovation and development accelerators. The economic role of educational institutions and the potential of public–private partnerships and institutional–corporate partnerships to propel growth are stressed (Youtie and Shapira, 2008). The New England Council and its collaboration with the Massachusetts Institute of Technology (MIT), Harvard University, and financiers to form the venture capital firm American Research and Development Corporation (ARD) in 1946 to commercialize inventions made at MIT and Harvard exemplifies this strategy (Etzkowitz, 2012: 769).

Manufacturing USA with its 14 specialized institutes for innovation in manufacturing, each one a public–private partnership, is similarly representative. One of the 14 institutes is Lightweight Innovations for Tomorrow (LIFT), which is based in Detroit, Michigan and operated by the American Lightweight Materials Manufacturing Innovation Institute (ALMMII). Funded by a broad consortium that includes federal and state agencies, manufacturers, professional organizations, and educational institutions, its goal is to revolutionize the process for manufacturing lightweight materials. The Advanced Robotics for Manufacturing (ARM) Institute in Pittsburgh, Pennsylvania, another of the 14 institutes of Manufacturing USA with a similar funding structure, seeks to spur the early, rapid adoption of robotic technologies in select manufacturing industries (e.g. textiles). Moreover, collaborative policies consider entrepreneurs stimulators of growth and call for investment in initiatives to attract and develop entrepreneurs (Hart, 2008). For example, former New York City Mayor Michael Bloomberg "issued a request for proposals, open to universities everywhere, to locate an engineering school with an entrepreneurial training component in [New York City]" as a means of generating new businesses and varied jobs (Etzkowitz, 2012: 766). The winning proposal came from Cornell University and the Technion – Israel Institute of Technology. Opened in 2017, Cornell Tech, which includes the Joan & Irwin Jacobs Technion–Cornell Institute, focuses on interdisciplinary research germane to the digital age, such as human–computer interaction, artificial intelligence, as well as data and modeling.

Specialization. This is a generic name for the cluster development strategy, which often comprises policies or initiatives intended to stimulate regional economic growth by identifying and further developing the clusters anchored in a select metropolitan area (Burfitt and MacNeill, 2008; Wolman and Hincapie, 2015; see also U.S. Cluster Mapping Project). Wolman and Hincapie (2015) list several policies and tools that scholars (Cortright, 2006; Feser, 2008; Mills et al., 2008; Rosenfeld, 1997) have suggested governments should use to support a cluster development strategy. These include "support cluster expansion through recruiting companies that fill gaps in cluster development";

"develop and organize supply chain associations"; and "represent cluster interests before external organizations such as regional development partnerships, national trade associations, and local, state, and federal governments" (Wolman and Hincapie, 2015: 141; see the same paper for a complete list). Examples that fall under this category include initiatives in Austin, Texas; Pittsburgh, Pennsylvania; and Los Angeles, California. The Austin Chamber of Commerce, the city government, and the University of Texas at Austin recruited high-tech firms, including Dell, Motorola, IBM, Advanced Micro Devices, and Applied Materials, to open branches or start their businesses in Austin (Youtie and Shapira, 2008: 1193). In Pittsburgh, the Allegheny Conference on Community Development is currently trying to create a manufacturing hub well-positioned within the natural gas supply chain as part of its initiative to expand and attract businesses to the metropolitan area and to create jobs (Allegheny Conference on Community Development, 2015). Another example is the automotive design cluster in Los Angeles: it is a consortium led by the Los Angeles County Economic Development Corporation, which established the Advanced Transportation Center of Southern California in response to emerging trends by promoting new, green technologies and autonomous vehicles (Los Angeles County Economic Development Corporation, 2017). The hope is that this center will lead to the creation of new, high-paying, high-skilled jobs. Finally, the industrial ecology cluster development policy plans to reduce industrial waste by establishing a loop in which one manufacturer uses the by-products of another (McManus and Gibbs, 2008). This often implies the construction of designated eco-industrial parks.

Balance. This strategy calls for using a set of policy tools to encourage the even spatial distribution of industry throughout a region (Labrianidis and Papamichos, 1990). It comprises many common policies that may be perceived as bread-and-butter economic development policies, including policies that incentivize investment in metropolitan areas' poorer communities, both in terms of prevailing socioeconomic conditions and lack of industrial assets and infrastruc-

ture. Policy tools include, but are not limited to, tax increment financing, tax-exempt bond financing, and the designation of special industrial zones or districts. For example, the city of Chicago assists businesses in distressed areas through tax increment financing (Chicago Department of Planning and Development, 2017), while the city of Houston has established Texas Enterprise Zones, distressed areas that it wants to revitalize by supporting businesses that have committed to these areas through rebates. Within the zones, the state of Texas and the city of Houston refund companies' state sales and use taxes on qualified expenditures in proportion to companies' capital investments and the number of local jobs they create (Texas Wide Open for Business, 2017).

Conversion. These strategies aim to convert industrial resources (e.g. land, facilities) within a region from one purpose (e.g. steel production) to another (e.g. the manufacture of aeronautics) or to the production of many different products. This was the strategy policymakers adopted in Mechanic Valley in southwest France (Guillaume and Doloreux, 2011: 1139–1141). Initiatives using these strategies include the issuing of Industrial Development Revenue Bonds by the city of Chicago. Proceeds from these tax-exempt bonds may be used to fund construction or renovation(s). Another example is the Power of 32 Site Development Fund, an initiative of Pittsburgh's Allegheny Conference on Community Development. The fund leads an effort to provide favorable mortgages for the preparation of select sites that have the potential to markedly affect the regional economy (Allegheny Conference on Community Development).

In addition to these existing policies, new policies are emerging in response to the Fourth Industrial Revolution. Most of them address the interlink between *labor* (society) and *production* (economy) (Autor et al., 2020; Helper et al., 2021). In terms of labor, emphasis is placed on: (1) skills and training supported by new technologies, including online instruction, AI-based guided learning systems, and virtual reality tools, which offer innovative ways to make training more ac-

PART I | FOR PRODUCTION'S SAKE

▰ Strategies in Industrial Development

Balance

Focus	|	Regional development
Aim	|	Encourage development in underdeveloped/underserved areas
Policies	|	Local context requirements, tax relief, financial incentives

Collaboration

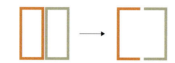

Focus	|	Regional innovation
Aim	|	Stimulate growth
Policies	|	R&D investment, university-led R&D, entrepreneurship

Specialization

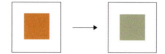

Focus	|	Cluster development
Aim	|	Develop a place-based expertise and make a place synonymous with an industry
Policies	|	Formation of trade associations; workforce development, marketing and branding, industrial ecology, eco-industrial parks

Conversion

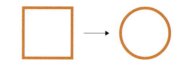

Focus	|	Industrial conversion
Aim	|	Redevelop disused industrial facilities and land
Policies	|	Tax relief, financial incentives

cessible, affordable, and engaging for students, workers, and job seekers at all stages of the lifecycle; (2) job quality improvement, with a focus on low-paid service jobs: cleaning and grounds keeping, food service, security, entertainment and recreation, and home health assistance (ibid.); (3) future labor and encouraging the next generation to embark on a manufacturing career through incentives like subsidized tuition for training and education in work-based learning such as apprenticeships. In terms of production, emphasis is placed on : (1) innovation expansion by generating economic growth, building areas of educational and research excellence, and spurring new work creation; (2) development of manufacturing ecosystems to create the positive spillovers that come from a regionally connected system for educating and training workers.

Governments often adopt strategies or policies that blend elements from these varied strategies. Thus, it is common to find strategies for developing clusters as part of a broader regional innovation approach. Tools that governments sometimes use when pursuing a regional development strategy or a strategy of industrial conversion include the establishment of local content requirements, or regulatory requirements that stipulate the "extent to which projects must use local products" (Johnson, 2015: abstract). Financial incentives, especially various forms of tax relief, are tools frequently used by governments when pursuing any of these strategies, but especially regional development. In short, the above strategies should not be seen as autonomous and/or standalone, but rather as dynamic strategies that are often used and adjusted simultaneously to develop a region.

In that respect, government policies do occasionally enhance and support new industrial urbanism, especially through economic development strategies for cultivating cross-sector collaborations and partnerships in metropolitan areas. Additionally, these strategies are sometimes used as a means to disperse industrial investment across a metropolitan area in a balanced way or to convert older facilities into new industrial uses.

The Future of Industry: From Parallel Initiatives to an Integrated Framework

Over the last decade, some cities, including Vancouver, Chicago, London, and San Francisco, to name a few, have been perspicacious in responding to changes in the manufacturing sector, the new opportunities that technological evolution presents, and threats to industrial land (Chicago Department of Planning and Development, 2014; Mayor of London, 2012; San Francisco Planning Department, 2002; Port of Vancouver, 2014). To be sure, these cities, with their industrial legacies, remind us that the role and configuration of industry in cities has been evolving for more than two centuries. Current trends are but another phase in this ongoing process.

There is no doubt that technology is a driving force behind many of the changes in the configuration and composition of cities. As in previous industrial revolutions, technology remains an influential force shaping the built environment, culture, the economy, and politics. From the perspective of society, it seems that there will be profound changes in the types of products available, and the ways in which they are manufactured and consumed. Technology will continue to dramatically change everyday life, including people's occupations and, relatedly, their socioeconomic status. Indeed, like prior revolutions in industry, progress belies problems: many people may be left behind by the changes of the Fourth Industrial Revolution, accelerating social fracture. As Schwab argues, in today's job market, there is "a strong demand at the high and low ends, but a hollowing out of the middle" and "this helps explain why so many workers are disillusioned and fearful that their own real incomes and those of their children will continue to stagnate" (Schwab, 2015).

From the perspective of development, the concepts of the Fourth Industrial Revolution, the industrial ecosystem, industrial urbanism, and industrial ecology are changing manufacturers' calculations with regard to the importance of location (i.e. center versus periphery) and community. These dynamics are leading manufacturers and civic leaders to question regulations, and this reflection is making adaptive and resilient land use regulations and building codes (i.e. form-based codes) highly desirable.

In addressing these trends, we should be concerned about two points. First, investigating the relationship between industrial cities' contemporary contexts (i.e. changing labor markets, innovation, and technological developments) and the regrowth of cities and metropolitan areas, in an effort to redesign the role of industry in the city. Second, a holistic view of city and industry should be adopted as a mean for producing a new understanding of the relationship between working and living. These evolving relationships call for conceptualizing a new approach that addresses urban land use strategies in the context of a wider economic framework, while also addressing development and workforce objectives as a way to minimize mismatches among workforce, community revitalization, and city-wide economic development goals (Mistry and Byron, 2011: 4). Thus, re-evaluating manufacturing should be a primary goal of planners, urban designers, and architects. Awareness of this goal is critical to the future development of cities worldwide.

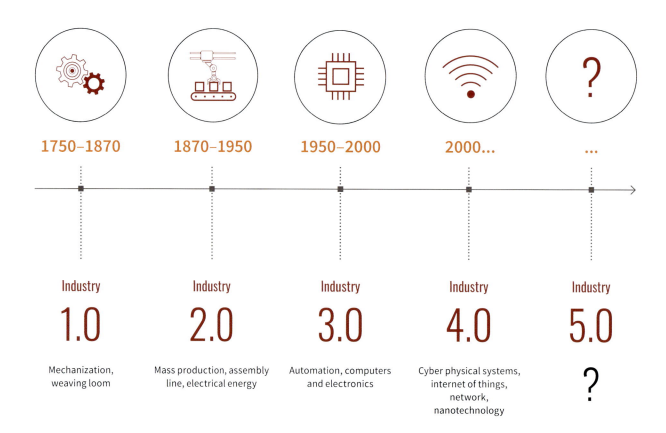

■ The Industrial Revolutions

C | THE WAY FORWARD

1908
Rhodes Manufacturing Co., Lincolnton, NC, USA 1908. Photo by Lewis Hine, U.S. Library of Congress.

1942
Consolidated Aircraft Corporation plant, Fort Worth, Texas, USA 1942. Photo by Howard R. Hollem, U.S. Library of Congress.

1957
An IBM 704 electronic data processing machine at NACA, Langley VA, USA 1957. Photo by NASA.

2020
Low-Energy Resolution Inelastic X-ray (LERIX) system at the Advanced Photon Source (APS), Argonne National Laboratory, Lemont, Illinois USA. Photo by US Department of Energy on Unsplash.

References

Ackermann, Kurt, and Michelle Spong. 1991. *Building for Industry*. Godalming: Watermark.

Allegheny Conference on Community Development. 2015. "Our Work: 2015–2017 Agenda: Connecting People to Opportunity." Allegheny Conference on Community Development. www.alleghenyconference.org/our-work/#Economy

Anderson, Stanford. 2000. *Peter Behrens and a New Architecture for the Twentieth Century*. Cambridge, MA: MIT Press.

Autor, David, David Mindell, and Elisabeth Reynolds. 2020. *The Work of the Future: Building Better Jobs in an Age of Intelligent Machines*. Cambridge, MA: MIT Press.

Barnes, Roy C. 2001. "The Rise of Corporatist Regulation in the English and Canadian Dairy Industries." *Social Science History* 25, no. 3: 381–406.

Berger, Suzanne. 2013. "An Overview of the PIE Study." Filmed September 20, 2013 at Production in the Innovation Economy Conference at the Massachusetts Institute of Technology, Cambridge, MA. Video, http://web.mit.edu/pie/america/index.html

Berger, Suzanne, and Philip Sharp. 2013. "A Preview of the MIT Production in the Innovation Economy Report." Task Force on Innovation in the Production Economy, MIT. Available at http://web.mit.edu/pie/news/PIE_Preview.pdf

Biggs, Lindy. 1996. *The Rational Factory: Architecture, Technology, and Work in America's Age of Mass Production*. Baltimore, MD: Johns Hopkins University Press.

Bradley, Betsy H. 1999. *The Works: The Industrial Architecture of the United States*. New York: Oxford University Press.

Burfitt, Alex, and Stuart MacNeill. 2008. "The Challenges of Pursuing Cluster Policy in the Congested State." *International Journal of Urban and Regional Research* 32, no. 2: 492–505.

Chicago Department of City Planning. 1965. *Basic Policies for the Comprehensive Plan of Chicago: A Summary for Citizen Review*. Chicago, IL: Chicago Department of City Planning.

Chicago Department of Housing and Economic Development. 2011. *Chicago Sustainable Industries*. Chicago, IL. www.cityofchicago.org/content/dam/city/depts/zlup/Sustainable_Development/Publications/Chicago_Sustainable_Industries/Chicago_Sustainable_Book.pdf

Chicago Department of Planning and Development. 2014. *Fulton Market Innovation District*. Chicago, IL. https://www.chicago.gov/content/dam/city/depts/zlup/Sustainable_Development/Publications/Fulton-Randolph%20Market%20Land%20Use%20Plan/FMID_Plan_Web.pdf

Chicago Department of Planning and Development. 2017. *Economic Development Incentives*. Chicago, IL: Chicago Department of City Planning. www.chicago.gov/city/en/depts/dcd/supp_info/economic_developmentincentives.html

Cohen, Peter, Mark Klaiman, and the Back Streets Businesses San Francisco Advisory Board to the Board of Supervisors and the Mayor. 2007. "Made in San Francisco." https://sfgov.org/sfc/bsbab/Modules/BStrRepor07__fbb0.pdf

Cortright, Joseph. 2006. "Making Sense of Clusters: Regional Competitiveness and Economic Development." The Brookings Institution. www.brookings.edu/research/making-sense-of-clusters-regional-

Costa, Xavier. 1997. "Lingotto." *Quaderns d'arquitectura i urbanisme* 218: 91–94.

Darley, Gillian. 2003. *Factory*. London: Reaktion Books.

Davis, Howard. 2020. *Working Cities: Architecture, Place and Production*. New York: Routledge.

De Backer, Koen, Isabelle Desnoyers-James, and Laurent Moussiegt. 2015. "Manufacturing or Services: That Is (Not) the Question." www.oecd-ilibrary.org/science-and-technology/manufacturing-or-services-

Deutz, Pauline, and David Gibbs. 2008. "Industrial Ecology and Regional Development: Eco-Industrial Development as Cluster Policy." *Regional Studies* 42, no. 10: 1313–1328.

Driemeier, Kale, Nathanael Hoelzel, Rahul Jain, Jodi Mansbach, Edward Morrow, Charlie Moseley, Shelley Stevens and Ermis Zayas. 2009. *A Plan for Industrial Land and Sustainable Industry in the City of Atlanta*. Atlanta, GA: School of City and Regional Planning, Georgia Institute of Technology.

Economist, The. 2012. "Special Report Manufacturing and Innovation: A Third Industrial Revolution." www.economist.com/node/21552901

Etzkowitz, Henry. 2012. "Triple Helix Clusters: Boundary Permeability at University–Industry–Government Interfaces as a Regional Innovation Strategy." *Environment and Planning C* 30: 766–779.

Ferm, Jessica, and Edward Jones. 2017. "Beyond the Post-Industrial City: Valuing and Planning for Industry in London." *Urban Studies* 54, no. 14: 1–19.

Feser, Edward. 2008. "On Building Clusters versus Leveraging Synergies in the Design of Innovation Policy for Developing Economies." In *The Economics of Regional Clusters: Networks, Technology, and Policy*, edited by Blien Uwe and Gunter Maier, 191–213. Cheltenham: Edward Elgar.

Flink, James J. 1988. *The Automobile Age*. Cambridge, MA: MIT Press.

Garnier, Tony. 1917. *Une cité industrielle: étude pour la construction des villes*. Paris: Auguste Vincent.

Gibbs, David, and Pauline Deutz. 2007. "Reflections on Implementing Industrial Ecology through Eco-Industrial Park Development." *Journal of Cleaner Production* 15: 1683–1695.

Giedion, Siegfried. 1992. *Walter Gropius*. New York: Dover Publications.

Guillaume, Régis, and David Doloreux. 2011. "Production Systems and Innovation in 'Satellite' Regions: Lessons from a Comparison between Mechanic Valley (France) and Beauce (Québec)." *International Journal of Urban and Regional Research* 35, no. 6: 1133–1153.

Hansen, Teis, and Lars Winther. 2011. "Innovation, Regional Development and Relations between High- and Low-Tech Industries." *European Urban and Regional Studies* 18, no. 3: 321–339.

Harrington, James, and Barney Warf. 1995. *Industrial Location: Principles, Practice, and Policy*. London: Routledge.

Hart, David M. 2008. "The Politics of 'Entrepreneurial' Economic Development Policy in the U.S. States." *Review of Policy Research* 25, no. 2: 149–168.

Hatuka, Tali. 2011. *The Factory: On Architecture and Industry in Argaman, Yavne*. Tel Aviv: Resling.

Hatuka, Tali, Roni Bar, Merav Battat, Yoav Zilberdik, Carmel Hanany, Shelly Hefetz, Michael Jacobson, and Hila Lothan. 2014. *City–industry*. Tel Aviv: Resling.

Hatuka, Tal and Eran Ben-Joseph. 2014. *Industrial Urbanism: Place of Production*. Exhibition Catalogue, Wolk Gallery, School of Architecture + Planning, Massachusetts Institute of Technology, 5 September–19 December.

Hatuka, Tali, and Eran Ben-Joseph. 2017. "Industrial Urbanism: Typologies, Concepts and Prospects." *Built Environment Journal* 43, no. 1: 10–24.

Hatuka, Tali, Eran Ben-Josef, and Sunny Menozzi. 2017. "Facing Forward: Trends and Challenges in the Development of Industry in Cities." *Built Environment* 43, no. 1: 145–155.

Hatuka, Tali, Gili Inbar, and Zohar Tal. 2020. "Synchronic Typologies: Integrating Industry and Residential Environments in the City of the 21th Century." [Hebrew]. https://drive.google.com/file/d/15sebgmX-VJHmjEAvydrNHnFeO7rOkNszY/view

Helper, Susan, Timothy Krueger, and Howard Wial. 2012. *Locating American Manufacturing: Trends in the Geography of Production*. The Brookings Institution. www.brookings.edu/research/reports/2012/05/09-locating-american-

Helper, Susan, Elisabeth Reynolds, Daniel Traficonte, and Anuraag Singh. 2021. *Factories of the Future: Technology, Skills, and Digital Innovation at Large Manufacturing Firms*. Cambridge, MA: MIT.

Herzberg, Fredrick. 1996. *Work and the Nature of Man*. Cleveland, OH: World Publishing.

Hoselitz, Bert. 1955. "Generative and Parasitic Cities." *Economic Development and Cultural Change* 3, no. 3: 278–294.

Howard, Ebenezer. 1898. *To-Morrow: A Peaceful Path to Real Reform*. London: Swan Sonnenschein.

Hurley, K. Amanda. 2017. "What Should Cities Make?" City Lab. www.citylab.com/work/2017/02/what-should-cities-make/516894/

Jaeggi, Annemarie. 2000. *Fagus: Industrial Culture from Werkbund to Bauhaus*. Translated by E.M. Schwaiger. New York: Princeton Architectural Press.

Johnson, Oliver. 2015. "Promoting Green Industrial Development through Local Content Requirements: India's National Solar Mission." *Climate Policy* 16, no. 2: 178–195.

Kalundborg Symbiosis. 1972. Business Strategy. www.symbiosis.dk/en/

Kim, Minjee, and Eran Ben-Joseph. 2013. "Manufacturing and the City." Paper presented at the Planning for Resilient Cities and Regions AESOP / ACSP Joint Congress. University College Dublin, July 15–19.

Kotkin, Joel. 2012. "Cities Leading an American Manufacturing Revival." *Forbes*, May 24. www.forbes.com/sites/joelkotkin/2012/05/24/seattle-is-leading-an-american-manufacturing-revival/?sh=-1c40e03a3230

Labrianidis, Lois, and Nicos Papamichos. 1990. "Regional Distribution of Industry and the Role of the State in Greece." *Environment and Planning C* 8: 455–476.

Lane, Robert, and Nina Rappaport, eds. 2020. *The Design of Urban Manufacturing*. London: Routledge.

Le Corbusier. [1923] 1970. *Towards a New Architecture*. 1st paperback edition. London: Architectural Press.

Leigh, Nancey Green, and Nathanael Z. Hoelzel. 2012. "Smart Growth's Blind Side." *Journal of the American Planning Association* 78, no. 1: 87–103.

Lever, W. F. 1991. "Deindustrialization and the Reality of the Post-Industrial City." *Urban Studies* 28, no. 6: 983–999.

Los Angeles County Economic Development Corporation. 2017. "Advanced Transportation." Los Angeles County Economic Development Corporation. http://laedc.org/our-services/initiatives/advanced-

Love, Tim. 2017. "A New Model of Hybrid Building as a Catalyst for the Redevelopment of Urban Industrial Districts." *Built Environment* 43, no. 1: 44–57.

Manyika, James, Jeff Sinclair, and Richard Dobbs. 2012. "Manufacturing the Future: The Next Era of Global Growth and Innovation." McKinsey Global Initiative and McKinsey Operations Practice. www.mckinsey.com/~/media/McKinsey/Business%20Functions/Operations/Our%20Insights/The%20future%20of%20manufacturing/MGI_%20Manufacturing_Full%20report_Nov%202012.pdf

Markillie, Paul. 2012. "A Third Industrial Revolution in The Economist." *The Economist*. www.economist.com/node/21552901

Massey, Doreen, and David Wield. 2004. *High-Tech Fantasies: Science Parks in Society, Science and Space*. London: Routledge.

Mayor of London. 2012. "Land for Industry and Transport: Supplementary Planning Guidance." www.london.gov.uk/what-we-do/planning/implementing-london-plan/supplementary-planning-guidance/land-industry-and

McKenzie, R.D. 1924. "The Ecological Approach to the Study of the Human Community." *The American Journal of Sociology* 30, no. 3: 287–301.

McManus, Phil, and David Gibbs. 2008. "Industrial Ecosystems? The Use of Tropes in the Literature of Industrial Ecology and Eco-Industrial Parks." *Progress in Human Geography* 32, no. 4: 525–540.

Mills, Karen, Andrew Reamer, and Elisabeth B. Reynolds. 2008. "Clusters and Competitiveness: A New Federal Role for Stimulating Regional Economies." www.brookings.edu/research/clusters-and-competitiveness-a-

Mistry, Nisha, and Joan Byron. 2011. "The Federal Role in Supporting Urban Manufacturing." www.brookings.edu/research/papers/2011/04/urban-manufacturing-mistry-

Mortensen, Mark, and Martine Haas. 2021. "Making the Hybrid Workplace Fair." *Harvard Business Review*, February 24. https://hbr.org/2021/02/making-the-hybrid-workplace-fair

Northam, Jackie. 2014. "As Overseas Costs Rise, More U.S. Companies Are 'Reshoring'." NPR. www.npr.org/sections/parallels/2014/01/22/265080779/as-overseas-costs-

Oxford English Dictionary. 2020. *Oxford English Dictionary*. Oxford: Oxford University Press.

Pike, Andy. 2009. "De-Industrialisation." In *International Encyclopedia of Human Geography*, edited by Rob Kitchin and Nigel Thrift, 51–59. Oxford: Elsevier.

Pisano, P. Gary, and Willy C. Shih. 2012. "Does America Really Need Manufacturing?" *Harvard Business Review*. https://hbr.org/2012/03/does-america-really-need-manufacturing

Plant, Robert. 2013. "The Experts: Will 3-D Printing Live up to the Hype?" *The Wall Street Journal*, June 14. www.wsj.com/articles/SB10001424127887324688404578541301662510978

Port of Vancouver. 2014. "Vancouver Fraser Port Authority Land Use Plan." www.portvancouver.com/wp-content/uploads/2015/06/port-metro-vancouver-land-use-plan-english.pdf

Porteous, J. Douglas. 1970. "The Nature of the Company Town." *Transactions of the Institute of British Geographers* 51: 127–142.

Powell, Kenneth. 2008. *Richard Rogers: Complete Works*. London: Phaidon Press.

Rappaport, Nina. 2011. "Vertical Urban Factory." *Urban Omnibus*. http://urbanomnibus.net/2011/05/vertical-urban-factory/

Rappaport, Nina. 2015. *Vertical Urban Factory*. New York: Actar.

Raushenbush, Carl. 1937. *Fordism, Ford, and the Community*. New York: League for Industrial Democracy.

Reynolds, Elizabeth. 2017. "Innovation and Production: Advanced Manufacturing Technologies, Trends and Implications for U.S. Cities and Regions." *Built Environment Journal* 43, no. 1: 25–43.

Rogers, Richard, and Richard Burdett. 1996. *Richard Rogers: Partnership Works and Projects*. New York: Monacelli Press.

Rosenfeld, Stuart. 1997. "Bringing Business Clusters into the Mainstream of Economic Development." *European Planning Studies* 5: 3–23.

San Francisco Planning Department. 2002. "Industrial Land in San Francisco: Understanding Production, Distribution, and Repair." http://sf-planning.org/sites/default/files/FileCenter/Documents/4893-CW_DPR_chapter5_2.pdf

San Francisco Planning Department. 2020. "Showplace/SoMa Neighborhood Analysis and Coordination Study." https://sfplanning.org/sites/default/files/documents/citywide/snacs/SNACS_Meeting02_Boards-021220.pdf

Schwab, Klaus. 2015. "The Fourth Industrial Revolution: What It Means and How to Respond." *Foreign Affairs*. www.foreignaffairs.com/articles/2015-12-12/fourth-industrial-revolution

Talbot, E. H. 1904. "Talbot's Industry and Railroad Map of Chicago." https://catalog.lib.uchicago.edu/vufind/Record/1583300

Taylor, Frederick Winslow. 1967. *The Principles of Scientific Management*. New York: The Norton Library.

Taylor, Michael, and Päivi Oinas. 2006. *Understanding the Firm: Spatial and Organizational Dimensions*. Oxford and New York: Oxford University Press.

Texas Wide Open for Business. 2017. "Tax Incentives." https://texaswideopenforbusiness.com/services/tax-incentives

Weber, Max. 1968. *Economy and Society: An Outline of Interpretive Sociology*. Edited by G. Roth and C. Wittich. Vol. 3. New York: Bedminster Press.

Weber, Max. [1927] 1981. *General Economic History*. New Brunswick, NJ: Transaction Books.

Wolman, Harold, and Diana Hincapie. 2015. "Clusters and Cluster-Based Development Policy." *Economic Development Quarterly* 29, no. 2: 135–149.

Youtie, Jan, and Philip Shapira. 2008. "Building an Innovation Hub: A Case Study of the Transformation of University Roles in Regional Technological and Economic Development." *Research Policy* 37: 1188–1204.

Goose Island, Chicago IL, USA. Photo courtesy City of Chicago

PART II

PLACES OF MAKING

PART II

Places of Making

"Places of Making" offers an overview of physical planning and design strategies for the development of industrial areas in cities and regions today. It addresses how technological change is altering manufacturing's physical footprint, architectural spaces, distribution processes and networks, access to transportation, and preferred geographical locations. In particular, this change is transforming the interactions between the location of labor and centers of research and development, markets, and highly skilled labor. What physical planning and design strategies do cities and regions pursue to retain, attract, and increase manufacturing activity? How do these strategies relate to other urban policies? Are these strategies part of a larger vision? In order to respond to these questions, this part addresses city-industry dynamics as an important factor in developing cities. These dynamics are particularly relevant today because of the rising costs of transportation and overseas labor as well as the urgent need to reassess domestic production and localize supply chains in cities worldwide.

Among the various planning strategies initiated in response to contemporary dynamics in industry, three approaches are explained and explored: *clustering*, *reinventing*, and *hybridity*. Using varied examples from the world, we emphasize the significance and implications of their physical and spatial strategies. Although the terminology in each case is context-sensitive, the term "industry" is generalized and unified for the purpose of this exploration. In this part, it refers to the more expansive definition of industrial activities, known as "production, distribution, and repair" (PDR), which includes functions such as construction, manufacturing, wholesale trade, transportation, warehousing, and additional activities that tend to be located in industrially zoned areas (Howland, 2010).

More specifically, Section 4, "Clustering New Industries," presents current trends in agglomeration. These trends evolve around industries such as food tech, biotechnology, and cyber technology that depend on resource- and knowledge-sharing. Consequentially, they benefit from the physical proximity of their main players, including academic institutions. Agglomeration allows for the sharing of services and infrastructure, and also encourages face-to-face interactions during which ideas are exchanged and innovation fostered. Using cases from Wageningen (the Netherlands), Hsinchu (Taiwan), Kista (Sweden), and Cambridge (Massachusetts, USA), this section presents the dominant features and spatial strategies of agglomeration processes, with a focus on management, culture, and place. Section 5, "Reinventing Industrial Areas," focuses on existing industrial sites and strategies of regeneration, reuse, and adaptation. The section includes cases from Jurong (Singapore), Hamburg (Germany), Brooklyn (New York, USA), and Los An-

▪ Key Approaches in Industrial/Urban Development

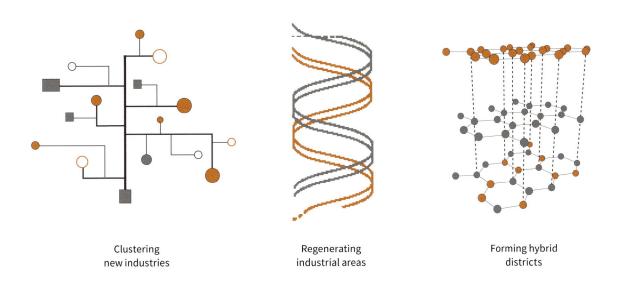

Clustering new industries · Regenerating industrial areas · Forming hybrid districts

geles (California, USA) and addresses their varied spatial approaches with emphasis on growth, culture, and place. Section 6, "Forming Hybrid Districts," is based on the premise that integration and mixing diverse uses is a primary policy for preserving and promoting industrial districts in cities. Hybrid industrial districts support a process of densification, the introduction of new building typologies, variety of land uses, and greater connectivity. Examples include lessons from Barcelona (Spain), Medellín (Colombia), Portland (Oregon, USA), and Shenzhen (China). The final section 7, "Industry and Place," offers a reflection on these three approaches, summarizes their shared premises and strategies and the possible ways they might influence future planning.

Clustering, reinventing, and hybridity do not represent a comprehensive list of approaches to the changing contemporary relationships between city and industry. Nor is the list of cases used to illustrate these approaches comprehensive. They represent the growing recognition of the role industry plays in the world's total economic activity. In addition, none of these approaches excludes any other, and one can find a mix of the three of them in the same location. Furthermore, their application will differ from one context to another. Although one can learn from the cases presented, these cases are not comparable as such, and their study can only suggest lessons to be learned. These cases teach us that industrial development is always contextual and culturally dependent, and it is these variants that contribute to the evolution of different types and forms of industrial ecosystems.

4

Clustering New Industries

Campus of Wageningen University and Research, Wageningen, Netherlands. Photo by Van Gooien (CC BY-SA 4.0).

4

Clustering New Industries

Features of Clustering Industries

Generally, the term "cluster" refers to a grouping of similar things or people positioned or occurring closely together (Malmberg, 2009). Although clusters are often presented in terms of ubiquitous creativity and global communications, they are very much rooted in particular places (O'Connor and Gu, 2010). This approach expands and complements the economic approach to clusters, which views a cluster as a "concentrated density of firms within a geographic region" (Donaldson et al., 2018: 56), characterized by a particular product or service, and often developing hierarchical relationships with other clusters that can span the world (Brown and Mczyski, 2009; Hutton, 2006; Rantisi et al., 2006). Economic perspectives on clusters tend to stress collaboration based on the *triple helix model*, which emphasizes the interactions among three key stakeholders: universities, industries, and governments (Etzkowitz and Leydesdorff, 1995; Etzkowitz, 2012). The triple helix is considered a means to enhance *cluster social networks* that encourage: (1) cross-sector relationships among academia, industry, and government; (2) cross-scale relationships among new entrepreneurs and larger established firms, as well as other, smaller firms; and (3) up- and down-

stream relationships between suppliers and producers (Hatuka et al., 2017).

The density of organizations and firms, the triple helix model, and the agglomeration of social networks allow a cluster to become highly specialized, and increasingly efficient and effective. Each firm hones a specific segment of production (i.e. one point on the supply chain), and companies within a given cluster typically depend on the greater network to which they belong in order to make possible other specialized segments of production (Brown and Mczyski, 2009). As Allen Scott writes, regional economic clusters are "caught up in structures of interdependency stretching across the entire globe" (Scott, 2000: 29). When competing on a global stage, non-codified or tacit knowledge becomes increasingly valuable, since it is difficult to (re)produce and impossible to imitate (Celata and Coletti, 2014).

One of the core features of industrial clusters is interdependency among firms and organizations. Interdependency relies on and strengthens network innovation and, in turn, enhances growth through collaboration (Cicerone et al., 2020). Economic development strategies often comprise policies or initiatives that seek to enhance these elements and other productive efficiencies in order to stimulate regional economic growth. These include supporting "expansion through recruiting companies that fill gaps in cluster development," organizing "supply chain associations," and representing "cluster interests before external organizations such as regional development partnerships, national trade associations, and local, state, and federal governments" (Wolman and Hincapie, 2015: 141).

Yet, as noted, over the last decade there has been a shift from the "economic" being the master signifier of clusters to the actual practices of industries in the city (O'Connor and Gu, 2010). Clusters benefit from and contribute to the image of the city, but they are also embedded in the social and cultural life of the city as place. From this perspective, the complex relationships between clusters of industries and place can evolve anywhere, in varied urban contexts, in mega cities, in smaller towns, and in rural areas. What counts in determining the potential of certain locations to support the growth of the creative economy is not the geography of the place, but rather the relationships among four dimensions of that place: infrastructure (e.g. transport, spaces, local amenities), governance (e.g. policy strategies), soft infrastructure (e.g. culture and identity), and markets (e.g. consumption) (Comunian et al., 2010). Furthermore, from an urban and geographical perspective, clusters are "a socio-spatial assemblage of people, buildings and activities without any necessary center, boundary or scale" (Wood and Dovey, 2015: 54). What is crucial are the *infrastructures* of the physical location. Firms in a given location typically benefit from efficiencies created by *shared infrastructure*, including transportation infrastructure; business networks; research facilities; academic institutions and training facilities; a critical mass of clientele; and complimentary industries and services. In addition, clusters' benefits from colocation include both production and consumption advantages; the mix of public and private actors; diverse leisure, retail, and entertainment offers; and a wider concern with their contribution to and benefit from the image of the city (O'Connor and Gu, 2010).

In addition to infrastructure, *physical proximity* plays a major role in developing a vibrant cluster. It increases the productivity of companies within a given network by driving innovation and stimulating new business. Physical proximity fosters personal relationships, creating a social environment in which it is "safer to take risks" thanks to the "socialization of sharing." Proximity is also associated with *density*, which makes face-to-face meetings easier, and increases the frequency of ad hoc, informal, and often chance encounters in public space (Katz and Shapiro, 1985: 424). Firms also derive advantage from being proximate to a diverse range of complementary industries (Wial et al., 2012). *Diversity* is considered an important, critical component of the system (Hansen and Winther, 2011). The underlying premise of the clustering approach is that proximity to firms in the same or related industries improves firms' access to "specialized workers, suppliers, and customers" as well as to the institutions that support their work, such as universities and research centers. *Social capital* is an especially important aspect of clusters. Sufficient supply of skilled labor and intellectual capital are among the most critical features of successful clusters. *Skilled labor*, too, becomes more specialized as a cluster develops. Training equivalent workforces in different locations becomes more difficult and costly, reinforcing the cluster's gravitational pull and industry dominance (Hatuka and Carmel, 2020).

Thus, proximity plays a leading role in the evolution of clusters, with different industries perceiving and experiencing different levels of "embeddedness" in local infrastructure, networks, governance, and markets (Comunian et al., 2010). As such, the pressing question is not *why* the cluster evolved in a particular location, but *how* the environment served as an incubator for its growth. In the search for an answer to this question, scholars point to the idea of "industrial ecosystems," which posits that production and innovation in a particular place form a multifaceted network, which encourages mutually beneficial relationships and exchanges between and among participating entities. Industrial ecosystems are often described with words such as "buzz," "feel," "atmosphere," and "character,"

4 | CLUSTERING NEW INDUSTRIES

■ Features of Clustering New Industries

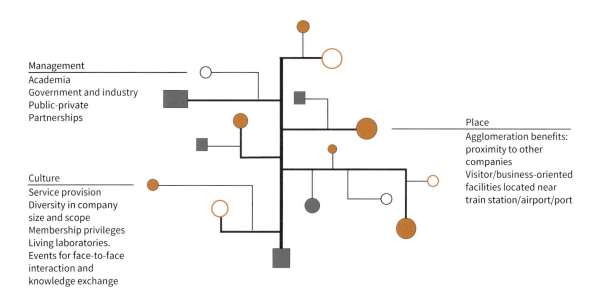

Management
Academia
Government and industry
Public-private
Partnerships

Culture
Service provision
Diversity in company
size and scope
Membership privileges
Living laboratories.
Events for face-to-face
interaction and
knowledge exchange

Place
Agglomeration benefits:
proximity to other
companies
Visitor/business-oriented
facilities located near
train station/airport/port

KISTA Science City, Sweden. Photo by
Google Maps.

Kendall Square and MIT, Cambridge, MA
USA. Photo by Google Maps.

Hsinchu Science Park, Hsinchu, Taiwan.
Photo courtesy of Taiwan Ministry of
Science and Technology.

85

all referring to the multilayered relations among people, practices, and built forms associated with their innovative clusters.

In sum, over the past decades, cluster conceptualizations evolve by introducing place into the more narrowly focused economic perspectives. Such growing recognition of the role of spatial contexts and urban morphologies means two things: (1) creative clusters are not randomly distributed; they are interwoven with the physical characteristics of particular places; and (2) clusters cannot be reduced to economics any more than they can be reduced to spatial patterns (Wood and Dovey, 2015: 52). This recognition does not suggest that each dimension in the environment directly influences the cluster, but rather that any cluster manifests the complex relationships among the social, spatial, cultural, and political (Foord, 2009). Context and location are crucial (Hatuka and Carmel, 2020).

Clustering is an adaptive process, which requires essential components for success. These include the presence of foundational institutions; attracting skills and talented workers; accommodating policy frameworks, culture of innovation, and physical infrastructure. Viewing context as a major actor in the evolution of clusters, the following part explores cases, from around the world, with an emphasis on three aspects: management, culture, and place. Regarding management, the focus is on the partnerships that nurture the growth of the cluster, what policies supported them and at what scale. Concerning culture, attention is given to policies and physical strategies that support diversity, social network, and shared infrastructures. Finally, the discussion of place details physical policies that support processes of agglomeration and enhance a cluster's visibility, identity, and growth.

The following section presents four snapshots of clusters: Wageningen Food Valley in the Netherlands, which is a rural agglomeration; Kista Science City in Sweden and Hsinchu Science Park in Taiwan, which are semi-urban agglomerations; and Kendall Square in Cambridge, Massachusetts, which is an urban agglomeration. In all of these cases, spatial relationships play

a significant role with policies and strategies defined and implemented to address the limits of existing conditions and enhance each place's unique strengths.

Food Valley, Wageningen, the Netherlands

Located some 85 kilometers east of Amsterdam, in the Province of Gelderland, Food Valley is a knowledge-intensive agri-food cluster that spans eight municipalities and is anchored by Wageningen University and Research (WUR). Food Valley can be considered a "regional innovation system" that takes advantage of the intersection of industry, a university, and government actors according to the triple helix model. "Food Valley" is the name that was given to the Wageningen food tech cluster as part of a marketing effort and after years of cultivating food companies and research organizations in the region. The development of the cluster started in the 1980s, when research and development companies were drawn to the area by Wageningen University's specialized labor force and the proximity to agricultural land. In 2004, the concept of Food Valley emerged within a virtual organization consisting of the Development Agency East Netherlands, Wageningen University and Research, and the Wageningen, Ede, Rhenen, and Veenendaal (WERV) municipalities. The Food Valley organization has since become a long-range program subsidized by the Netherlands Ministry of Economic Affairs.

Spread throughout its 10-kilometer radius, Food Valley boasts over 1,500 food and agriculture companies. These companies include a wide array of both public and private institutions ranging from tiny start-ups of food geneticists and researchers, to established food producers (Crombach et al., 2008). Among the varied companies there are a few which serve as anchors and attract other businesses. For example, in 2002, dairy giant Campina decided to concentrate its R&D in Wageningen so that researchers, product developers, and marketing experts could work together in close physical proximity. In addition, the decision of the Dutch baby food company Numico to locate its research arm in Wageningen and the creation of the Top Institute for Food and Nutrition – a research collaboration created by food tech businesses, universities, and the Dutch government – served as important steps in the consolidation of the cluster. In 2011, the Biopartner Center Wageningen, an incubator facility, created an environment where start-up companies could work side-by-side with existing companies. This mix of enterprises and variety of companies is typical in cluster development, and often contributes to its expansion and success.

Cluster growth is often supported by designated policies and strategies. In the case of the Food Valley, dominant stakeholders and foundational institutions decided to follow the triple helix model by bringing together scholarship, government, and industry. In this triple dynamic, Wageningen University (WUR), which is considered one of the best agri-food, academic, and contract research organizations in Europe, serves as the anchor for the cluster. First, the university is a merger of academia and industry, including Wageningen University, the Van Hall-Larenstein Polytechnic, and the Dutch government's applied research laboratories in agriculture and animal husbandry. Second, the university, besides being a knowledge catalyst, also plays a major role in providing the region with human capital and produces knowledge through research. Wageningen University, incidentally, is a small university but attracts more than 50% of its students from all over the world (Kourtit et al., 2011). A number of large businesses made the commitment to establish R&D facilities in the cluster (such as Numico and Unilever), which helped solidify the cluster. These businesses benefit from the role played by the central government in the development of the cluster and its decision to prioritize national business efforts, including financial and logistical support. In this triple dynamic, academia, government, and industry each plays an active role, each responding to the needs of the other, thus enhancing the growth of the cluster.

The cohesive relationships between the three sectors owe their success to recognizing the role advanced knowledge plays in the agri-food industry. There is an expanding spectrum of knowledge areas and competences involved including health, nanotechnology, process production industry, and logistics. This growing demand, in turn, increases the need for pre-competitive cooperation. The coordination among the various actors coalesced as the Food Valley organization, which represents the interests of all three and serves as a central body to support the interests of the cluster. This coordination, which also has a national appeal, benefits the Dutch agri-food industry, and resulted in partnerships across different levels of government and national sectors. The province, for example, decided to adopt the knowledge economy as its main engine of regional growth.

This cooperation among the dominant stakeholders and the success of the cluster also contributed to a culture of research and reciprocation, supported by varied organizations. The Food Valley Consortium provides services such as coaching for spinning-off new start-ups by connecting them with business coaches, financing of pre-seed loans to entrepreneurs to develop their business ideas, and professional assistance for patenting to protect intellectual property. Furthermore, research programs supporting industry in Food Valley are developed as public–private partnerships (PPPs). PPPs are a critical part of these programs as they bring research support from a conglomerate of industries, the government, and research institutes, resulting in a stable stream of funding to carry out competitive research.

Marketing helps to expose the products and successes of the companies in the cluster. For example, the cluster organizes a yearly conference to bring attention to developments in the area through press coverage and by bringing together various players in the field. A series of publications in journals and magazines including *Nature* and *New Food* have also helped to build the reputation of Food Valley and bring it to the attention of parties and leaders at the national level (Barnhoorn, 2016).

Place and geography pose major challenges in the development of the cluster. The Food Valley is located in the midst of low-density agricultural land. Although remote from Amsterdam, it still benefits from a solid transportation infrastructure and easy local connections, offering opportunities for greater R&D engagement with the surrounding area. While the location of Food Valley is ultimately far from a large urban center, companies have located there because of the critical mass of benefits inherent in targeted clustering, including a captive, specialized labor force, land ripe for research, and opportunities for knowledge exchange among key industrial players.

An additional challenge is related to the form of the cluster itself. The Food Innovation cluster is not a concentrated, dense agglomeration, but rather an 11-kilometer-long strip – an axis that runs from the municipality of Ede in the north to Wageningen in the south – of companies, institutes, and government buildings. Along the axis lie Wageningen University and the Wageningen Business and Science Park, the Ede Knowledge Campus, and the World Food Center in Ede. The physical closeness of the companies, institutes, and governmental agencies fosters effective cooperation. In addition to the support of the industrial cluster by the local governments, the eight surrounding municipalities have worked together to ensure the development of the built environment. Their aim has been to improve its accessibility and the living environment of the area to attract more residents (and companies).

Studies of Food Valley and other similar clusters have shown that the innovation process of clusters results in the promotion of the region as an attractive living and working area for highly qualified employees (Garbade et al., 2013). But most of all, "knowledge synergy through spatial connectivity and industrial or institutional networks appears to be a critical success factor" (Kourtit et al., 2011: 159). Going beyond the local-global performance of Food Valley in the Wageningen region, it is important to place it as part of a larger innovation system in the eastern Netherlands that includes three successive cluster initiatives around

the three themes and three regions: Health Valley (Nijmegen region), Technology Valley, and Food Valley (Wageningen region). The geographic connectivity between the regions is a vehicle for generating added value from the thematic, complementary clustering of innovative activities and initiatives, which are naturally rooted in these regions and are not externally "parachuted" in (Kourtit et al., 2011: 159).

The Food Valley in the Netherlands is an outcome of various interlinked strategies with a focus on institutions, physical infrastructure, and culture. What is also evident from the cluster's development is the ongoing responsive actions to agro and food tech innovation. This was possible with the formation of an organization that could formally coordinate among stakeholders, municipalities, businesses, and the university. It also gave a name and identity to the clustering phenomenon that could be marketed to the rest of the world, promoting the idea of Food Valley at the forefront of novel developments in food technology.

Kista Science City, Sweden

Development in the area of Kista, 10 kilometers north of Stockholm, began in 1905 as a military training ground in Järvafältet. In the 1960s, as part of Sweden's Million Homes Program, the government established Kista Municipality and initiated the construction of 100,000 homes between 1965 and 1974 (Hall and Vidén, 2005). But the economic recession and oil crisis in the early 1970s prevented its immediate development; then, three large companies decided to move to Kista in 1975: Ericcson, RIFA, and IBM. This move was a shift in its development and already in the early 1980s, the city of Stockholm, the Royal Institute of Technology (KTH), and the Ericsson Company had collaboratively envisioned and developed the place as an electronics center. As a result, Kista started becoming known as "Sweden's Silicon Valley." In 1985, the key actors established a collaborative organization bringing together the city government, academic research institutes, and private industry known as the Electrum

Foundation. This dynamic contributed to the attraction of the place, and many companies relocated their offices – including Apple, Microsoft, Nokia, and Sun – forming a critical mass. Collaboration continued to develop and in 2000, Kista and Akalla combined their business centers and formed Kista Science City. Two years later in 2002, the Royal Institute of Technology (KTH) and Stockholm University jointly founded the IT University Campus there. In the same year, the Kista Galleria shopping center opened and the start-up incubator STING (Stockholm Innovation and Growth Organization) began its business program. Companies in the city range widely in size, from start-ups to multinational corporations. Most companies in the cluster are involved in the ICT sector, including software production, R&D in IT, telecommunication, hardware production, and consulting/computer services. To date, Kista is the largest ICT cluster in Northern Europe and is second only to California's Silicon Valley globally. It is home to approximately 1,400 companies and 300 ICT companies, such as Ericsson, IBM, Microsoft, Samsung, Oracle, and Intel (Yigitcanlar and Inkinen, 2019).

The history of Kista tells a story of an underdog that became a favorite. Much of its success is connected to the presence of foundational institutions, attracting skills and talent, accommodating policy frameworks, physical infrastructure, culture, and, significantly, demand for the product. A key step in its success was the establishment of Electrum Foundation, whose board includes the President of KTH University, the Mayor of Stockholm, and CEOs of major technology and real estate companies. Five councils operate under Electrum, each dedicated to a specific component of the Science City – higher education, innovation, infrastructure, marketing, and research – in order to identify problems and form task forces to implement actionable solutions. In addition, the foundation established two Electrum-owned subsidiaries, the STING business incubator and Kista Science City AB,[1] which also provide support to innovation development. STING offers incubator and accelerator assistance, such as coaching,

office space, and access to investment networks in order to nurture emerging entrepreneurs. Kista Science City AB acts as a non-profit organization that promotes economic development through managing potential investors and facilitating negotiations between real estate developers and the city of Stockholm.

The development of place was a means of enhancing Kista's attractiveness as an industrial development. In addition, public investment focused on both transportation and technological infrastructure. Improvements to commuter rail and the airport enabled access to regional and international labor; and investments in fiber-optic networks facilitated technologies dependent upon connectivity. Furthermore, social programs aimed at promoting technological adoption, and entrepreneurship cultivated a population equipped for innovation and comfortable with technology.

In 2000, the Kista changed its name from Kista Science Park to Kista Science City and, in doing so, expressed its ambitions to mature beyond its standing as an innovation center. With its success, Kista also faced new challenges. First, it needed to create urban vibrancy, since it was identified as professional and competent, but also boring and nerdy. Many young entrepreneurs and knowledge workers indicate that they would not consider living there, but strongly prefer the vibrancy and atmosphere of the Stockholm city center. This has led to investing in cultural events and centers, student housing, high-end apartments, more attractive and lively walking routes and improved transport connections with the city center and the airport. Another challenge is keeping the Kista brand strong, marketing the location as a science city, and lastly attracting human capital. Addressing these shortages is a challenge for Kista's universities as well as for the municipalities' housing policy (Van Winden et al., 2012).

Kista boasts foundational institutions that have played a significant role in sustaining the cluster's success. The efforts of those foundational institutions have been successfully funneled through the Electrum

---

1 AB is the Swedish abbreviation for "Aktiebolag," a private limited liability company.

Foundation, which coordinates efforts as a whole. Nonetheless, as opposed to other case studies that might highlight the convenient location, the internal culture, or the physical clustering of industry, Kista's comparative advantage lies in the placement of major, large players in the cluster that draw the center of the ICT world away from an urban core and into the city's industrial park.

Finally, the case of Kista is part of a wave of science cities that are based on a set of strategic projects in existing cities, with a focus on city-wide strategies rooted in partnership and inclusion. Science cities shifted from the production of science in order to drive economic development to social and economic development for the benefit of the wider population. This approach emphasizes community beyond the people working in the labs and industry. Vision plays a critical role in the development of science cities as a means to pursue future agendas of mutual agreement (Charles, 2015).

Hsinchu Science Park, Taiwan

Hsinchu Science Park (HSP) was established in 1980 by the Taiwanese National Science Council as an important component for encouraging high-tech industry in Taiwan. Prior to the establishment of the park, Hsinchu was known primarily for its agriculture and the manufacturing of light bulbs and was not considered an important industrial region. However, the county-level city of Hsinchu became a significant industrial region when National Tsing Hua University and the National Chaio Tung University relocated in the late 1950s after the Kuomingtang (KMT) government retreated to Taiwan, and since then has been considered an important higher education hub and natural location for a high-tech science area.

Modeled after Stanford Industrial Park in Palo Alto, CA, the science park was conceived to leverage existing higher educational institutions, new R&D institutions, and private capital to elevate Taiwan's industries from labor-intensive manufacturing to high-tech

industries (Chen, 2013). Castells and Halls describe it as "a national Government demonstration project to foster the so-called 'co-operation triangle' between government research institutes, universities, and private high-technology firms, under the auspices of the Ministry of Economy" (Castells and Hall, 1994: 100). Different from other countries that have been established to create science parks within the private sector, Taiwan set out to create its core, high-technology capabilities within the public sector, and then to use these institutions, such as the Industrial Technology Research Institute (ITRI), as engines for the rapid diffusion of technological capabilities to the private sector. The Taiwanese approach also departed from the conventional view that sees industrial innovation in terms of new firms developing new products or processes. Instead the Taiwanese jumped to the second stage, namely, the diffusion of the new product or process knowledge to other firms (Chen and Ju Choi, 2004; Saxenian and Jinn-Yuh, 2001).

This departure point also influenced one of the central functions of HSP – attracting overseas capital and expertise for high-tech development. This has also produced an important conduit for a reverse brain drain. In addition, the Ministry of Finance created an institutional framework for venture capital in the early 1980s to provide funding for the R&D work it was targeting in HSP. Early beneficiaries included the company Acer. The appeal of HSP for attracting returnees included its proximity to Taipei, the surroundings, and its high-quality residential and living areas, and publicly funded bilingual primary and secondary education facilities (Saxenian, 2004).

The cluster includes a major anchor firm, The Semiconductor Manufacturing Corporation (TSMC) – the most successful semiconductor company in Taiwan and the world's largest independent semiconductor foundry. The business model of the company is to focus solely on manufacturing products as specified by customers. "By choosing not to design, manufacture or market any semiconductor products under its own name, the company ensures that it never competes directly with its customers" (TSMC, 2020).

One of the prime strategies in developing the park was the establishment of the Industrial Technology Research Institute (ITRI) by the Taiwanese government in 1973. This public R&D institution, funded by the Ministry of Economic Affairs & Industry and the National Science Council, aimed to "raise the level of TW's industrial technology." Many key companies such as UMC and TSMC are spinoffs from ITRI. In addition, the Hsinchu Science Park Administration (HSPA) itself, which is authorized by the central government, administers and provides many services including: land requisition, public facility and infrastructure development, a program to bring in high-tech industries, product market development, investment promotion operations, R&D innovation program subsidies, transportation and logistics, tax incentives, residential services, and financial services.

While HSP is a major state-led project, it differs from the classic East Asian developmental state models that rely on a tight relationship between a strong state and large conglomerates (e.g. Japanese and Korean industries). Instead, Taiwan's IT sector, although heavily subsidized by the state, is "entrepreneurship-led." This is an outcome of the Taiwanese industrial policies from the 1980s that have privileged small and medium-size enterprises (SMEs) rather than large transnational firms. It is also linked to the model of the Silicon Valley, which served as an inspiration. The Taiwanese engineers studied Silicon Valley by traveling and communicating with policymakers, a process that informed the design of HSP and assisted in establishing important business and capital ties with Silicon Valley.

In terms of fiscal incentives, HSP is unique. It enjoys more fiscal incentives than other companies in Taiwan, including a five-year tax holiday, maximum income tax rate, duty-free imports of machinery, equipment, raw materials, and semi-finished products, and capitalization of investors' patents and technology as equity shares. Lastly, companies located in HSP are not restricted to selling in the domestic market.

The vision for industry was accompanied by a master plan that designed it as a new high-tech town that includes industrial, residential, and recreational zones in the periphery of Hsinchu City and close to the two national universities. The park's residential areas include single-sex dormitories, family housing, and also private development parcels. There are also high-end villas for managerial and executive staff in addition to retail, hotels, and other hospitality establishments. The central government has also established dedicated national-level public education facilities for primary and secondary education for returnees and employees of the park. The master plan, known for emulating a California-inspired suburban development model, was implemented and is currently in its third phase of expansion.

In terms of its proximity to national infrastructure, HSP is adjacent to the National Freeway 1, Taiwan's first freeway, completed in 1978, with a designated off-ramp into the park. While HSP is not directly adjacent to port facilities, the Taoyuan International Airport is only 40 minutes away by car and the National Freeway system facilitates easy access to major port facilities in Keelong to the north and Kaohsiung to the south. In addition to national infrastructure, HSP is also well-connected at the regional level. The High Speed Rail Station completed in 2007 is an approximately 15-minute drive away and connects to Taipei City within 30 minutes. There is also a dedicated customs house within the park to facilitate imports and exports, a logistics center, and dedicated banking facilities as well. Locally within HSP there are four internal shuttles that circulate throughout the park and connect to major public transportation facilities in the region. HSP also has an internal wastewater treatment facility and dedicated freshwater and electricity utilities. There is a "one-stop-shop" approach to approvals of investors in addition to dedicated training facilities for workers.

HSP has also played an important role in the transformation of the region. It transformed the region from being a central place on the local level to a successful high-tech urban region renowned on a global scale. The multiple forces in the region, including international forces in electronics that are linked to Western countries and governmental interventions in the infrastructural and institutional constructions, altered and influenced the geography and spatiality of the region (Chou, 2007). While Hsinchu City already existed prior to the establishment of the park, additional infrastructure and increased employment in the region have spurred secondary real estate development primarily along major highways and roads. Although this development accommodates lower-end residential needs, there is also significant high-end real estate development especially close to the high-speed rail station in Chubei. This enhanced development and demand is attributed not only to the location of Hsinchu City and the improved connectivity to Taipei, but also to the economic flourishing of Hsinchu City, which has become one of the highest income per capita places in Taiwan. This success also created new challenges. The interconnected forces of various geographical scales caused by this polycentric development have led in turn to governance contradictions and conflicts (ibid.). "In particular, the fragmented political system and associated local competition have increasingly facilitated the local governments to pursue their property-led competitive strategy by expanding urban development plans, dismantling collaboration possibilities raising a common regional agenda for the spatial development" (ibid.: 1400).

Kendall Square, Cambridge, Massachusetts, USA

In the 1960s, Kendall Square was considered by many to be a blighted area. Manufacturing and businesses were moving out to the suburbs and the anchor institution – NASA's mission control center – was soon to be moved to Houston, Texas, leaving large land parcels empty and abandoned. The Massachusetts Institute of Technology (MIT) worked to expand towards Kendall Square in order to fill the gap left by local industry. This dynamic was interrupted during the 1970s, when

advances in science and genetic research particularly caused a national public and regulatory debate about how to limit genetic interventions. Cambridge became an actor in this debate because it was home to the new scientific start-up industry, and a number of new life sciences companies were born in Cambridge including Biogen and Genzyme. The debate benefited Cambridge, which became associated with the biotechnology industry, a trend that strengthened rapidly in the ensuing decades. As the district neared the new millennium, the MIT Investment Management Company – the real estate arm of the Institute – started to focus its efforts on Kendall Square. A number of real estate developments offered prime real estate to large companies and start-up ventures alike, setting the stage for today's Kendall Square innovation district. As Boston's other famous innovation ecosystems began to decline (notably Route 128), many companies started looking to Kendall Square as the new innovation hub for the region.

Today, Kendall Square, dubbed by some as "the most innovative square mile on the planet" (Owuor, 2019), boasts 25 biotech and life sciences companies, ranging from Biogen to Pfizer to Novartis. The area also plays host to extensive laboratory and start-up spaces, designed to launch high-potential life-science and biotech start-ups. This trend has also been supported by the Broad Institute of MIT and Harvard, an institution that encourages collaboration among researchers from both institutions and from affiliated hospitals in the greater Boston area. The development of the district also contributed to expanding the type of industries located in Cambridge, and in addition to its life sciences and biotech cluster, Kendall Square is also one of the country's leading tech hubs. It serves as a major hub to many of the world's powerhouse tech players – among them Google, Amazon, and Microsoft. The Cambridge Innovation Center houses more than 400 start-up businesses – many of them in the tech industry – as well as a number of venture capital firms.

Many clusters evolve around an anchor institution, which plays a major role in connecting various stakeholders. In the case of Kendall Square, MIT viewed the ties between academia and industry as a prime interest. The Institute encourages and supports the development of industry in close proximity to the campus and for that reason promotes development in the Kendall Square area. The municipality also played a major role in developing progressive policies to attract companies to Cambridge. For example, the initial companies that helped to initiate the area's first cluster in life sciences were direct spinoffs of research conducted at MIT. These companies were able to do business as an immediate result of lenient laws adopted by the Cambridge City Council which allowed DNA experimentation. This allowed for the creation of the earliest companies in the field in the city, including Biogen – a company that is still based in Cambridge today. Cambridge has since continued to encourage innovation through accommodating policies as well as improvements in livability in order to help companies attract and retain the talent that is essential to their operations.

The city of Cambridge and the academic institutions played complementary roles. The city initiated key policy and logistical support for the district, while MIT and Harvard University cultivated life sciences and biotech research, and collaboration with industry. These efforts were supported by the Broad Institute which coordinates the interests and activities of both universities, and strengthens the research and its output through collaboration. Furthermore, the State of Massachusetts has also played a large role in supporting the development of the Kendall Square cluster through a number of efforts, including 31 state-owned incubators and the investment of over $700 million in the industry over the past decade through a number of development programs.

The advantage of the area is the availability of human capital. The density of universities throughout the Greater Boston region, and particularly in the city of Cambridge, creates a natural talent pipeline that is enviable for other clusters around the globe. The result is an area with start-up companies that have been

spun off from the universities' research. In addition, the life sciences, biotech, and data-heavy industries are dependent on skilled workers, and Cambridge is a city that spawns much of that talent, drawing companies to the source. The State of Massachusetts helps to streamline the process through a number of events that seek to connect larger companies to talent. At these "partnering" days, big companies can meet potential employees and connect with early-stage start-up companies, entrepreneurs, and more.

In 2008, with the growth and success of the cluster, the Kendall Square Association was founded to coordinate among stakeholders and key actors. The association serves as a central body that coalesces the interests of Kendall Square's industries, and its goal is to help different players within the cluster "connect and exchange ideas" while supporting livability improvements in the district.

In the case of Kendall Square, the first businesses in the area were skill-intensive industries that naturally rely heavily on proximity to university research and talent creation. Nonetheless, the district boasts a number of urban planning interventions and policies that helped to ensure that the initial companies sparked a larger trend of clustering that is still thriving to this day. A number of early policies allowed, for example, for the creation of businesses that didn't yet have the legal rights to establish themselves elsewhere in the state of Massachusetts. The Kendall Square Association has helped to steer the efforts of the key players of the district in a direction agreeable to all (Budden and Murray, 2015). In addition to its immediate adjacency to MIT, the Kendall Square cluster is conveniently located on Boston's Red Line, which offers easy connections to Harvard and the city's many other academic institutions. Many have pointed to this easy transportation access as a key strength that sets the Kendall Square cluster apart from many of its competitors. Nonetheless, Massachusetts ranks near the bottom of all of the states in the United States with regards to road quality and commuting times. The challenge of reducing congestion is one of the tasks that the Kendall Square

PART II | PLACES OF MAKING

WAGENINGEN Food Valley
Gelderland, the Netherlands

Wageningen Food Valley in the Netherlands is a knowledge-intensive agri-food cluster that spans eight municipalities in a 10-kilometer radius. The area is home to a number of science, business, and research institutes all of which are focused on food. Initiated and anchored by Wageningen University and Research (WUR). The Food Valley serves as an example of an autonomous, rural cluster that thrives on a specialized labor force and on R&D-intensive activities.

LINEAR |
Connective knowledge-industry cluster in a 10-kilometer radius

94

4 | CLUSTERING NEW INDUSTRIES

PROTOTYPE |
Autonomous

INDUSTRY PROFILE

Program	Food tech
Spatial form	Autonomous, rural agglomeration
Industrial typologies	Varies
Largest employers	Unilever, Heineken, Vion, Friesl and Campina
Anchor institution	Wageningen University and Research
Cluster catalyst	Specialized labor force and rural experimentation

STRATEGIES |

Management

The Food Valley draws on a trifecta of foundational institutions, that are part of the triple helix model: academia, government and industry. Academia serves as the anchor for the cluster: businesses started naturally springing up around WUR's strong agricultural program, drawing on the resultant talent pool and research expertise.
The Netherlands' government has declared food tech a priority for national business efforts, and offered both financial and logistical support for the cluster. A number of large key businesses also made a commitment to establish R&D facilities in the cluster, playing a key role in its solidification.

Culture

Wageningen University and Research is considered to be one of the best agri-food academic and contract research organizations in Europe. It has approximately 6,500 employees and 9,000 students. It is a merger of Wageningen University, the Van Hall-Larenstein Polytechnic, and the Dutch government's applied research laboratories in agriculture and animal husbandry. WUR provides the region with human capital as well as producing knowledge through research.
Eight surrounding municipalities have worked together to ensure a suitable supply of housing as well as easy transportation access to local urban areas, creating what the Food Valley calls "the front door in the city and the back door in the countryside." The initiative has national appeal as a direct result of its potential to benefit the Dutch agri-food industry and its adjacent research areas through expansion and innovation. This has resulted in partnerships across different levels of government and national sectors.

Place

Food Innovation Strip is an 11km long cluster of companies, institutes, and government agencies, along an axis that runs from the municipality of Ede in the north to Wageningen in the south. The physical closeness of this network of companies, institutes, and governmental agencies fosters effective cooperation. To address the changing research needs in the realm of food tech, where lab configurations, experiments, and research initiatives are in constant flux, laboratories on the campus are designed to be flexible, and can also easily be converted to other uses. Wageningen also boasts one of the first autonomous shuttles, which operates on a public road within the cluster.

PART II | PLACES OF MAKING

KISTA Science City
Stockholm, Sweden

The Kista district north of Stockholm, Sweden consists of commercial, production and residential areas. The commercial enterprises are mainly Information and Communications Technology (ICT) businesses. Most companies in the cluster are involved in the ICT sector, including software production, R&D for IT, telecommunication, hardware production or consulting/computer services. It is considered the largest ICT cluster in Northern Europe, and is sometimes referred to as referred to as Europe's "Silicon Valley".

CENTRAL | Supporting elements (housing) on periphery

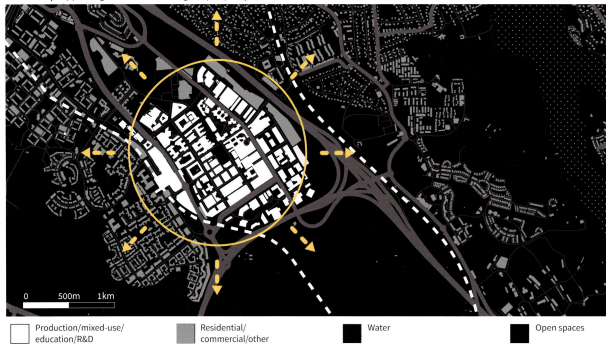

4 | CLUSTERING NEW INDUSTRIES

PROTOTYPE |
Autonomous

INDUSTRY PROFILE

Program	Information, communications, and technology
Spatial form	Autonomous, semi-urban agglomeration
Industrial typologies	Varies
Largest employers	Ericcson, IBM, Microsoft
Anchor institution	Electrum Foundation
Cluster catalyst	Large anchor companies

STRATEGIES |

Management

Kista Science City AB is a non-profit organization that promotes economic development by managing potential investors and facilitating negotiations between real estate developers and the City of Stockholm.
Electrum Foundation is an organization that embodies the triple helix model. Board members include the President of KTH Royal Institute of Technology, the Mayor of Stockholm, and CEOs of major technology and real estate companies. Five councils operate under Electrum, each dedicated to a specific component of Kista Science City – higher education, innovation, infrastructure, marketing, and research – in order to identify problems and form task forces to develop actionable solutions.

Culture

Two Electrum-owned subsidiaries, the STING business incubator and Kista Science City AB, support innovation development. STING provides assistance, training, and access to capital for newly-formed businesses with a mission to support technology companies. STING has been extremely selective with its program. From 2002–2013, only 92 out of 1,134 companies that applied gained admission, but it accounts for 228 million euros in value.
In 1994, Stockholm constructed the world's largest open-fiber network with almost 100% of businesses and 90% of homes tapping into that infrastructure by the beginning of the 21st century. Kista Science City has boosted it connectivity and bandwidth even higher, to support its production.

Place

Kista's development of mixed-used buildings and cultural amenities attempts to address a lack of urban life. Moreover, continued plans for providing civic space and strategically designing areas for interaction also coincide with larger efforts to address social issues in the region, such as spatial segregation and immigration policy. Kista's reputation as "Wireless Valley" created a strong identity that helps attract talent and economic development. Improvements to commuter rail service and the airport enable access to regional and international labor; and investments in fiber-optic networks facilitate technologies dependent upon connectivity. Furthermore, social programs aimed at promoting technological adoption and entrepreneurship cultivate a population equipped for innovation, and comfortable with technology.

PART II | PLACES OF MAKING

HSINCHU Science Park
Taiwan

Hsinchu Science Park (HSP) was established in December 1980 by the Taiwanese National Science Council as an important component for encouraging high-tech industry in Taiwan. Previously, Hsinchu was known primarily for agriculture and manufacturing lightbulbs, and was not considered an important industrial region. Hsinchu Science Park occupies over 650 hectares, and houses almost 400 tenant companies with more than 150,000 employees.

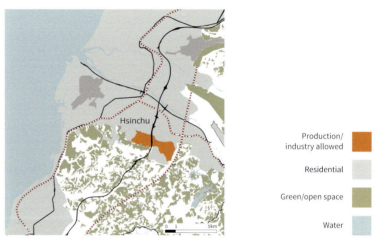

EDGE | Integration of industry with education and housing

98

4 | CLUSTERING NEW INDUSTRIES

PROTOTYPE |
Adjacent

INDUSTRY PROFILE

Program	Telecommunications, integrated circuits, opto-electronics, biotechnology
Spatial form	High-tech growth pole / industrial cluster / knowledge transfer
Industrial typologies	Acer, TSMC, Philips, Logitech, UMC, Holtek, AU Optronics, Epistar
Largest employers	Industrial Technology Research Institute (ITRI), National Tsing Hua University,
Anchor institution	National Chiao Tung University
Cluster catalyst	Taiwanese National Science Council

STRATEGIES |

Management	Culture	Place

The Hsinchu Science Park Administration (HSPA), authorized by the central government, provides: land requisition, public facilities, and infrastructure development, a program to attract high-tech industries, product market development, investment promotion operations, R&D innovation program subsidies, transportation and logistics, tax incentives, residential services, and financial services.
HSP enjoys fiscal benefits, including a five-year tax holiday, favorable income tax rate, duty-free imports of machinery, equipment, raw materials, and semi-finished products, and capitalization of investors' patents and technology as equity shares. Lastly, companies located in HSP are not restricted to selling in the domestic market.

Industrial Technology Research Institute (ITRI) is a public R&D institution established in 1973 by the Taiwanese government. It is funded by the Ministry of Economic Affairs and Industry and the National Science Council. Many key companies such as UMC (1980) and TSMC (1987) are spinoffs from ITRI.
Taiwan's IT sector, although heavily subsidized by the state, resembles that of Silicon Valley and is "entrepreneurship-led." Taiwanese industrial policies in the 1980s privileged small and medium size enterprises (SMEs), rather than large transnational firms.

Hsinchu Science Park was master planned as a new, high-tech town that includes industrial, residential, and recreational zones on the periphery of Hsinchu City, and near two national universities. HSP is currently in its third phase of expansion, and is known for emulating a California-inspired suburban development model in Taiwan.

HSP is located adjacent to National Freeway 1, Taiwan's first freeway completed in 1978, from which there is a designated off-ramp into the park. The Taoyuan International Airport is 40 minutes away by car and the National Freeway system facilitates easy access to major port facilities in Keelong to the north and Kaohsiung to the south. The High Speed Rail Station is an approximately 15-minute drive away, and connects to Taipei City within 30 minutes.

PART II | PLACES OF MAKING

KENDALL Square,
Cambridge, Massachusetts, USA

Adjacent to the Massachusetts Institute of Technology (MIT), Kendall Square's business district and adjacent areas near the MIT campus are home to many global technology players, ranging from Amazon to Google and Microsoft, as well as key biotechnology and pharmaceutical companies such as Genzyme, Pfizer, Novartis and Sanofi. The area relies heavily on MIT's human capital as an anchor resource, but the business district has grown beyond the university and forms a self-sustaining cluster of dynamic businesses.

Production/industry allowed
Residential
Green/open space
Water

Diffused | Industry integrated with education

Production/mixed-use/education/R&D
Residential/commercial/other
Water
Open spaces

4 | CLUSTERING NEW INDUSTRIES

PROTOTYPE |
Integrated

INDUSTRY PROFILE

Program	Life sciences, biotech, and high tech
Spatial form	Integrated, urban agglomeration
Industrial typologies	Varies
Largest employers	Pfizer, Novartis, Amazon, Google
Anchor institution	Massachusetts Institute of Technology
Cluster catalyst	Academia-intensive industries in natural urban cluster

STRATEGIES |

Management

The Kendall Square Association serves as a central body that coalesces the interests of key industries in Kendall Square. The density of universities in the Greater Boston region, and particularly in the city of Cambridge, creates a natural talent pipeline that is envied by other clusters around the globe. The life sciences, biotech, and other data-heavy industries are heavily reliant on skilled workers; and Cambridge is the location that nurtures a lot of that talent, which draws companies to the source.
MIT and Harvard University are key players in the life sciences and biotech, and thus are also key players in the development of the district. It boasts many start-up companies that have spun off from the universities' research. The Broad Institute, for example, helps to coordinate the interests and activities of both universities, and strengthen the research and its output through collaboration.

Culture

The city of Cambridge serves as a key foundational institution for the cluster, providing key policy and logistical support for the district throughout its development over many decades. In the late 1970s, when genetic research was first emerging, the Cambridge City Council was one of the first in the country to allow DNA experimentation. Cambridge has since continued encouraging innovation with accommodating policies and livability improvements in order to help companies attract and retain the talent that is essential for their operations.

Cambridge's early, accommodating policy framework served as the key catalyst in paving the way for the creation of Kendall Square's unique innovation cluster.
The State of Massachusetts has also played a large role in supporting the development of the Kendall Square cluster, and has invested over $700 million in industry there over the past decade through a number of development programs.

Place

The urban character of the cluster plays a significant role in retaining talent. Kendall Square companies capture the young talent when they graduate from the universities, and then offer incentives for them to stay in the area, due to the stability provided by the high density of businesses and the perks of living in a thriving urban area.
The location of the cluster in an urban area also offers the benefits of greater connectivity and ease of transportation to areas throughout the Greater Boston region. Kendall Square is located on Boston's red line transit, which offers easy connections to Harvard and many other academic institutions.

101

PART II | PLACES OF MAKING

Clustering New Industries: Program, Spatiality and Catalysts

	WAGENINGEN Food Valley Gelderland, Netherlands	**HSINCHU Science Park** Hsinchu, Taiwan
Morphology	Linear	Edge
Program	Food tech	Telecommunications, integrated circuits, opto electronics, biotechnology
Spatial form	**Autonomous** Rural agglomeration	**Adjacent** Semi-Urban agglomeration
Catalysts	Specialized labor force and rural experimentation	Taiwanese National Science Council

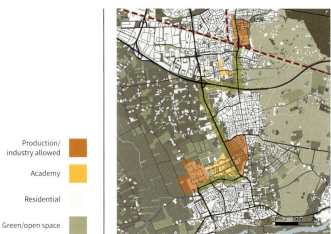
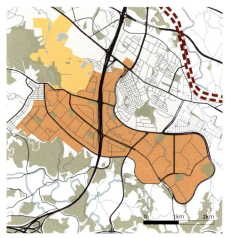

Production/industry allowed
Academy
Residential
Green/open space

102

4 | CLUSTERING NEW INDUSTRIES

KISTA Science City
Stockholm, Sweden

Central

Information
Communications and technology

Autonomous
Semi-urban agglomeration

Large, anchor companies

KENDALL, Cambridge
Massachusetts, USA

Diffused

Life sciences, biotech and information communications and technology

Integrated
Urban agglomeration

Academia-intensive industries in urban cluster

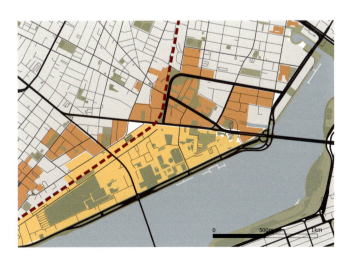

Association has listed as among its top priorities in helping to shape the district's future.

One of the cluster's largest assets is its urban character. The development of the Kendall Square area is characterized by a mixed-use approach, and innovation spaces are included as a zoning requirement for the planned development of the area (Bevilacqua and Pizzimenti, 2019). The Kendall Square Urban Renewal Plan (KSURP) includes a major, urban, mixed-use project on a 24-acre site within the 42-acre Kendall Square Urban Renewal Area, directly across the Charles River from downtown Boston. The Cambridge Redevelopment Authority (CRA) assembled properties, prepared the site for development, and constructed public improvements. Through a public competition, the CRA selected Boston Properties as the master developer that continues to facilitate development. The Master Plan provides for over 4 million square feet of new development in 19-plus buildings across three development blocks. The project accommodates a wide range of complementary uses: office space and biotechnology laboratory space; hotel and retail space; more than 150,000 square feet of major public open space, parks, and plazas; and new residential buildings (Cambridge Redevelopment Authority, n.d.).

The urban atmosphere or "buzz" plays a significant role in retaining talent. Kendall Square companies capture the talent young as they emerge from universities and then offer incentives for individuals to stay in the area thanks to the stability created by the high density of businesses and the perks of living in a thriving urban area.

Clusters depend on anchor institutions and the infrastructures to support them. Kendall Square has both. It has established academic institutions and progressive governments at the state and local levels, which develop policies to connect companies and individuals that are already in close proximity to each other. It also has vibrant urban physicality which has been further developed and enhanced. These two assets may explain why clustering has happened gradually and naturally, on a collaborative, progressive basis.

The Industry–Place Nexus in Developing Clusters

To be sure, paths and trajectories in developing clusters can vary greatly. A cluster can grow organically, or be grown intentionally by local governments. Whether they evolve from the top down or the bottom up, clusters are always grounded in the built environment that influences a place's production and appeal. There is, therefore, no ideal spatial or morphological form of clustering, and the cases discussed exemplified four different morphological-spatial manifestations.

The first cluster, Wageningen Food Valley, a *linear-autonomous cluster*, is a rural agglomeration based on the agricultural assets of the place and the specialized labor in the region. The second cluster, Hsinchu Science Park, an *edge-adjacent cluster*, is a semi-urban agglomeration, which national policies strongly support. The Kista Science City, a *central-autonomous cluster*, is a semi-urban agglomeration based on large anchor companies surrounded by a housing development. The last cluster, Kendall Square, is a *diffused-integrated* urban agglomeration. Diffusion in this case characterizes not only the cluster's physical and spatial features but also the collaboration between industry and academia. Although it is often common to think about clusters as condensed central agglomerations, their morphology varies. Whether linear, central, or diffused, or located at the edge or the center of the city, clusters are nonetheless connected (if not attached) to the existing city and have the requisite relevant physical features to further enhance their links and connectivity to it.

Two points can summarize this discussion:

1. Clustering is an ongoing political process and it does not suit all situations. The clustering approach requires concentrations of specialized activity, collaborating with research and/or educational institutions, interacting with complementary industries and/or services, and having access to a skilled labor pool. Furthermore, clustering is a process, and it is based on

institutional building, partnerships, and funding. Once evolved, a key task is to sustain it and further develop it, through a dynamic vision that does not rely solely on economic development but also on social development at the regional scale.

2. Clustering is about nurturing a socio-spatial ecosystem. Hypothetically, clusters can evolve anywhere, in a rural, a semi-urban, or a dense urban environment. But clustering is contextual and relies to great extent on human capital and community. The spatial form of the cluster is a manifestation of both the spread of the industrial anchors, the lifestyle of the community in place, as well as the policies and spatial strategies used to support and/or alter the cluster's growth and identity. In general, clustering leans on developing supportive physical infrastructure; on constructing built form that supports face-to-face interaction; and on cultivating social culture and spatial character.

In sum, industry and place are codependent in clustering development, and urban planning and zoning are driving factors in supporting the innovation-oriented demands of socioeconomic and physical transformation (Bevilacqua and Pizzimenti, 2019). As illustrated, clusters are often located in established, high-income places. The epicenter of each cluster is a large, diverse urban environment with a developed transportation network. Policy, both national and local, plays a key role in the development of the cluster. National policies tend to be more specifically directed towards industry itself, and local policy, emanating from municipal government, tends to support innovative industry in general, by initiating programs, projects, and incentives that influence the environment and local culture. Thus, to better understand clusters, it is crucial to consider how zoning and urban planning tools might bring about a better connection between policy, place-based innovation, and knowledge convergence that activates informational spill-overs (Bevilacqua and Pizzimenti, 2019).

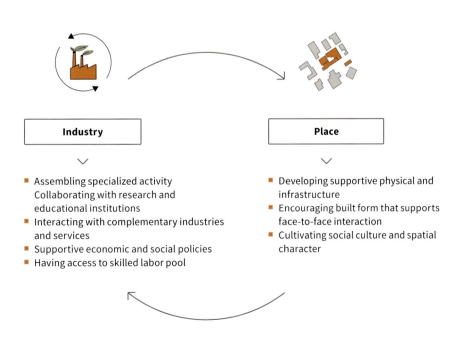

■ Industry - Place Nexus in Clustering Development

5

Reinventing Industrial Areas

Brooklyn Navy Yard, Brooklyn NY, USA. Photo by Ian Bartlett (CC BY-SA 4.0).

5

Reinventing Industrial Areas

Features of Reinventing Industrial Areas

"Reinventing," "rejuvenating," and "regenerating" are concepts that promote processes that boost existing uses and reverse possible urban decline by improving physical infrastructure, protecting and enhancing current land use, and building on the urban character of industrial areas. These processes are tightly related to the contestation over industrial land, resulting from the rapid growth of the office and retail sectors as well as the population in comparison with the slow growth of the industrial sector (Howland, 2010). This contestation, although mainly discussed in the context of cities, also influences the suburbs that have experienced industrial job loss and industrial decline as a result of the further decentralization of manufacturing to rural areas and offshore locations (ibid.).

Contestation over industrial land relates, in part, to the process during which vacant or underutilized factories and warehouses were converted into non-industrial uses such as loft apartments or living/work spaces for artists. Leigh and Hoelzel observe that the view of urban industrial areas as unproductive and unattractive dominates the discourse on smart growth. This narrow view, in turn, provides little incentive to consider local industrial policies (Leigh and Hoelzel,

2012: 91). The irregular industrial spaces that remain as a result of these processes are often insufficient to accommodate large or unique building footprints. Yet, the paradox is that cities' public works departments need urban industrial land, especially to execute environmental initiatives, including recycling programs. But despite the factors that make urban areas attractive locations for manufacturing, the planning efforts to preserve industrial land for industrial uses continue to shrink (Lester et al., 2013). This is not a new claim. The literature on industrial displacement dates back to the late 1980s and finds strong links between the conversion of industrial land – especially older, multi-story loft buildings – and residential gentrification (Curran, 2007; Giloth and Betancur, 1988; Lester and Hartley, 2014).

This process of cities converting their industrial areas to other uses is highly debated. Scholars keep warning that industrial activities are critical to the economic health of metropolitan areas. Marie Howland (2010) lists seven reasons: (1) the industrial sector continues to be an important source of jobs; (2) many industrial activities are critical to the operation of government; (3) industrially zoned areas house back-office activities critical to other sectors; (4) industrially zoned areas are home to many of the activities that support the local population, such as auto repair shops, household repair services, and warehousing of consumer products; (5) industrially zoned areas provide low-cost space that is critical for high-tech start-ups and incubators, making industrially zoned areas important to a healthy and vital economy in the long run; (6) industrial employment provides relatively good jobs for workers with lower levels of formal education than does the service sector, because it pays higher wages (Howland, 2010); and finally, (7) after years of industrial activity, some parcels carry a legacy of contamination. For such properties, industrial activity is often the highest and best use. For these reasons, scholars have emphasized the indirect role of manufacturing firms and the industrial land they occupy in enhancing the health of the overall urban economy (Chapple, 2014).

Additional arguments supporting manufacturing in cities arise from the manufacturers. Their site selection decisions are based on the speed of delivery to customers; manufacturers are increasingly choosing locations based on labor availability and transportation access, which influence the speed of delivery, rather than on land costs. This priority suggests that manufacturers are willing to compete for purchasing land in mixed-use zones that permit industrial uses. Furthermore, the storage and distribution practices and regulations, e.g. freight transport via truck and plane, the use of tractor-trailer trucks, containerization, and the deregulation of the trucking industry, which "minimize[s] [costs] when goods [are] shipped from a national location that [minimizes] distance to all customers," often make extra-urban sites more attractive. Cities cannot exile industry to the hinterland (Leigh and Hoelzel, 2012: 88). The need for "warehouse space that supports the efficient distribution of products specifically created for inner city markets" and "firms that produce products more easily transported on smaller trucks (due to small size or small volumes) [and which] can also use inner-city warehouse space" remains (Leigh and Hoelzel, 2012: 88). Nonetheless, land use, zoning regulations, and building codes continue to prevent manufacturers of various types of products (from pharmaceuticals to foodstuffs) from including manufacturing uses and building factories in cities.

Recognizing the need to address the gap between land use regulations and growing needs for industrial production, and after decades of declining industrial jobs and large inventories of industrial land, many cities are now at a critical juncture (Lester et al., 2013). On the one hand, vacant industrial properties do not generate revenue and may limit the potential for the type of high-density residential and commercial development that creates vibrant urban places; on the other hand, if cities do not maintain their industrial lands, they may be overlooked by manufacturing companies (Lester et al., 2013: 303). As a result, the task for many cities is to develop strategies to support the growth of manufacturing firms and related industrial businesses in the city and to modify some standards and policies to support smart industrial growth. Although smart growth standards and policies are meant to strengthen and diversify local economies, these standards and policies fail to protect industrial land from encroachment and do not call for urban land to be reserved for industry (Leigh and Hoelzel, 2012: 87).

Bridging this gap between needs and regulations requires conceptualizing the city in a way that situates it within the broader, regional economy. It requires viewing the center and the periphery, or the metropolitan area, as an innovation-production ecosystem that cultivates production along an "advanced manufacturing continuum" through a regional advanced manufacturing strategy (Reynolds, 2017). Identifying and developing sites that are appropriate for manufacturers at various stages (e.g. the maker stage, the start-up stage, the scale-up stage, the small and medium-sized enterprise stage), based on regional strategic objectives (e.g. the growth of a particular sector), is viewed as encouraging the return of industry to the city (ibid.).

Two complementary trends are associated with the return of industry to the city and with regenerating industrial areas: sustainability and heritage. Sustainability is associated with the efforts to clean up, improve, and reinvent areas of contaminated land in post-in-

5 | REINVENTING INDUSTRIAL AREAS

■ **Features of Regenerating Industrial Areas**

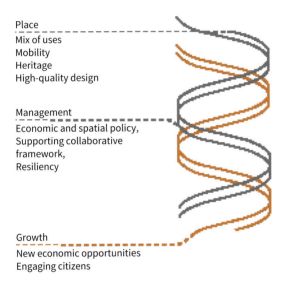

Place
Mix of uses
Mobility
Heritage
High-quality design

Management
Economic and spatial policy,
Supporting collaborative
framework,
Resiliency

Growth
New economic opportunities
Engaging citizens

Jurong area, Singapore. Photo by Edsel Little (CC BY-SA 2.0).

HafenCity district, Hamburg, Germany. Photo by Jorge Franganillo (CC BY 2.0).

Garment District, Los Angeles, California USA. Photo by Levi Clancy (CC BY-SA 4.0).

111

dustrial cities (Kitheka et al., 2021). For example, Santa Barbara in Tuscany initiated a new sustainable and environmental vision. This vision was a necessary first step toward a redevelopment process capable of overcoming the loss of mining activities without losing the historical, economic, and social roles that Santa Barbara has played in the Valdarno territory since the end of the 19th century (Bozzuto and Geroldi, 2020). Santa Barbara is just one example of the implementation of green concepts in production and manufacturing organizations with allied processes and practices. Indeed, although not all manufacturing inputs (i.e. materials, machines, human beings) can be green, manufacturing processes can nonetheless implement concepts and practices of going green (Agarwal et al., 2020).

Reinventing is embedded in the history and heritage of the place. Local and regional governments throughout Europe, the United States, and other countries have undertaken initiatives to conserve and adapt heavy industrial complexes in the belief that their efforts will generate economic benefits for distressed industrial regions and offer these regions a role in increasingly service-oriented national economies (Peterson, 2017). These projects cannot be reduced to their physical detritus, as they all have a social context. "As labor-intensive enterprises, heavy industrial complexes tend to loom large in the lives of workers and their families, as well as in local and regional histories" (Peterson, 2017). Projects that repurpose historic heavy industrial complexes can become powerful impetuses for environmental remediation and the cultivation of the natural landscape. The North Duisburg Landscape Park in Duisburg, Germany, for example, conserves the historic Thyssen Ironworks, which operated from 1903 until 1985. Another example is Parque Fundidora, a 350-acre public park and cultural and entertainment center in Monterrey, Mexico, built at what once was the site of the Fundidora Monterrey steel foundry company. These types of projects require substantial long-term planning processes and often involve more of a central planning or top-down initiative to revamp and generate new economic and urban vitality. What characterizes successful projects is a shared, holistic, envi-

ronmental, transformative journey; the improvement of the quality of life of residents in the city/region; and the intentionality in building partnerships and fostering citizen engagement (Kitheka et al., 2021).

The ideas of sustainability and heritage as a framework for regenerating manufacturing and industrial areas in cities are constantly questioned. Not all cities favor preserving manufacturing in the city, and not all efforts by cities are conducive to preserving manufacturing in the city. Dominant competing paradigms of regeneration processes focus on the smart city, the resilient city (Hatuka et al., 2018; Lester et al., 2013: 303), or the creative city, for example, as concepts that support smart growth while paying little attention to industry in cities. Furthermore, regenerating industrial areas is a process that posits multiple environmental, social, and planning challenges; it requires substantial resources and an undertaking of physical-urban design planning. Although it is unclear whether industrial preservation policies and regulations within cities are entirely beneficial and efficacious (Davis and Renski, 2020), more than before cities are initiating regenerating processes of industrial areas.

Despite deindustrialization processes in the Western world and the shrinkage of industrial land in cities, central cities still maintain a large number of manufacturing firms and a large inventory of industrial land. Cities that host industry within their juridical boundaries and rely on industry in their economic development are strategic about their industrial land inventory. In keeping their competitive advantage in economic development, they are also designing strategic land use policies that take into account the needs of each industry in order to craft processes of regeneration that enhance the area's mixed uses, accessibility, and identity.

Generally, regenerating industrial areas takes into account interlinked growth, management, and place. Growth involves policies that trigger new economic opportunities as they engage the private sector and the citizenry. Management involves having policies to support collaborative frameworks and social resiliency. In regenerating place, the core planning strategies include maintaining a sense of heritage and place, providing for mobility, offering new economic opportunities, engaging citizens, including a mix of uses, offering high-quality design, ensuring that the regeneration adheres to sustainable principles, and remaining resilient over the long term.

The cases presented in this section initiated reinventing processes in existing industrial areas. In each case, the history of the place is briefly introduced followed by the most important strategies that supported its creation. In this set of cases, the urban context and relevant stakeholders played a major role in the design of the reinventing strategy: Jurong, in Singapore; HafenCity, in Germany; Brooklyn Navy Yard in New York; and the Fashion District in Los Angeles.

Jurong, Singapore

Singapore has increasingly faced land limitations. As a result the country has been forced to be creative in its approach to densification and expansion. Despite the growing demands for land for residential and commercial uses, Singapore has continued to cultivate its manufacturing sector as a key sector for job growth. Viewing manufacturing as a priority dates back to the 1960s when the government determined that industrialization was the best way to strengthen Singapore's struggling economy, and the petrochemical industry was identified as an industrial cluster capable of contributing significantly to the economic growth of Singapore (Yang and Lay, 2004). The government turned its sights to Jurong, a set of islands with Malay villages in the southeast part of the country, and proposed constructing an industrial estate in the area. The first industries to locate on these islands were petrochemical and steel companies – industries that required some space buffer from the mainland. Three oil companies developed their facilities on three of the islands – Esso in Pulau Ayer Chawan, Singapore Refinery Company in Pulau Merlimau, and Mobil Oil in Pulau Pesek (Yang and Lay, 2004). Two decades later, in the

1980s, faced with an increasing lack of industrial land on the mainland, decision-makers decided Jurong could serve a much larger purpose. They forged plans to connect the islands in order to form a contiguous area of industrial land. The process of land reclamation began in 1995, and in 2000 it was completed and the area opened.

The plan was to accompany industrial growth with the development of residential and commercial uses by growing the area to include the greater Jurong districts. Responding to the growing needs and increase in development pressure, Singapore has had to strategically redesign the greater Jurong districts to accommodate both industry and residential needs, and has worked to optimize space in order to maximize both quality of life and productivity. Today, the Jurong area boasts a diversity of businesses, including a wide array of eco-friendly and clean tech businesses as well as a number of vibrant start-up businesses cultivated in Jurong's Innovation District formed near Nanyang Technological University, and the number of lighter manufacturing businesses is currently growing rapidly.

Governance lies at the crux of the successful redevelopment of the Jurong area. With its strong executive body, Singapore has a top-down governance structure which is closely involved in the planning of economic development and urban design. The process for Jurong has proven successful thanks to several factors including innovative ways of designing its policies. First, policymakers set creative classifications for industry, going beyond the traditional categories of heavy and light industry, to put in place a nuanced range of industrial classifications in order to help support better integration of residential and commercial uses with safe industrial uses (Stouffs and Janssen, 2016). This classification system set aside land for non-polluting industries and businesses that engage in research and development (R&D) and high-tech and knowledge-intensive activities. The planning authority also created up-to-date guidelines for e-businesses and the media industry, including descriptions of core activities and the allowable land types where industries can be located. Second, policymakers enhanced flexibility of site development as means to integrate the industrial sector with civic life. To achieve this goal, Singapore's planning authorities and the Urban Redevelopment Authority (URA) defined a zoning category labeled as "white site zoning." This category provides developers the flexibility to respond to the market demand and supply conditions more effectively by instantly adjusting and optimizing space and sites for different uses. Within the industrial zoning business designation, white sites make it possible to integrate uses such as commercial services or even residential uses. This flexible approach to land uses incentivizes developers to attract clean industry and to integrate it with more lucrative residential and commercial uses.

In terms of place development, Singapore has typically used a Planned Unit of Development (PUD) as the basic logic to organize land uses at a larger scale. Under the PUD scheme, each residential community is organized around a centrally located service center which provides multiple services for the nearby residents. To strengthen the attractiveness of Jurong, the Jurong Town Corporation (JTC) decided to extend the logic of organizing residential units according to the PUD to Jurong in order to activate the industrial areas. The fundamental planning proposition is reorganizing the mix of industries. The idea is to densify the service network and infrastructure network as a means to attract clean industries, and in turn replace the previous, heavily polluting industries thereby attracting new population and civic activities.

On top of these efforts in 2008, Singapore's URA identified Jurong as a key cog in the development of its clean tech industry and a site for the creation of a green business – a hybrid concept between green buildings and the agglomeration of conventional industry (Hwang et al., 2017). The CleanTech Park (CTP) in Jurong was meant to position Singapore as a global test-bed and preferred site for early adoption of clean technology products and solutions for urbanized settings in the tropics. It houses a community of organizations and companies focusing on the research and development

of clean/alternative energy. The Park itself is designed according to a unique framework of social, economic, and environmental considerations and has already attracted a number of green manufacturers.

In short, by the early 2000s, Jurong had established itself as a heavy industry and manufacturing hub. It boasted a wide array of high-profile companies in the petrochemical and steel industries. Still, with Singapore's rapid population growth, the island was also starting to see an influx of residents and smaller/lighter manufacturers. As a result, the government needed to adopt a policy for better integrating industrial and residential uses; the goal was to allow for overall densification and greater compatibility among differing uses. The efforts have been successful largely because they have been adopted from a number of different angles: policies have allowed developers greater flexibility to integrate uses; the design of housing and industry has become more aligned with residential densification; and the government has built out infrastructure to attract next-generation industries such as clean tech and green manufacturers.

HafenCity, Hamburg, Germany

The city of Hamburg has long been famed for its industrial port and for being a key player in the Hanseatic League as far back as the 13th century. More specifically, it is best known for its shipbuilding industry and active maritime trade, with Hamburg's waterfront serving as a center of industrial and urban economic growth. Nevertheless, with the decline of heavy industry in Germany in the late 20th century, Hamburg, too, saw a falling-off in its economic prosperity.

After the city experienced a considerable loss of jobs and industry in the early 1970s, the city government first attempted to attract new heavy industry to the area. This approach was unsuccessful because of the high cost of labor and land. Subsequent high unemployment and accompanying unrest led to a new policy dubbed "enterprise Hamburg," which focused instead on attracting new, skills-based industries. The city simultaneously invested in infrastructure, making it attractive to new industry. This approach proved successful, and between 1985 and 1990 the new industry created an impressive 16,000 new jobs in the city.

As a casualty of this dynamic the port area has significantly declined. In response, Hamburg has initiated a revitalization project for the port and its surroundings, covering nearly 28 square miles. The aim of the project, approved in 1998, is to allow the city center to expand and, at the same time, integrate with the port, beyond the Elbe, which for decades has been increasingly relegated to the southernmost part of the town (Sepe, 2013). The project, named HafenCity, is coordinated by HafenCity Hamburg GmbH, a new institution that remains publicly owned by the city but operates with the responsiveness of a privately managed corporation. The HafenCity Hamburg GmbH is a state-owned enterprise (SOE) tasked with the redevelopment of a city-owned, former harbor area. HafenCity Hamburg GmbH declines to charge the maximum possible price for the land but in return demands that potential investors and developers contribute to the broader planning vision of HafenCity, thereby further increasing the value of new plots of land (Bruns-Berentelg et al., 2020). This allowed the city to play a significant role in determining the parameters of development within the district and to build long-term value, rather than attempt to fully develop the district all at once (Lepore et al., 2017).

With this approach, Hamburg took a risk and invested in infrastructure development in the district in advance of land value increases (which have since justified the investment). The renewal of the waterfront was carried out in several stages. The first focused on water as the element around which the town's economy would be developed. This stage was followed by the development of the port, the waterfront, and the river, expanding towards new sectors (Sepe, 2013). The development of the eastern part of HafenCity had to take into account existing industrial uses that coexist with the new residential and retail activities.

To achieve this mix of uses and achieve sustainability, an agreement between the industrial companies and the housing developers was needed. It demanded that industries reduce their nighttime activities, and also lessen the noise. It also demanded that housing developers use materials that reduce acoustic pollution. Furthermore, when projects advertised in the market, all residential spaces were required to disclose the location of nearby industry.

In terms of urban planning, HafenCity was designed as a mixed-use area from its inception. The top-down masterplan aimed at strengthening the residential role of the city center and created a variety of new jobs and opportunities in retail, education, culture, entertainment, and tourism (HafenCity Hamburg GmbH, 2006). In particular, HafenCity was envisioned as a business location, with some 50% of the available floor space for companies rendering services, ranging from small local enterprises to big multinationals. In many parts of HafenCity, retail stores and eateries are prevalent at ground level (Praticò, 2015). In order to establish an independent identity for the district, HafenCity boasts a number of unique buildings, and calls for design innovation. The design of the Marco Polo Tower apartments, for example, is distinctive and curved – and already iconic; the Dockland is an office building shaped like a ship jutting into the water along the city's waterfront. It is a direct result of the redevelopment formula of the district: from its inception, the city of Hamburg called for design proposals for development and granted plots to the developers with the most innovative designs.

The architectural innovation is supplemented by urban design and infrastructure projects. Although not fully finished, HafenCity expects to include more than seven miles of seaside promenades. Each building is required to incorporate commercial space at street level to enliven the streets. In addition, the district has prioritized inclusive housing growth as part of its mission. This program, for example, takes advantage of federal legislation to cap rent increases and prioritizes faster planning and approval processes. In the redevelopment of the HafenCity district, the city was able to partner with private developers to transform a brownfield site wedged among manufacturing districts into a dynamic, mixed-use district. Rather than prioritizing development on the fringes of the city, the planned redevelopment of HafenCity shows a commitment to densification and long-term sustainability. The design requirements of the district as well as the division of parcels across different developers have ensured that Hamburg has maintained control of the direction of the district and has hence been able to prioritize the public interest throughout the process.

The success of the district is also the result of an economic program and the creation of the Hamburgische Gesellschaft für Wirtschaftsföderung (HWF), a joint public–private development corporation. Instead of depending solely on federal funds to support development, Hamburg relied on public–private partnerships and city-focused economic strategies. Since the city has maintained control over the development process it has prioritized public engagement and feedback on the progress of the development and its ongoing use through interviews with residents and research on the use and experience of the residents who moved into the area.

Finally, the district has been very effective at integrating new development with existing industry. It did not gradually push out the surrounding heavy industry; instead developers and officials have emphasized the cohabitation of the new development with existing industry through a number of agreements and requirements imposed on both parties.

The HafenCity project is part of a growing trend to transform old harbors into waterfronts with offices, housing, and recreation (Røe and Andersen, 2016). These retrofitting efforts may lead to long-term benefits for the city and its residents, but the motivation behind any particular act of entrepreneurial urban development is by nature at least partly about creating conditions to attract incoming investment, skills, and most importantly (hopefully) to retain or bring about new industry (Bruns-Berentelg et al., 2020).

Brooklyn Navy Yard, New York City, USA

Located directly across from Manhattan in New York City's Williamsburg neighborhood, the Brooklyn Navy Yard (BNY), built in 1802, boasts a rich history of maritime industrialism. Originally, the Navy Yard operated as a port and ship manufacturing site. While long well-respected, the yard nickname "Can Do Shipyard" had its heyday during World War II, when 70,000 employees constructed warships for the country, operating around the clock. At the end of World War II, the site had exhausted its purpose. The Navy Yard eventually shut down in 1966 and the largest portion of its 300-acre site, with complex, extensive utilities and infrastructure as well as its drab, massive dock buildings, was sold to the city of New York in 1969 for reuse as an industrial park (Kimball and Romano, 2012). The economic and social goals of the revival efforts that began in the 1970s focused on converting the site into an industrial complex that would provide 30,000 new local jobs.

The revitalization process of the BNY was not straightforward; it was complex but offers a lesson on management structure. After the original Navy Yard with its maritime focus closed, management was at first turned over to a non-profit organization named CLICK, which focused on anchor tenants for the area. The project failed after one of the anchor tenants filed for bankruptcy, leaving a prevailing attitude that "industry is dead" (Oden et al., 2003: 40). After CLICK's failure, the Brooklyn Navy Yard Development Corporation (BNYDC), a mission-driven not-for-profit, took over management of the space. While maintaining a similar overall model (a non-profit holding a long-term lease from the city), the approach was quite different. Instead of focusing on specific anchor tenants, the BNYDC subdivided building plans and re-imagined single-factory spaces to host many small businesses. Rather than seeking tenants through commercial brokers, it put out ads in local newspapers, targeting small businesses that could operate without the building and infrastructure standards required by big companies. At the time, the BNY could not offer a cheap rent or a redeveloped area and the site lacked adequate parking, funds to renovate buildings, repair streets, string utility lines, and other types of infrastructure. What they could offer was tax-free rent in exchange for small businesses building out their space independently. The BNYDC established close relationships with each tenant. It offered business strategy, administrative, and legal guidance. It hosted biweekly lunches for tenants to network with one another. And the benefits were mutual – the BNYDC accumulated contacts of businesses either supporting or supported by existing tenants. They then set out to relocate these businesses in the BNY, effectively establishing an agglomeration economy on the site. Today, the citywide Industrial Business Zones (IBZ) program operates as the BNY's main strategic plan.

Once the model proved successful and the area attracted international interest, the city of New York stepped in to assist the BNYDC in its efforts. For example, the city invested in basic infrastructure to help make the area more attractive for potential new tenants. The agreement between the BNYDC and the city allows the yard to reinvest profits into the district as opposed to paying them to the city in the form of rent. The partnerships between the city and the yard have allowed the yard to leverage tax credit programs and diverse financing resources to engage in large-scale construction and expansion projects. In addition, the long-term lease between the BNYDC and the city ensures greater stability for the small businesses which need not fear eviction.

In terms of physical strategies, and while the tenants are responsible for building out and designing their space, the area itself has preserved its historic industrial character. Many former naval bases have been converted to mixed-use activities; the Brooklyn Navy Yard is one of only a few examples that are still committed to industrial activity. Furthermore, the BNYDC is committed to sustainable infrastructure and green buildings, for example installing solar street lamps, creating a roof-mounted urban farm, implementing building-mounted wind turbines, and more. These ef-

forts have in turn attracted green industry and manufacturing. As urban areas in New York city deindustrialize, the yard also serves as a safe haven for intensive industries: in the walled-off industrial park, tenants are allowed to use trucks at all hours and engage in loud or noisy activities, without disturbing residential or office neighbors. It is important to note that the area's redesign – the subdivision of the existing large industrial plots – played a key role in helping small businesses populate the space. In many ways, the Navy Yard is a successful mixed-use industrial zone that is well-diffused with its surrounding neighborhoods in an increasingly post-industrial New York City.

The story of Brooklyn Navy Yard is a unique example of an industrial redevelopment success in which the area was converted into exclusively next-generation industrial activities. When the maritime needs of the nation declined after the end of World War II, the Brooklyn Navy Yard's new non-profit management cleverly diversified into a variety of different industries to ensure long-term stability. It presents a model adept at pursuing synergies between historic resources and the kind of economic regeneration that is spurred by more than market values alone. This type of synergistic model is centered in the status of BNYDC as a mission-oriented corporation, an emerging type of public–private partnership (La Porte, 2020). The key concepts of sustainability and sustainable development, led by BNYDC with a focus on reuse, triggered economic development activities, social regeneration, ecological efficiency, and cultural heritage preservation. Its success, in turn, caught the attention of the city of New York, which has since been an important actor in helping to sustain the success of the yard through infrastructure investments and tax credits. Over the next several years, for example, the city will be making improvements in transportation in the form of Bus Rapid Transit (BRT) extensions and ferry landings, bike paths, and green and recreational spaces.

These ongoing management and revitalization efforts proved successful and helped convert the area into a vibrant, next-generation industrial complex. By 1998, the area had a 98% occupancy with over 3,000 employees. Today, the Brooklyn Navy Yard boasts more than 275 local businesses in a wide variety of industries, hosts 6,400 employees, and has more than 4 million square feet of leasable space. The yard has an impressive waiting list of over 100 businesses seeking to locate there in the future.

The Navy Yard is often viewed as a model of 21st-century manufacturing, with businesses ranging from maritime activities to media, high-end crafts, and medicine. Many industries focus on design and high-tech manufacturing to produce luxury goods, for example, while others use the low-rent space for storage and warehousing close to Manhattan destinations or even as standard office space. Recent investments in green infrastructure within the industrial area have attracted a growing cluster of green manufacturers as well. Today, one of the big challenges of the area is the gentrification process taking place in adjacent neighborhoods, combined with land use modification allowing for mixed-use development. These competitive processes of industry versus residential land uses have resulted in factory conversions to housing and office space, and the loss of industry in the areas immediately adjacent to the yard.

Finally, to achieve a successful outcome in post-industrial redevelopment two complementary dimensions should be pursued: first, preservation of a harmonious relationship between the project and its surroundings with attention to cultural, environmental, and aesthetic assets; and second, the social and economic interests of the benefited community (Loures, 2015).

The Fashion District Los Angeles, California, USA

LA's Garment District first established its reputation as a center for fashion over 100 years ago. The evolution of the district was dynamic. It experienced substantial growth between 1920 and 1950 when it became a center for sportswear and women's clothing. In the 1990s,

with contributions from workers hailing from Korea to Iran, the Garment District gradually grew into a well-known innovation cluster for fashion. Even so, during this time, and echoing a trend seen in many cities around the United States, the area suffered negative migration with many residents and businesses leaving the central part of the city in favor of newer, more accessible, and often cheaper locations at the periphery.

In order to address these challenges and preserve the fashion industry in LA, key players came together from both the public and private sectors forming the LA Fashion District Business Improvement District (BID). This type of organization has been widely adopted in the USA as a means of enhancing service provision and guaranteeing greater impacts from regeneration efforts. Although the operation of BIDs can be problematic, they do offer means of delivering limited objectives for city center renewal. In the case of LA Fashion District BID, it became one of the most important players in the upgrade of the district, having been established and organized by a group of business and property owners in 1995, and is "dedicated to helping the community be a clean, safe, and friendly place to work, shop, live, and do business." Its 60-member Clean and Safe Team works to maintain a positive public environment for the community, including providing business and property owners, residents, and visitors with Emergency Contact Cards to help them feel safe. The BID has also collaborated on several commercial, residential, and mixed-use developments to boost the value of the district.

The public sector, meanwhile, has been working to stem the reduction of industrial land in downtown Los Angeles. For example, LA's Department of City Planning released the ILUP Project (Industrial Land Use Policy Project), which recommended four categories of industrial land with different strategies and policies. Other players, such as the Industrial Development Policy Initiative and the Community Redevelopment Agency (CRA), played crucial roles in helping the government and the public be aware of the significance of industrial land use.

These efforts evolved around re-assessing zoning and dealing with the competition around land uses. As in many other cities across the country, LA adopted traditional zoning approaches aimed at pushing out noisome uses to the city's periphery. This led to a significant loss of industrial land in downtown areas. Like farmland, industrial land is hard to reclaim once replaced by other functions. The repercussions of this trend first started gaining the attention of the public sector in 2003. The Industrial Development Policy Initiative (IDPI), started by the Mayor's Office of Economic Development, found that over 29% of the total workforce in Los Angeles worked in industrial factories, whereas only 12% of building permit valuations were for industrial uses. Around 26% of the industrial zoned land, moreover, had been replaced by non-industrial uses, which was found to be more serious in urban transitional areas such as the Garment District. As a result, the municipality started looking inward to regenerate and maximize existing industrial land uses.

Working closely with the Mayor's Office of Economic Development and the Community Redevelopment Agency (CRA), the IDPI helped the government and the public realize the significance of industrial land as a source of jobs for LA's citizens and as an economic driver for the city. The IPDI highlighted the negative impacts of industrial land loss in Los Angeles and stressed the economic value of industrial land. By establishing the IDPI, the Mayor's Office both indicated that preserving industrial land was a priority for the administration and created a body that could help efforts to coordinate and support the preservation of industrial space. With purposes similar to those of the IDPI, the Department of City Planning (DCP) launched the ILUP that recommended a variety of strategies to ensure the sustainability of industrial lands for subsequent generations. These included the creation and innovation of a number of different districts with the goal of preserving industrial land uses, including employment protection districts, industrial mixed-use districts and transition districts. The new mixed-use districts allowed developers to construct non-industrial buildings and allowed for new live/work units in

addition to spaces reserved for productive uses by industrial businesses, and ensured the preservation of key industrial activities (Los Angeles Mayor's Office of Economic Development, 2004).

LA's Fashion District offers a number of lessons from its long and storied past. Although long famed for its role in influencing the fashion industry, it fell on hard times in the 1990s as safety concerns and a reduction in land zoned for industrial uses threatened to reduce both patrons and suppliers alike. To reverse those trends, both the public and private sectors intervened with creative and, significantly, long-term solutions. Businesses in the district banded together to increase safety and improve the aesthetics of the district.

New zoning strategies, such as a hybrid-industrial ordinance, were an essential part of these efforts. Such ordinances provide a set of development standards that preserve and protect the current characteristics of the area. They ensure that future development preserves the surrounding industrial and artistic character of buildings, enhances street-level activity, maintains a consistent urban street wall, and orients buildings toward streets. Overall building heights and minimum floor-to-ceiling height requirements maintain the industrial functionality of the buildings. Additionally, ordinances include floor area incentives for adaptive reuse projects. In short, they initiated physical standards that contributed to shaping the identity of the district to ensure its continuity.

After more than 20 years of experiments, iterations, and efforts, the LA Fashion District has become a design, production, and distribution cluster of the fashion industry (clothing, accessories, fabric, etc.) with more than 4,000 businesses and around 1,500 showrooms. Mega clothing companies such as American Apparel and Andrew Christian have manufacturing homes in the district, and the district boasts a number of high-profile events throughout the year, including LA Fashion Week, with designers, celebrities, models, and media visiting the district to learn about the latest trends (Brown, 2019; LA Fashion District: Urban Place Consulting Group, 2018). With these multifaceted

PART II | PLACES OF MAKING

JURONG
Singapore

Located in the southwest region of Singapore, Jurong covers various planning areas and a few offshore islands. In the 1960s, Jurong was developed as Singapore's first large-scale industrial district. Today, the district also boasts many residential and commercial uses, parks, universities and research and development centers. Recent policies and design initiatives have aimed at better integration of its diverse uses.

CONNECTIVITY | Linkages through logistical routes + proximity

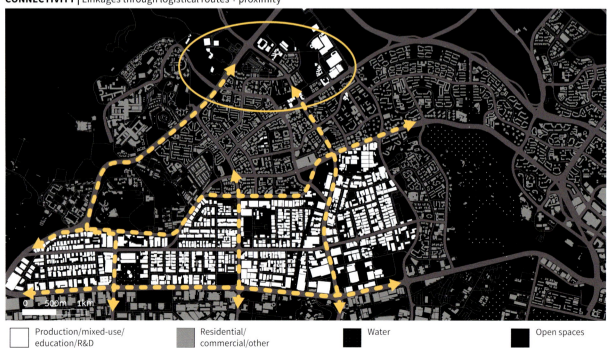

5 | REINVENTING INDUSTRIAL AREAS

PROTOTYPE |
Adjacent

INDUSTRY PROFILE

Program	Industrial redevelopment and innovation district adjacent
Spatial form	Industrial agglomeration
Industrial typologies	Diverse industries, and Research and Development (R&D)
Key actors	JTC Corporation (formally Jurong Town Corporation), Urban redevelopment authority (URA)
Redevelopment catalyst	Top-down redevelopment and redesign

STRATEGIES |

Growth

Initially known as the Jurong Town Corporation JTC was established in 1968 to oversee the development of the area and launch Singapore's industrialization effort. In 2008, Singapore's Urban Redevelopment Authority identified Jurong as a key component in the development of its clean tech industry. As part of this effort the CleanTech Park (CTP) was located in the area to position Singapore as a global testbed for early adoption of clean technology products and solutions for urbanized settings in the tropics. The park houses a community of organizations and companies focusing on the R&D of clean/alternative energy with well-developed transportation infrastructure to ease commuting.

Management

The Singapore government is closely involved in planning its economic development and urban design. The government first initiated the industrial development of Jurong in the 1960s, and has spurred subsequent redevelopment of the region as well. The process has proven successful due to a number of factors including economic incentives and innovative policy tools.

Singapore created a nuanced scale of industrial classifications in order to help support better integration of residential and commercial uses with harmless industrial uses. A new industrial land category, "business park," was created specifically to set land aside for non-polluting industries and businesses that engage in R&D and high-tech, high value-added and knowledge-intensive activities. It has also created updated guidelines for e-business and the media industry, including descriptions of core activities and the allowable land types where these industries may be located.

Place

Singapore has often used Planned Unit of Development (PUD) as the basic logic for organizing land uses at a larger scale. To increase the attractiveness of Jurong, JTC extended the rationality of PUD to the area in order to revitalize the industrial uses. The fundamental strategy is to densify the service and infrastructure networks. These new service centers are intended to attract clean industries that can, in turn, replace the previous, heavily polluting uses, and thus attract more population and civic activities.

Another innovation for better integration of the industrial sector is the creation of "white site zoning," which gives developers more flexibility in the use of the sites. Developers are given flexibility for responding to market demand and supply conditions by instantly adjusting and optimizing the space among different uses. "White sites" allow the integration of uses including commercial services (such as hotels) or even residential areas in business parks. This incentivizes developers to attract clean industry, and integrate it with residential and commercial uses.

121

PART II | PLACES OF MAKING

HAFENCity District
Hamburg, Germany

In second half of the 20th century, Germany's second largest city Hamburg found itself in decline due to significant job losses in heavy industry and manufacturing. Yet a combination of economic policies and design initiatives have helped the city reverse course. One such example is the city's HafenCity district. The area's plan has productively integrated new forms of industry with old ones, while creating a vibrant, mixed-use area that has successfully attracted residents and industry alike.

Production/industry allowed
Residential
Green/open space
Water

ECOSYSTEM | Interdependent sub-areas

Production/mixed-use/education/R&D
Residential/commercial/other
Water
Open spaces

5 | REINVENTING INDUSTRIAL AREAS

PROTOTYPE |
Integrated

INDUSTRY PROFILE

Program	Waterfront redevelopment
Spatial form	Integrated, urban agglomeration
Industrial typologies	Heavy industry juxtaposed with services economy
Key actors	HafenCity Hamburg GmbH, Hamburgische Gesellschaft für Wirtschaftsföderung
Redevelopment catalyst	Government-led initiatives

STRATEGIES |

Growth

The economic strategy implemented in the late 20th century focused on sustainable economic development and is a result of the creation of the Hamburgische Gesellschaft für Wirtschaftsföderung (HWF), a joint public-private business development corporation. Rather than depending on federal funds to support development, Hamburg instead relies heavily on its public-private partnerships and city-focused economic strategies. The city has also prioritized public engagement and feedback on the progress of the development through ongoing qualitative interviews with residents and research on the use of the public spaces.

Management

HafenCity Hamburg GmbH is responsible for the development, and has focused on building long-term value. More directly, Hamburg accepted the risk of infrastructure development in the district prior to the increase in land value (which has since justified the investment). All proceeds from completed sales were invested in the infrastructure and economic development of the district. Further, parcels were spread out among different developers to ensure that the city remained the primary actor and convener in the district. To achieve the mix of uses, it was necessary for the industrial companies and the housing developers to reach an agreement:
1. Industries agreed to reduce their nighttime activities to reduce noise;
2. Apartment projects agreed to set architectural guidelines for a) interior spaces and b) using materials that reduce acoustic pollution; 3. Advertising for all residential spaces must disclose the location of nearby industry.

Place

The district is planned and designed as a mixed-use area, with diverse housing, offices, street-level commerce, and amenities. It also attempts to establish an independent identity by boasting a number of unique building designs such as its iconic concert hall.

PART II | PLACES OF MAKING

BROOKLYN Navy Yard
New York City, USA

Built in 1802 as a ship manufacturing site, the Brooklyn Navy Yard found itself in decline together with the national maritime industry by the late 20th century. The Brooklyn Navy Yard Development Corporation (BNYDC) stepped in during the 1980s, and invited diverse, smaller businesses to repopulate the space. Since then, the Brooklyn Navy Yard has proven itself a model of next-generation industrial development. With over 100 businesses waiting for a space within the industrial park, the Brooklyn Navy Yard has grown to house over 6,000 workers and more than 200 businesses.

DIFFUSION | Interdependent yet interlinked to surrounding neighborhood

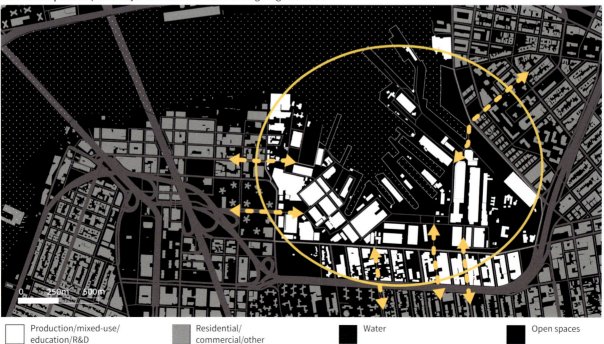

124

5 | REINVENTING INDUSTRIAL AREAS

PROTOTYPE |
Integrated

INDUSTRY PROFILE

Program	Waterfront redevelopment
Spatial form	Integrated, urban agglomeration
Industrial typologies	Small industrial businesses
Key actors	Brooklyn Navy Yard Development Corporation, City of New York
Redevelopment catalyst	Bottom-up small business development

STRATEGIES |

Growth

The Brooklyn Navy Yard is viewed as a model of twenty-first century manufacturing, with businesses ranging from maritime activities to media, high-end crafts and medicine. Recent investments in green infrastructure within the industrial area have notably attracted a growing cluster of green manufacturers as well. The yard has an impressive waiting list of more than 100 businesses seeking to relocate there in the future. Urban regeneration efforts include maintaining a sense of heritage and place, providing for mobility, offering new economic opportunities, engaging citizens, accommodating a mix of uses, offering high-quality design, and ensuring that the regeneration adheres to principles of sustainability, and is resilient over the long-term.

Management

Brooklyn Navy Yard Development Corporation (BNYDC)–a mission-driven, not-for-profit organization–subdivided building plans and imagined how single-factory spaces could host many small businesses. BNYDC establishes close relationships with each tenant and offers business strategy, administrative, and legal guidance. They host biweekly lunches for tenants to network with one another, effectively establishing an agglomeration economy within the site. Once the model proved successful and the area attracted international interest, the City of New York stepped in to assist the BNYDC in its efforts.

Place

While the tenants are responsible for building and designing their space, the area itself has preserved its historic industrial character while integrating new architecture. The BNYDC has committed to sustainable infrastructure and green buildings by, for example, installing solar street lights, creating a rooftop urban farm, installing building-mounted wind turbines and more. These efforts have in turn attracted green industry and manufacturing.

125

PART II | PLACES OF MAKING

FASHION DISTRICT,
Los Angeles, USA

The Fashion District in downtown Los Angeles has a rich heritage in the fashion industry. It was neglected during the 1990s, and faced a range of challenges including safety concerns, ineffective marketing, and a lack of development. As a direct result of efforts by the LA Fashion District Business Improvement District (BID), the Mayor's Office of Economic Development and several organizations and initiatives, the district has since been renovated into a culturally, socially, and economically diverse community covering more than 100 blocks. Today, it is known as the most successful innovation area for the fashion industry on the West Coast.

CONTINUITY | Retaining an existing urban fabric

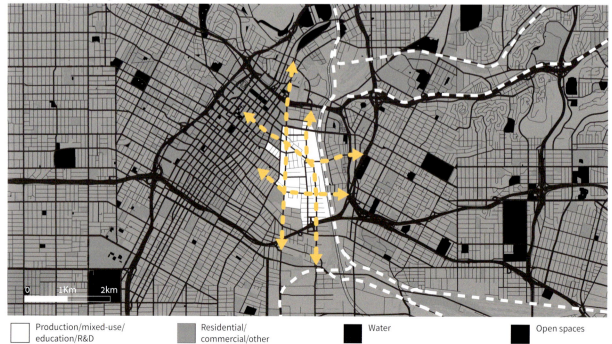

126

5 | REINVENTING INDUSTRIAL AREAS

PROTOTYPE |
Integrated

INDUSTRY PROFILE

Program	Mixed-use industrial district
Spatial form	Integrated, urban agglomeration
Industrial typologies	Light industry, commercial, residential
Key actors	City of Los Angeles, LA Fashion District Business Improvement District
Redevelopment catalyst	Community and government-led initiatives

STRATEGIES |

Growth

LA's Fashion District established its reputation as a center for fashion over 100 years ago. The district experienced a substantial growth between 1920 and 1950 when it became a center for sportwear and women's clothing. With contributions from diverse workers hailing from Korea to Iran, the Garment District gradually grew into a well-regarded innovation cluster for fashion until the 1990s. At that time, industrial uses (including the fashion industry) were being pushed out of urban centers in favor of other uses, such as residential or commercial.

The LA Fashion District Business Improvement District (BID), one of the most important players in the upgrade of the district, was established by a group of business and property owners in 1995. At that time the LA city government has been working to stem the reduction of industrial land in downtown Los Angeles. For example, the ILUP Project (Industrial Land Use Policy Project), recommended four types of industrial land with different strategies and policies. After more than 20 years of experiments, iterations, and efforts, the District remained a design, production, and distribution cluster for the fashion industry with more than 4,000 businesses and around 1,500 showrooms.

Management

The Industrial Development Policy Initiative (IDPI), started by the Mayor's Office of Economic Development, found that over 29% of the total workforce in Los Angeles worked in industrial factories while only 12% of building permit valuations were for industrial uses. Also, around 26% of the industrial zoned land had been replaced by non-industrial land uses, which was considered more serious in urban transitional areas like the Garment District. As a result, the municipality started setting its sights inward, in order to regenerate and maximize existing industrial land uses.

Working closely with Mayor's Office of Economic Development and Community Redevelopment Agency (CRA), the Industrial Development Policy Initiative helped the government and public realize the significance of industrial land as a key source of jobs for LA's citizens and as an economic driver for the city. The initiative highlighted the negative impacts of industrial land loss in Los Angeles, and argued for the economic value of industrial land. By establishing the IPDI, the Mayor's Office indicated that preserving industrial land was a priority for the administration and created a body that could help to coordinate and support efforts towards preserving industrial space.

Place

The LA Department of City Planning (DCP) adopted a variety of strategies to ensure the sustainability of industrial lands for subsequent generations. These included creating and renewing several different districts with the goal of preserving industrial land uses, including employment protection districts, industrial mixed-use districts, and transition districts. The new mixed-use districts allowed developers to construct non-industrial buildings and allowed for new live/work units, but also reserved spaces for productive uses by industrial businesses, and ensured the preservation of key industrial activities.

As a local non-profit organization, LA's Fashion District BID aims to create "a district that is evolving into a future that will include residential and creative opportunities while maintaining its roots in fashion." Its 60-member Clean and Safe Team works to maintain a positive public environment for the community, including providing emergency contact cards to business and property owners, residents, and visitors, to help them feel safe. The BID has also collaborated on several commercial, residential, and mixed-use developments to boost the value in the district.

PART II | PLACES OF MAKING

■ Regenerating Industrial Areas: Program, Spatiality, and Catalysts

	JURONG Singapore	**HAFENCity** Hamburg, Germany
Morphology	Connectivity	Ecosystem
Program	Industrial redevelopment	Waterfront redevelopment
Spatial form	**Adjacent** Industrial agglomeration	**Integrated** Urban agglomeration
Catalysts	Top-down redevelopment and redesign	Government-led initiatives

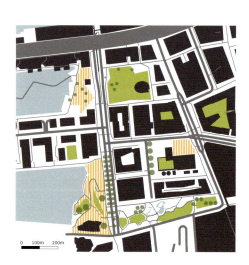

128

5 | REINVENTING INDUSTRIAL AREAS

BROOKLYN Navy Yard
New York City, New York, USA

Diffusion

Waterfront redevelopment

Integrated
Urban agglomeration

Bottom-up small business development and government support

Fashion District,
Los Angeles, USA

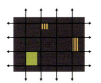

Continuity

Mixed-use industrial district

Integrated
Urban agglomeration

Community and government-led initiatives

activities, these companies have established their own distinct qualities that have allowed the LA Fashion District to emerge as a multifaceted design and manufacturing hub. Finally, this case illuminated that agglomerations are not just foci of economic activity but also places with definite cultural and social identities that can be turned to competitive advantages (Scott, 2000).

Industry–Place Nexus in Reinventing Areas

There is no such thing as a vacuum in a city. The neglected and abandoned sites are filled with new actors and uses. Neglected industrial areas often go through a process of redevelopment that focuses on housing and offices. Yet, many cities find out, sometimes too late, that they have lost their industrial base and with it the city's income. One of the main challenges is not how to sustain the industrial area but how to reinvent it in a way that will suit the needs and lifestyle of the 21st century. A major component in the reinvention plans of industrial areas is connectivity; that is, linking what has been separated in new ways. Connectivity implies both linking the varied actors, public and private, and connecting industrial land uses to other amenities in the city.

The reinvention approach is about using the existing urban fabric as a means of enhancing economic growth and the well-being of the residents in the city. It is about using what exists as a way to re-envision a new future by integrating economic, social, and physical interests. The cases discussed are all projects of reinvention. Jurong, in Singapore, uses *connectivity* to bring together industry and to increase Jurong's attractiveness. Jurong Town Corporation extended the rationality of the Planned Unit of Development (PUD) and used it as the basic logic for organizing land uses at a larger scale in order to revitalize the industrial uses. Another innovation for better integration of the industrial sector is the creation of "white site zoning," which gives developers more flexibility in the use of the sites. HafenCity forms an *ecosystem*: The district is planned and designed

as a mixed-use area, with diverse housing, offices, street-level commerce, and amenities, in an attempt to establish an independent identity by boasting a number of uniquely designed buildings such as its iconic concert hall. Brooklyn Navy Yard in New York uses a *diffusion* scheme to tie and connect its existing buildings and infrastructure to the surrounding neighborhoods while promoting sustainable infrastructure and green buildings. Los Angeles uses *continuity*, recommending a variety of strategies to ensure the sustainability of industrial lands for subsequent generations. These included creating and renewing several different districts with the goal of preserving industrial land uses, including employment protection districts, industrial mixed-use districts, and transition districts.

Building on what already exists, a reinvention process is based on three tiers: management, sustainability, and conservation. The first tier, management, is central to industrial reinvention processes. In general, there are three models of management structures (Darchen, 2017). First, private governance is more common in North America, where limited public funding is available for redevelopment, and thus the governance of this process has been more of a private type with a major role played by BIDs in the renewal of central areas. Second is bottom-up and grassroots reinvention, associated with artists and cultural entrepreneurs, often generating an organic, unplanned, evolving process. Third, consensus building and network governance describe a joint governance process where a wide array of stakeholders are involved in decision-making. In addition to these more common models, there is the entrepreneurial city model, where the municipal government acts like a private investor. The second tier is sustainable development which encourages a mix of uses, and promotes green environmental strategies and integration of high-quality design. Similar to clustering, regenerating processes are building on agglomeration strategies, and offer economic opportunities and incentives to stakeholders. The third tier is conservation: maintaining a sense of heritage and place, by taking a surgical approach to identifying industrial areas that merit preservation and reinvention and then initiating a broad urban economy vision for the place.

Reinventing degraded urban and industrial areas in cities is also viewed as enhancing a city's adaptability and resiliency "by increasing the surface area that is biologically active. Among the activities which increase the city's resilience in response to climate change there is also the revival of degraded ecosystems in cities, and the development of ecosystem-related services" (Gorgoń, 2017: 24). Above all, the redevelopment of vacant or abandoned industrial land can promote social cohesion, bring a sense of belonging to the area, and also improve the welfare of local residents in addition to improving the physical environment (Chan et al., 2019).

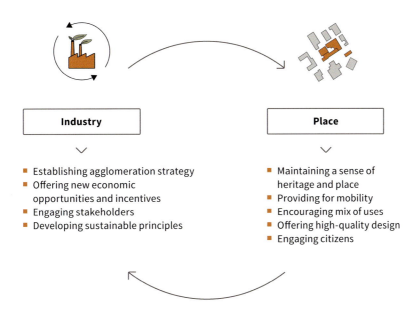

■ Industry–Place Nexus in Regenerating Industrial Areas

6

Forming Hybrid Districts

Ruta N & Innovation District, Medellín, Colombia. Photo courtesy of Ruta N.

6

Forming Hybrid Districts

Features in Generating Hybrid Districts

Hybridity is about encouraging the creation of heterogeneous environments that include diverse activities in industrial areas. This process, supported by the rapid development of information technologies, has broad social and environmental effects and influences planning policies. Current strategies for designing industrial areas advocate creating a mix of uses (e.g. employment and commerce), diversifying production activities (e.g. manufacturing, research, and development), and designing varied programmatic characteristics (e.g. zoning, size of plots and the relationship among them). Planners use a variety of tools to support these strategies (Hatuka and Weinberg, 2016). First, *supporting employment mix*: creating a useful combination of industry for craft, offices, as well as commerce and recreation. Second, *integrating diverse industrial activities*: encouraging varied activities and planning the industrial area so that a complete production chain is possible, from research and development through production to logistics, management, factory stores, and visitor centers. Third, *developing specialized complexes for manufacturing, logistics, and offices*: allocating specialized complexes for various activities and dispersing them throughout the indus-

trial area in a way that avoids nuisances and mutual disruptions on the one hand and produces functional logic on the other. Fourth, *combining public uses that serve the employment area and its environment*: encouraging communal activities and utilization that serve the industrial area, such as education (vocational education and training), health (occupational clinic), and employee welfare (sports center, day care centers). Fifth, *encouraging residential integration as part of the employment area and its surroundings*: planning of industrial areas adjacent to residential areas while considering the point of contact between the two areas, subject to environmental constraints (ibid.).

Hybridity, different from the clustering and regenerating that are advocated by economic policymakers and city planners, emerged from the fields of architecture and urban design. The concept of hybridity focuses on spatial and architectural expressions, as a result of a growing recognition that most existing land use and planning regulations do not advance current manufacturing trends. Hybridity is also a reaction to the maker movement, viewed as the result of shifts in both technology and consumption behavior (Anderson, 2012; Dougherty, 2012; Hatch, 2013). The accessibility of open-source design software and rapid-prototyping technologies such as three-dimensional printers reduce the resources necessary to engage in product design and fabrication (Wolf-Powers et al., 2017). Pallets and stocking/stacking systems in shipping and storage also mean that the multi-story factory is once again set to be a practical competitor of the common single-story factory (Rappaport, 2015). Arguments in favor of the multi-story factory include: the need to reconsider the advances in building technology; to maximize the supply of urban land zoned for industry; and to develop a building typology that will fit better into cities' existing urban fabrics. Furthermore, in anticipation of small and medium-sized advanced manufacturers' needs, policymakers encourage and support renovating and partitioning old urban factories originally designed for a single large manufacturer's use (Mistry and Byron, 2011: 7). Cities, it is argued, need to develop "metropolitan export strategies" to help "local firms market their goods, services, and expertise, including newly fashioned advanced manufacturing products, beyond regional borders" (ibid.: 5–6) – which might require building, redesigning, or updating transportation systems.

In its essence, the hybrid approach emphasizes locality and the opportunities created for the inhabitants and users of the area. The premise of this approach is that a mix and variety of employment uses address a range of professional abilities and aspirations of the area's residents, and possibly increase their employment opportunities. In addition, just like the benefits of mixing uses in city centers, the mixing of uses in industrial zones increases the chance of making the area an active and living place, for more varied use and longer hours. Advocates of this approach perceive hybridity as a spatial framework for preserving industrial districts in cities with a growing shortage of industrial and "back-of-house" real estate. Architect Tim Love, for example, suggests that mixed-use industrial development cross-subsidizes the construction of new industrial spaces with non-industrial and higher-value uses on upper floors and supports densification that results in hybrid buildings (Love, 2017). This approach may improve the walkability of industrial areas, and promote alternative transportation modes and neighborhood retail (ibid.). More concretely, hybridity re-

jiggers the regulations in industrial districts to allow light manufacturing, R&D, commercial, and live/work tenants on the upper floors. The development of hybrid buildings or vertical urban factories (Rappaport, 2017) is not limited to the individual building, but can also be aggregated at the district scale, and helps to connect real estate and economic development issues with a specific approach to land use planning (ibid.). These ideas are based on the normative premise that a new hybridity – both spatially and economically – might lead to more productive and vital cities. In other words, by integrating manufacturing at the building scale in multi-story buildings and at the city scale in mixed-use areas, a new hybrid can contribute to a sustainable city – economically, socially, and ecologically (Rappaport, 2017).

It is important to note that the integration of the living space and the work space is not new. Prior to the first Industrial Revolution, most people worked in or near living space. But, with the transition to mass production in factories and its environmental consequences, the separation of uses took hold. The return to hybridity in the late 20th century is associated with regeneration bottom-up processes in industrial areas in decline, as is the case of SoHo, New York. SoHo began with an illegal conversion of an industrial area into an area with housing and commerce. Later, new buildings began to be built as a combination of residence and work in the same unit. Following this move, young urban professionals entered the industrial area. With the change in local character and rising real estate values, more and more affluent settlers arrived (including families), and the areas stabilized as residential neighborhoods. At first, this successful dynamic was identified by real estate developers and municipal planning departments worldwide as a means of reviving industrial areas in cities that had deteriorated as a result of a shrinking manufacturing sector. Later, a more critical approach emerged and this phenomenon became known as "residential reversion" (Cutting Edge Planning & Design, 2015), and poses a challenge for planners and architects, namely how to protect lower-value industrial uses from competing with housing.

6 | FORMING HYBRID DISTRICTS

■ **Features of Hybrid Districts**

Place
Preservation and enhancement of existing assets
Organic growth and minimal tactical interventions
Flexibility
Mix requirements and regulations
Patchwork

Culture
Community engagement
Live/work
Affordable housing and commercial spaces
Innovation from the margins

Leadership
Local advocacy
Public/private partnership
Government and public agencies

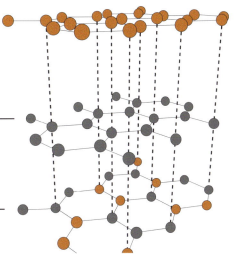

22@DISTRICT Barcelona, Catalonia, Spain. Photo by Thomas Nemeskeri (CC BY-NC-ND 2.0).

Huaqiangbei area Shenzhen, China. Photo by Jack Tanner (CC BY-NC-ND 2.0).

The Fair-Haired Dumbbell building, Central Eastside Portland OR, USA. Photo courtesy of Peter Eckert.

137

Still, advocates of hybridity argue that cities do not have to choose between strategies that support either compact, mixed-use development or "urban industrial development"; instead, they need approaches that explicitly safeguard productive urban industrial land and discourage industrial sprawl. To build livable cities with robust economies, policymakers must integrate their economic development, industrial policies, and environmental policies (Mistry and Byron, 2011: 6). Moreover, policymakers can "develop a new narrative about manufacturing and metropolitan economies," and "urban, industrial land use strategies should be linked to wider economic development and workforce objectives and should minimize mismatches among workforce, community revitalization, and city-wide economic development goals" (Mistry and Byron, 2011: 4). These tensions, between aspirations to create a more mixed city, moving away from the separation of land uses, and the realities of industrial sites on the ground, will continue to occupy planners and policymakers, along with the need to protect lower-value industrial uses from competition with housing (Ferm and Jones, 2016).

Hybridity reflects a new trend towards developing industrial and employment-based living environments, adapted to contemporary lifestyles and relying on new technologies. These built environments are based on synchronizing the industrial and the living in a way that could not have been promoted before. This approach is still in its infancy, and new structural approaches and typologies are expected to develop.

Implementing the concept of hybridity requires leadership, the involvement of multiple government and public agencies as well as local advocacy. The framework of hybridity relies a great deal on a place's culture, community engagement, live/work lifestyle, and a dynamic environment that also supports affordable housing. Leadership and the culture of the place are key in supporting hybridity as a framework, which implies a mix of requirements and regulations accompanying a view of the urban fabric as evolving organically and as a patchwork rather than with a top-down vision of economic development. In the following section, four cases – Barcelona (Spain), Medellín (Colombia), Portland (Oregon, USA), and Shenzhen (China) – exemplify varied paths in achieving hybrid industrial districts.

22@ District, Barcelona, Spain

Founded in 2000, Barcelona's 22@ District was a government initiative aimed at reinvigorating a dilapidated industrial area on the periphery of Barcelona's downtown. The area, also known as San Martí, first rose to prominence in the mid-18th century with the arrival of a new railway line, connecting it to the city center of Barcelona. In the latter half of the 18th and during the 19th century, the number of factories increased fourfold, making it the unofficial industrial center of the city. The area boasted factories in many diverse industries, including textiles, construction, food and wine, and agriculture. Even so, after World War II, the city of Barcelona established a new area of industrial activity closer to the city center – a move that started to drain the San Martí district of its industrial prowess; by 1990 the area had lost more than 1,000 factories.

A major shift in this dynamic is linked to the 1992 Olympic Games, which brought about an extensive infrastructure build-out, including key investments in transportation. These investments included ring roads connecting the district with the rest of the region. When this infrastructure was finally finished in 1999, government officials started to brainstorm about the future of the district. Although there was considerable pressure to rezone the area for residential development following the Olympic Games, the City Council of Barcelona chose instead to adopt a more nuanced strategy that encompassed a number of different land uses. The result was a plan for the 22@ District, and in 2000, the government of Barcelona unanimously approved a master plan for the area: it focused on industrial refurbishment and novel zoning strategies to encourage economic development.

The key idea of the plan was to replace traditional industries with the most advanced economic activities. The project aimed to create a cluster of knowledge-based firms, and is viewed as one element in the city of Barcelona's shift towards positioning the city in the knowledge economy (Duarte and Sabaté, 2013). The success of the plan was based on a set of complementary policy actions. First, a redevelopment of the urban landscape and the change of zoning classification. The classification 22a (i.e. exclusively for industrial purposes) was replaced with a new classification, 22@, which allowed a mixed use of the land in the district (all economic industries could be located there, together with housing and public services uses) (Viladecans-Marsal and Arauzo-Carod, 2012). To increase the knowledge-based undertakings, any developer wishing to increase land profitability could choose to create spaces devoted exclusively to 22@ activities, defined as those related to the information, communication, and technology sector, with research, design, culture, and knowledge (ibid.: 381). The adoption of an innovative zoning allowed for both economic densification and the diversification of land uses. Instead of emphasizing one kind of land use over another, the zoning amendments encouraged the gradual development of a stable mix of land uses as a means to achieve urban renewal, economic renewal, and social renewal. This offered a more inclusive approach to urban development which helped to establish a model that would both spur economic development and social growth (Gianoli and Henkes, 2020).

Second, the redevelopment of an infrastructure network re-urbanized and modernized 37 kilometers of streets in the district. The city invested in public amenities, and 220,000 square meters were dedicated to new public facilities and green spaces as well as residential development; 3.2 million square meters were set aside for office space in order to create the critical mass needed for economic clustering. Furthermore, design also played a role in developing the district's identity, and internationally renowned architects were brought in to develop iconic designs, including the Edificio Forum, which quickly became an architectural landmark.

In addition, the master plan broke down the district's 115 city blocks into five small clusters that would be appealing areas to both work and live in – MedTech, Design, Media, ICT, and Energy. In supporting this idea, the district boasts a number of organizations and activities brought together to create opportunities for interaction and collaboration among companies within the district. The 22@ Staying in Company program, for example, connects university students with local businesses to retain homegrown talent. Other programs include regularly hosted breakfasts that foster exchanges of ideas, an Urban Cluster Day symposium to present research findings, and a networking body that connects individuals across different companies. All these programs and activities contributed to the clustering culture.

This top-down, strategic development program also included a management organization that was tasked with supervising the creation and the maintenance of the district. The organization played a key role by enacting aspects of the master plan, issuing zoning permits, coordinating activities, and engaging in effective and consistent branding initiatives.

The 22@ District is an example of top-down planning and management in the creation of a hybrid district that sustains residential, commercial, and industrial activities. "Urban regeneration projects are characterized by a high degree of uncertainty, conflict, and complexity, as they are usually developed within a long-term perspective where situations of asymmetry of information and power among actors are frequent" (Gianoli and Henkes, 2020: 2). The adaptive governance principles offered solutions to the challenges inherent in urban regeneration projects.

Indeed, through a number of innovative approaches and very clearly delineated tactics, the city of Barcelona was able to convert the area from a struggling industrial area to a dynamic economic district. Yet, there are also critical voices that point to the gentrification

PART II | PLACES OF MAKING

processes in the area and the expropriation of cheap public housing (Duarte and Sabaté, 2013; Rowe, 2006). These controversies point to tensions between economic growth that supports knowledge-based urban development and society's needs.

Medellínnovation District, Medellín, Colombia

The second largest city in Colombia, Medellín served as the country's industrial capital throughout the mid-20th century. The city's proximity to agricultural lands made it the home and support-center for the country's coffee industry. But from the mid-20th century until the 1970s, the city faced many challenges caused by the inner migration of farmers and agricultural workers around Colombia and especially in Bogotá. City limits quickly grew past the ones envisioned by the city's master plan and city officials struggled to provide for the populations that were flooding into the city. In turn, the city's crime rate and violence grew rapidly, and it became one of the murder capitals of the world. However, in the last two decades, as a result of a number of government investments in transportation infrastructure and social urbanism programs that help connect the city and spur economic growth, the city was able to turn around its bleak past. The city built a safe and efficient metro system as well as a cable car that links some of the city's poorest neighborhoods with the city center. It has also made significant investments in research centers and facilities such as the University Research Building.

This change is also part of a public–private management initiative. In 2009, the city of Medellín and the public-utility and telecommunications company EPM-UNE launched Ruta N Medellín, a public organization with a mission to transform Medellín into a knowledge city (Morisson and Bevilacqua, 2019). As one of its first major initiatives, Ruta N Medellín announced a plan to create an innovation district in the northern part of the city in 2012, which had historically been a very impoverished area. The area housed a number of actors

necessary to spark innovation, including a number of universities, hospitals, and research centers (i.e. the University of Antioquia, the National University, the Hospital San Vicente de Paul, the Parque Explora, and the Botanical Garden of Medellín, two metro stations, the Ruta N innovation center) and was consequently viewed as a good location for development. It also boasted strong existing infrastructure, including crucial transportation nodes that connected it with Medellín's city center.

Similarly to 22@ in Barcelona, the Medellínnovation District is a result of a top-down development approach, initiated by key public entities within the city and with the aid of international experts. In 2012, experts from 22@ Barcelona came to Medellín as consultants to help structure the strategy for the Medellínnovation District; in 2013, urban planning professors from MIT (Dennis Frenchman and Carlo Ratti) designed the masterplan for the Medellínnovation District (Morisson and Bevilacqua, 2019). The vision was to integrate all the actors in the district and to develop an innovation district planned around the Ruta N innovation center, a 33,140-square-meter complex that houses Ruta N offices, EPM-UNE research laboratories, the ViveLab animation learning center, international companies, and international start-ups (Morisson and Bevilacqua, 2019). The complex includes three buildings, gardens, and access to transportation nodes. The buildings themselves are connected and designed to spark interactions between and among residents and visitors. They house several large companies, including Hewlett Packard, established public entities such as UNE Telecommunications and EPM group, and Medellín's major universities.

In pushing the vision forward, Ruta N teamed up with a number of different research groups to help plan this new innovation district (Ratti, 2014). This strong top-down leadership played a key role in helping to spur new initiatives within the district, to ensure its successful development, and assist in integrating the district into the existing community. The core procedure was to attract knowledge-intensive international start-ups in the areas of ICT, health, and energy. The programs developed and implemented by the innovation district division at Ruta N can be regrouped into two categories: attraction and absorption (Morisson and Bevilacqua, 2019). Attraction refers to programs that appeal to different incubators, start-ups, and companies through the early-stage development process. The programs also integrated the district with the existing area and cultivated exchanges among the companies, organizations, and start-ups located there. The city also offered tax breaks to companies located within key knowledge clusters to attract them to the complex (EU University Business Cooperation, 2019). Absorption programs aim to convert residents of the Medellínnovation District into full participants in the development of the innovation district – by, for example, incorporating extensive community feedback into its process, or ongoing programs such as DistritoLab, which encourages start-up development among local high school students – and works to incorporate the surrounding community into the district itself.

While it is still growing and developing, the district has played a key role in earning the city accolades for its economic development initiatives and in attracting new companies to the city as well as spurring endogenous growth. Furthermore, this case study serves as an example of efforts to integrate economic development with existing communities and attempts to include those communities in the ensuing growth (Auschner et al., 2020). However, it has also been argued that in public–private partnerships (PPPs) in Latin America (including Medellín), emphases on economic goals have sometimes trumped ecological, equity, and engagement marks. This has resulted in recommendations to restructure PPPs to more meaningfully integrate more people's perspectives, particularly lower-income and historically disenfranchised communities (Franz, 2017; Irazábal and Jirón, 2020). In addition, due to set-up costs and the lack of appropriate office and housing sites in the neighborhood, firms established themselves within the Ruta N Complex but not in the district at large. The characteristics of the neighborhood have, to some extent, limited the influx

of businesses and talent, therefore minimizing their potential transformational effect (Arenas et al., 2020). Consequently, if strategies for community outreach are not introduced, the debate and criticism may manifest themselves in a more intense and organized manner in the future (ibid.).

Central Eastside, Portland, Oregon, USA

Portland, like many other cities, includes several historic industrial districts developed in the early 20th century around railroad and waterfront infrastructure. These older industrial areas are typically located close to central business districts and are characterized by smaller blocks and older loft-style factory buildings. Another aspect of these districts is that due to their proximity to downtown areas they are also impacted by gentrification and the expansion of office development.

Central Eastside (CES) is one such industrial district. Developed as a railroad-based warehouse center and light manufacturing zone, the area became one of Portland's first industrial districts when it was incorporated into the city in 1891. For the following decades, it continued to prosper as an industrial base for the city. While most of Portland's industrial districts have gone through land use changes, Central Eastside has benefited from the city's industrial sanctuary zoning, which has helped retain the industrial base in the city center despite the turnover of manufacturing firms (Abbott et al., 1998). Today, this area is a dynamic and evolving part of Portland. It is seen as a planning success story, playing an important role in the city's economic and job growth.

In the mid-20th century, the Central Eastside industrial base was rapidly growing while shifting its early focus. Due to lack of efficient road infrastructure and unsuitable building types, some of the industry relocated to suburban locations while other, smaller firms moved in. While the economic base remained strong, providing employment opportunities in close proximity to downtown, it also brought about negative environmental impacts (Minner, 2007: 14–15). In the early 1980s, the Central Eastside Industrial Council asked 1000 Friends of Oregon, a land use planning watchdog organization, to author a report that would address the obstacles to revitalization of the district. The document, entitled "Central Eastside Industrial District: Benefactor of Portland's Economy," emphasized both the importance of industry in the district and its fragility. As a result of these efforts, as well as other reports by the city and its consultants, Portland's 1988 Central City Plan directly addressed the inclusion of the district, and its functions, policies, and visions. CES was adopted as an official district of the Central City in order to preserve it as an industrial sanctuary, and various zoning tools were used to promote industrial uses throughout the district. These included: (1) encouraging the formation of incubator industries in the district; (2) reinforcing the district's role as a distribution center; (3) allowing mixed-use developments, which include housing, in areas already committed to non-industrial development; (4) preserving buildings that are of historical and/or architectural significance; (5) developing Union and Grand Avenues as the principal north–south connection and commercial spine in the district for transit and pedestrians; (6) continuing implementation of the Central Eastside Economic Development Policy (Minner, 2007: 19).

These zoning tools were used to promote industrial uses throughout the district. For example, the dominant zone designation, General Industrial 1 (IG1), allowed a minimum amount of office and retail uses by right, with the ability to earn substantially more floor area through conditional use procedures. Some of the industrial codes were also amended to create a performance-based code to allow for flexibility and the changing nature of industry (Minner, 2007: 29). In 2006, the City Council created an Employment Opportunity Subarea (EOS) in portions of the Central Eastside. Within this subarea, zoning provisions were adopted that provided more flexibility in terms of the maximum amount of retail as well as offices permitted in the IG1 zone. Most importantly, these regulations were

intended to protect existing industrial operations in the district, while providing more flexibility for new emerging industrial sectors seeking incubator space to start their businesses in the district.

To maintain the viability of the zoning for industrial uses, the area has protections from non-compatible land uses through the Industrial Disclosure Statement. This document (signed by all local landowners) acknowledges the normalcy of industrial uses within the neighborhood and shields compliant industries from complaints by neighbors. Owing to the high potential of conflicts within mixed-industrial zones, neighborhood transitions are managed through urban design guidelines that orient residential and commercial blocks towards mixed-use corridors, while orienting loading zones and other functions that support industrial uses towards the industrially zoned areas.

Growth in the area is managed by encouraging higher-density, mixed-use development in the portions of the district best served by transit and active transportation. This is done through the creation of an overlay EX (Central Employment) zone which allows for taller and denser development within the IG1 zone. This zone also permits a broader mix of uses, including residential, commercial office, retail, institutional, as well as light industrial uses. It notably provides for a higher degree of change and diversity in areas where existing industrial uses are either not located or are not the dominant land use pattern. This applies to station areas, for example, which require higher-density employment for activity and safety and also to support transit ridership (Portland, 2021).

In addition, heritage and identity play a role in the development of the area. The area boasts a unique collection of historic industrial buildings as well as a centralized location near Portland's business core. These strategies contributed to the diversification of industrial types, which also influence the need and development of the transportation modes used to move both employees and products. The city has helped to capitalize on this latter opportunity through substantial public investment in multimodal transportation infrastructure, such as light rail, streetcar, and bike and pedestrian facilities. The Portland–Milwaukee Light Rail (PMLR) line, which opened in 2015, for example, includes two stations within the district next to several larger redevelopment opportunity sites, which could accommodate growth of existing businesses or attract new industries and employment to the district (Chilson, 2017).

The investment in expansive mobility infrastructure is a direct result of the need to reduce conflicts between transport modes as a result of the area's diverse (and intense) land uses. Moving freight is particularly important for industry: the district solves potential conflict with active modes by providing prioritized routes and infrastructure to improve truck circulation and by converting select routes into one-way streets, increasing the number of traffic signals and improving signage. The pedestrian and bicycle infrastructure, meanwhile, has also been developed into a route, the "Green Loop," which connects existing attractions, open space, recreational amenities, and central city districts (Portland Bureau of Planning & Sustainability, 2017).

The success of Portland's Central Eastside can be attributed to a number of creative zoning and land use strategies that established a context in which a mix of uses could grow and thrive. Unlike other successful hybrid districts, which are managed closely from above, Portland's CES is evidence of bottom-up success in which a strategic groundwork was laid for hybrid uses to grow naturally. It is important to note that the zoning strategies themselves did not operate in a vacuum, but were supported through a number of design initiatives that improved the quality of life in the district and increased its attractiveness for alternative uses. Clear transportation planning and design strategies in particular created a context in which industry, commercial and residential uses alike could thrive.

The evolution of the Central Eastside into an industrial area has shaped the urban form that exists today. With each successive era, the types of buildings and transportation infrastructure in the district have changed to meet evolving business needs. Where old-

er buildings used to house a single product distribution company, for example, they now house numerous small-scale manufacturing, industrial services, and industrial office users. To date, the CES is home to more than 1,100 businesses and 17,000 jobs – more than any other district in the Central City outside of the downtown core. This is largely because industrial uses and creative businesses sit side-by-side, as the area becomes an emerging location for cross-industry exchange – from film and digital enterprises, to food, creative services, and craft industries. While employment in other Central City areas decreased during the recent economic downturn, jobs increased in this district – in part because of a growing presence of traded sector industries that reinforce and form a symbiotic relationship with each other, creating an industrial ecosystem (Portland Bureau of Planning & Sustainability, 2014).

Portland's approach to urban revitalization, in the form of industrial sanctuary designation implemented through a flexible regulatory framework, protects existing manufacturing use and is a powerful tool for keeping the gentrification of industrial uses and their potential displacement from city centers in check (Abbott et al., 2004). One of the goals of the Portland Metro Region through the 2040 framework and functional plans is "to designate the best places for more intense concentrations of housing and businesses and to protect industrial and employment lands that are the backbone of the regional economy and provide high paying jobs" (Portland, 2021). With its prime location, Central Eastside, has managed to provide valuable employment opportunities for inner city neighborhoods and allows industrial firms to locate in a more compact and mixed urban form.

Huaqiangbei, Shenzhen, China

Shenzhen was established as a special economic zone (SEZ) in 1979 and was an important experiment in industrial policy in China's reform era economy. Urban planner Zhang Jun (2017) describes the evolution of

Shenzhen's industrial policy in four phases. Phase 1 (~1986) focused on low cost manufacturing (mainly assembly) and the establishment of an industrial park. Until 1986, industrial development relied on cheap land and labor, with industrial zones concentrated near convenient transportation. During this time, major industries in the city included electronics, textiles, and construction material industries. Shangbu Industrial Park, established in 1982, where the Huaqiangbei Electronics Market is located (Chen, 2017), was the first area that specialized in electronics assembly in China. Phase 2 (1987–1997) included a physical expansion of industrial zones and the formation of second-generation IT and high-tech clusters. During this period, the number of low cost manufacturing and highly polluting industries moved towards other parts of the Pearl River Delta (Guangzhou and Dongguan) while Shenzhen recruited businesses in telecommunications, the new materials industry, and the biotech industry. As early as 1988, Shangbu Industrial Park began to develop a strong communications industry and professionally oriented market. By 1994, the site resembled a commercial district instead of an industrial zone. However, Chinese industrial policy – different from Western tech clusters – did not cultivate higher education and R&D facilities as a catalyst for the site development but focused instead on high-tech manufacturing. Phase 3 (1998–2008) was about accelerating high-tech industries and the emergence of local innovation. During this period, heavy industries and labor-intensive industries moved away from Shenzhen, and accordingly much of the new development involved redevelopment of older industrial zones and land reclamation. Industrial policy – specifically the "Shenzhen Municipality High-Tech Industrial Belt Development Plan" of 2001 – specified areas dedicated for high-tech, industrial development, and intentionally phased out other forms of industrial production. These planned areas were located on the outskirts of the established cities, but other high-tech zones (such as Huaqiangbei, Shekou, and Chegungmiao) also organically emerged as hybrid commercial and industrial zones. Phase 4 (2009 onwards) was about the formation of innovation

districts and industrial ecology. During this time, there has been significant growth in local innovation in Shenzhen, with 17 new comprehensive development zones in the city including commercial, residential, industry, and multifunctional, planning to cater to a different type of labor in the city. Shenzhen also began to play the role of a regional hub for innovation and high-tech industries, with many of the large factory/manufacturing spaces moving north and west within the Pearl River Delta, maintaining administration and R&D facilities in Shenzhen.

Geographically, Huaqiangbei is located in the Futian District of Shenzhen; more than 1.45 square kilometers of land has been transformed into an industrial area. In terms of industry this area is known as "China's first electronics street" or the "Silicon Valley of Hardware," and it is China's largest electronics hub, accounting for over 50% of China's electronics sales (Sun, 2018). It also serves as a center for China's high-tech maker movement.

Historically, Shangbu Industrial Zone was established in 1982 by Huaqiang – a Guangdong Provincial Level State-Owned Enterprise. At the time, the central government played a big role in its development, especially as various national level SOEs entered into the zone; for instance, subsidiaries of the Ministry of Aviation set up several electronics factories here (Chen, 2017). In the 1990s, with Shenzhen's deindustrialization strategies (see phase 2 above) many primary manufacturing tenants in the zone left for other parts of the PRD and the zone then transformed into an electronics wholesale district with suppliers at a range of levels – national level wholesale distributors to small stalls in commercial centers. When a local flea market closed, many small electronics vendors moved in along Huanqiang North Road, which is the forefather of the current Huaqiangbei electronics market. However, this transformation was largely bottom-up and the Shenzhen municipal government sought to centralize the planning in the mid-1990s – but in vain.

By the early 2000s, rising land prices had forced most manufacturing to leave the district but showrooms and vendors remained in the electronics market. During this time, China's e-waste economy also played an important role in shaping Huaqiangbei's electronics market as many components were recycled back into retail or extracted and shipped to other processing facilities (Chen, 2017: 168). However, this early involvement in e-waste also points to how Huaqiangbei's electronics did not cater to a high-end market, but rather to a low-end or second-hand electronics market. During this time, the architectural typology of the electronics market emerged. Vendors occupied small stalls (0.5–6 square meters) in high-rise buildings often organized as component types (Chen, 2017: 170).

The dense electronics market and high volume of products have facilitated the tech maker movement in Shenzhen, which is known for rapid prototyping of products and now also product design. It relies on an intricate ecosystem of informal and formal manufacturers and entrepreneurs. It has also facilitated a vibrant fashion retail and food/beverage district adjacent to the electronics market.

In its essence, and from an industrial perspective, Huaqiangbei and Shenzhen's manufacturing ecosystem relies on a reciprocal relationship between state-led policies and grassroots industry – also known as the Shanzhai (山寨 in Chinese) system. Four processes influence this ecosystem. First, national policy prioritizes of developing an electronics industry in Shenzhen. In particular, the Ministry for the Electronics Industry set up an SOE that is now known as "Shenzhen SEG" in 1985, which included more than 100 electronics subsidiaries. This was the forerunner of the largest electronics market in Huaqiangbei, SEG plaza (Sun, 2018). Second, during this time global circuit board manufacturing started entering into China, and Huaqiangbei served as a key site for circuit board trading. Third, mobile phones proliferated in the mid-2000s when China relaxed regulations on the manufacturing of cell phones. Low-cost mobile phones, especially from Taiwanese manufacturers, flooded the Chinese market and naturally found a home in Shenzhen and Huaqiangbei. Fourth and last, a national innovation

and entrepreneurship policy in 2015 enabled the proliferation of innovation districts throughout China.

Although the origins of Huaqiangbei are rooted in traditional large-scale SOEs, its later evolution has dissolved into a significantly fragmented, horizontal, and grassroots organization. With very few exceptions, the majority of the operations in Huaqiangbei are very specialized and small scale, and it is an extensive interpersonal network and physical proximity that enable rapid prototyping, component sourcing, and eventually mass production to occur (Hallam, 2019). These efforts have been bolstered by China's 2015 policies to support mass entrepreneurship and innovation through preferential tax policies, resulting in the proliferation of creative spaces, innovation districts, and incubator spaces throughout China (State Council Information Office, 2015). The program particularly targets electronics and high-tech industries, and makes available subsidies and mechanisms for venture capital as well as knowledge transfer by encouraging foreign entrepreneurs or overseas Chinese to return. Last but not least, this policy aims to reinforce intellectual property rights in China. The 2015 national entrepreneurship and innovation program enabled a strong producers' movement in Shenzhen. This producers' movement is a convergence of the open-source ethic of Shanzhai and global tech entrepreneurship. It has been observed that many of these Shanzhai producers are not global elites nor do they possess technical expertise, rather some are provincial entrepreneurs that seek assistance in Shenzhen to develop a product and then distribute it back in their hometowns elsewhere in China, or other less developed economies (Stevens, 2019).

The outcome is "Shanzhai," a less formal manufacturing ecosystem comprised of a horizontal web of component producers, traders, design solution houses, vendors, and assembly lines. They operate through an informal social network and a culture of sharing (Lindtner et al., 2015). This ecosystem includes out-of-town entrepreneurs, industrial designers, electronic markets, and factories (Stevens, 2019).

PART II | PLACES OF MAKING

22@ DISTRICT,
Barcelona, Spain

Founded in 2000, Barcelona's 22@ District was a government initiative aimed at reinvigorating a dilapidated industrial area on the periphery of Barcelona's downtown. Under the guidance of strong leadership and with the help of several innovative land use policies and clustering strategies, the district has succeeded in attracting more than 4,500 new companies. Its 500 acres house five clusters of expertise: media, energy, MedTech, ICT, and design. The district's success was achieved through an integrated model of growth that included urban, economic, and, significantly, social renewal.

Production/industry allowed
Residential
Green/open space
Water

FORMALITY | Axes as connectors

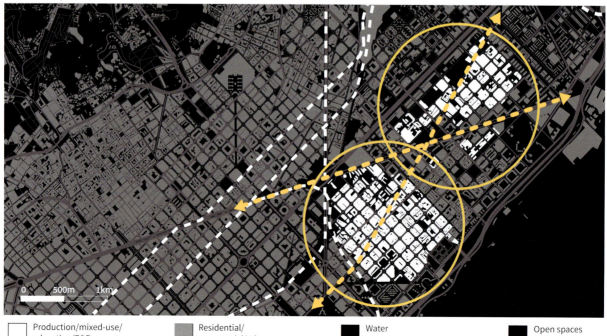

Production/mixed-use/education/R&D
Residential/commercial/other
Water
Open spaces

146

6 | FORMING HYBRID DISTRICTS

PROTOTYPE |
Integrated

INDUSTRY PROFILE

Program	Innovation district
Spatial form	Integrated, urban agglomeration
Land use typologies	Light industry, commercial, residential
Key actors	Ajuntament de Barcelona

STRATEGIES |

Leadership

The 22@ District was initiated by the city of Barcelona as a top-down, strategic development program. The city was responsible not only for creating a Master Plan that offered a comprehensive strategy for the area, but also for creating an organization that was tasked with supervising the creation and maintenance of the innovation district. The latter in particular has played a key role throughout the district's existence, issuing zoning permits, implementing key aspects of the master plan, coordinating activities and engaging in effective and consistent branding initiatives. The overall strategy was one of "urban renewal, economic renewal and social renewal," which offered a more inclusive approach to urban development that helped establish a model that would spur both economic development and social growth.

Culture

The district boasts a number of organizations and activities aimed at creating opportunities for interaction and collaboration among companies within the district. There are five designated clusters: MedTech, Design, Media, ICT, and Energy, which the district works actively to support and cultivate. The 22@ Staying in Company program, for example, connects university students with local businesses to retain homegrown talent. Other programs include regular, hosted breakfasts that foster idea exchanges; an Urban Cluster Day symposium to present research findings; and a networking organization that connects individuals in different companies. The 22@ District is often regarded as a model for clustering culture.

Place

Design played an essential role in planning for the success of the district. The district was an impressive 115 city blocks; the master plan broke the area into smaller clusters to create appealing areas to both work and live. In the district, 220,000 square meters were dedicated for new public facilities and green spaces as well as residential development; 3.2 million square meters were set aside for office space in order to create the critical mass needed for economic clustering. Internationally-renowned architects were brought in to develop iconic designs, including the Edificio Forum, which quickly became an architectural landmark. The district's planners viewed design as a key aspect of creating a district that would increase both livability and economic productivity.

PART II | PLACES OF MAKING

INNOVATION DISTRICT,
Medellín, Colombia

After being dubbed "the murder capital of the world" in the 1990s, Medellín is now lauded as one of the world's most innovative cities. At the center of this turnaround lies a strong emphasis on economic growth and inclusive development efforts. Established in 2012, the innovation district in Medellín embodies this strategy. Located in an impoverished area within the city, the Medellínnovation District has succeeded in both attracting international companies and nurturing domestic ones. A strong emphasis on design combined with top-down strategies for endogenous incubation, albeit still in progress, is showing signs of success.

CENTRAL | Remaking a new core

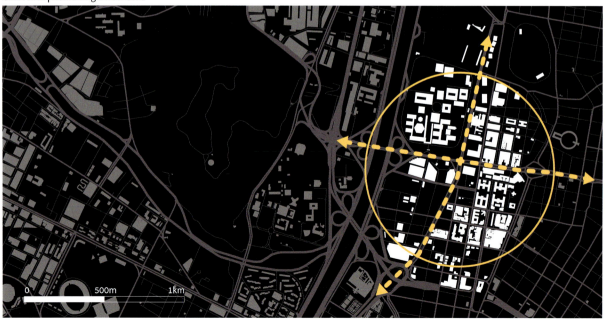

148

6 | FORMING HYBRID DISTRICTS

PROTOTYPE |
Integrated

INDUSTRY PROFILE

Program	Innovation district
Spatial form	Integrated, urban agglomeration
Land use typologies	Light industry, commercial, residential
Key actors	Hewlett-Packard, EPM, UNE

STRATEGIES |

Leadership

The creation of Medellín's innovation district was guided by Ruta N Medellín, a public entity formed through a partnership between the city of Medellín and UNE EPM (the city's public utility and telecommunications company). Ruta N led the development of a master plan for the district, and continues working to help guide the evolution of the district. This strong top-down leadership plays a key role in helping to spur new initiatives within the district. The core strategy of the district is to attract knowledge-intensive international startups in the areas of ICT, health, and energy. The Ruta N complex offers varied incubator and start-up programs to help usher companies through the early-stage development process. Notably, the city also offers tax breaks to companies.

Culture

The district emphasizes several different programs to both integrate the district into the existing area, and cultivate exchanges among the companies, organizations, and startups located there. The master plan and the subsequent development in the area incorporated extensive community feedback in its process, for example, and there are ongoing programs, such as DistritoLab, which encourages start-up development among local high school students, and works to incorporate the surrounding community into the district itself.

Place

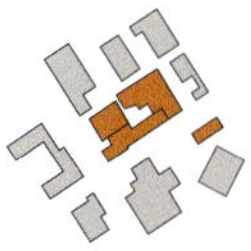

The Ruta N Complex is at the core of the innovation district. The complex includes three buildings, gardens, and access to key transportation nodes. The buildings themselves are integrated with each other, and carefully designed to spark interactions between and among residents and visitors. They house several large companies, including Hewlett Packard, key public entities such as UNE Telecommunications and EPM group, and Medellín's major universities.

149

PART II | PLACES OF MAKING

CENTRAL EASTSIDE,
Portland, Oregon, USA

The success of Portland's Central Eastside (CES) can be attributed to an unwavering insistence on industrial protection. Zoning has played a significant role in that success. The city effectively created a symbiotic industrial ecosystem through diversification of industries and businesses. One approach for arriving at that end goal was a varied overlay zoning strategy that allowed for consistent renewal and reinterpretation of some areas, the integration of new forms of mobility, and making provisions for an evolving character.

DIFFUSION | Enhancing an existing urban fabric

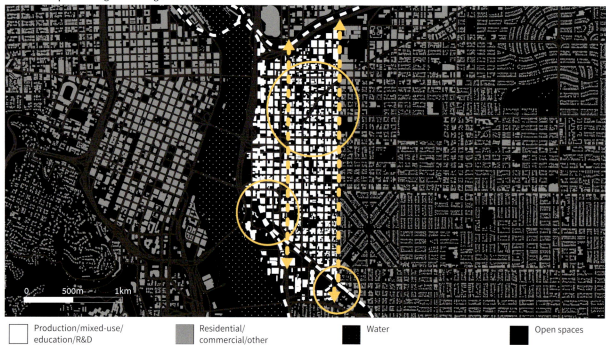

6 | FORMING HYBRID DISTRICTS

PROTOTYPE |
Integrated

INDUSTRY PROFILE

Program	Mixed-use industrial district
Spatial form	Integrated, urban agglomeration
Land use typologies	Heavy and light industry, commercial, residential
Key actors	City of Portland, Central Eastside Industrial District (CEID)

STRATEGIES |

Leadership

In 2006, the Portland City Council created an Employment Opportunity Subarea (EOS) in portions of the Central Eastside. Within this subarea, zoning provisions were adopted that provided more flexibility in terms of the maximum amount of retail and offices permitted in the industrial zone. This zone also allows a broader mix of uses, including residential, commercial office, retail, institutional, and light industrial use. Most importantly, these regulations were intended to protect existing industrial operations in the district, while providing more flexibility for new, emerging industrial sectors seeking "incubator" space to start businesses in the district.

Culture

The CES is home to more than 1,100 businesses and 17,000 jobs. This is largely due to industrial uses and creative businesses sitting side-by-side, as the area becomes an emerging location for cross-industry exchange, from film and digital enterprises to food, creative services, and craft industries. Employment in this district has been strong in part because of a growing presence of traded sector industries that form a symbiotic relationship, and reinforce each other, creating an industrial eco-system base.

Place

The area boasts a unique collection of historic industrial buildings as well as a centralized location near Portland's business core. The city has helped to capitalize on this latter opportunity through substantial public investment in multi-modal transportation infrastructure, such as light rail, streetcar, bicycle, and pedestrian facilities. The Portland-Milwaukee Light Rail (PMLR) line, which opened in 2015, for example, includes two stations within the district, adjacent to several larger redevelopment opportunity sites, which could accommodate growth of existing businesses or attract new industries and employment to the district. Pedestrian and bicycle infrastructure, meanwhile, has also been developed into a route dubbed the "Green Loop" that connects existing attractions, open space, recreational amenities, and Central City districts via a continuous bicycle and pedestrian pathway.

PART II | PLACES OF MAKING

SHENZHEN
Guangdong, China

Shenzhen's Huaqiangbei is a globally significant high-tech and innovation district – also known as the "Silicon Valley of Hardware". The district was originally an industrial zone and then, with the outward movement of manufacturing in the 1990s, it became a large market for electronic components and "shanzhai" products – originally referring to fake or copycat electronics but now synonymous with a grassroots producers movement. Huaqiangbei is a hub for a grassroots ecology of electronics assembly, recycling and repair, prototyping and testing, logistics, branding, product design and sales.

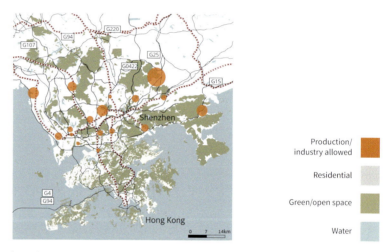

ORGANIC ECOSYSTEM | Validating and building on informality

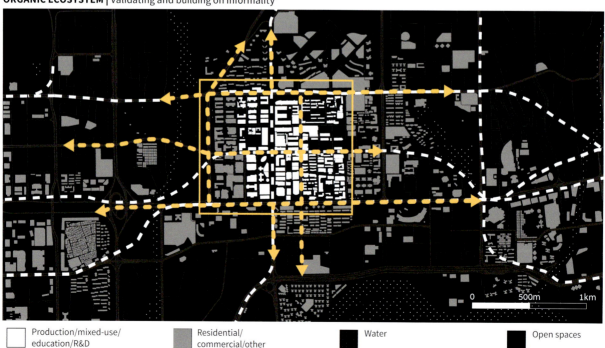

152

6 | FORMING HYBRID DISTRICTS

PROTOTYPE |
Integrated

INDUSTRY PROFILE

Program	Innovation district
Spatial form	Integrated
Land use typologies	Electronics market, commercial, residential
Key actors	Bottom-up entrepreneurship, Shenzhen municipality

STRATEGIES |

Leadership

Shangbu Industrial Zone was established in the early 1980s as a planned electronics industry hub in the newly established Shenzhen Special Economic Zone. The industrial zone housed several important state-owned enterprises, and after a planned exit of manufacturing from the inner core of Shenzhen in the 1990s, their expertise and spaces were transformed into the series of high-rise electronics markets that characterize Huaqiangbei. Around the same time, Huaqiangbei became a key site for global circuit board trading. In the mid-2000s when the regulations on mobile phone manufacturing were relaxed, Huaqiangbei became known for low-cost mobile phones and copy-cat electronics – which later evolved into the shanzhai manufacturing ecosystem. In 2015, the Chinese government implemented a national innovation and entrepreneurship policy for planned innovation districts, supposedly modeled after Huaqiangbei's successful shanzhai system.

Culture

Although the origins of Huaqiangbei are rooted in traditional, large-scale SOEs, its later evolution has devolved into a significantly fragmented, horizontal, grassroots organization. With very few exceptions, the majority of operations in Huaqiangbei are very specialized and small-scale; its extensive interpersonal network and physical proximity enables rapid prototyping, component sourcing, and eventually mass production. The 2015 national entrepreneurship and innovation program facilitated a strong maker's movement in Shenzhen where local tech incubators Seeed Studio and Chaihuo x. factory began to organize the annual Maker Fair Shenzhen. This producers' movement is a convergence of the open-source ethic of shanzhai and global tech entrepreneurship. These incubators provide space and networks for global entrepreneurs to develop products, prototypes, and eventually mass produce and distribute their new products.

Place

There have been a few attempts to redevelop the area. A 1999 master plan by the Shenzhen municipality proposed a pedestrian-oriented outdoor mall, but was not implemented due to opposition of major landlords and tenants of the district. Instead, a piecemeal renovation that accounted for the logistical needs of the zone was implemented with small-scale streetscape upgrades, and additional parking facilities. A second masterplan in 2000 sought to consolidate some of the spaces, and remove walled residential and old factory spaces. A denser street network was constructed in order to allow more commercial and retail frontage.

153

PART II | PLACES OF MAKING

■ Forming Hybrid Districts: Program, Spatiality and Land Uses

	22@ DISTRICT Barcelona, Spain		**INNOVATION DISTRICT** Medellín, Colombia	
Morphology	Formality		Central	
Program	Innovation districts		Innovation district	
Spatial form	**Integrated** Urban agglomeration		**Integrated** Urban agglomeration	
Catalysts	Light industry, commercial, residential		Light industry, commercial, residential	

Legend:
- Production/mixed-use
- Residential
- Green/open space

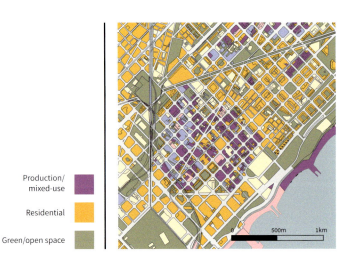

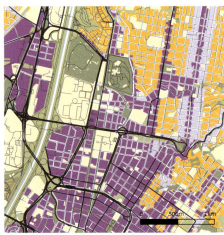

154

6 | FORMING HYBRID DISTRICTS

CENTRAL EASTSIDE
Portland, Oregon, USA

Diffusion

Mixed-use industrial district

Integrated
Urban agglomeration

Heavy and light industry, commercial, residential

SHENZHEN
Guangdong, China

Organic ecosystem

Innovation district

Integrated
Urban agglomeration

Electronics market, commercial, residential

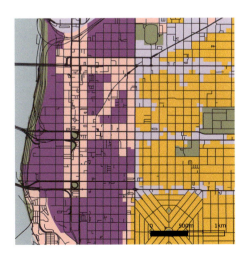

155

There have been a few attempts at redevelopment in the area. A first master plan in 1999 by the Shenzhen Municipality (primarily a pedestrian-oriented, outdoor mall) was not implemented due to the opposition of major landlords and tenants in the district. Instead, a piecemeal renovation that accounted for the logistical needs of the zone was implemented with small-scale streetscape upgrades and additional parking facilities. A second master plan in 2000 sought to consolidate some of the spaces and remove walled residential and factory spaces that were built in the 1980s. A denser street network was implemented in order to allow for more commercial and retail frontage. However, subsequent planning attempts were largely met with opposition of the local community – including an urban design competition for "vertical streets" throughout the zone and other urban visions – because there was no consideration of how major landowners and tenants would be restructured in the new plans (Chen, 2017: 180–182).

Shenzhen, founded under China's "open door" policy, has experienced dramatic urban development over the past 30 plus years (Goodling et al., 2015). It was the first Chinese city to adapt the capitalist world's urban development practices to an indigenous, centrally controlled land management system. This growth and unique fusion of top and bottom development processes is manifested in the hybrid district area of Huaqiangbei.

Industry–Place Nexus in Forming Hybrid Districts

Hybridization aims to create a new mix between industrial employment (light manufacturing structures, arts and crafts, small high-tech firms), affordable housing and public realm improvements. Hybridity is about economic growth, spatial flexibility, and compactness, offering a new adaptable lifestyle model for the future. The development of hybridity supports related aims: (1) new economic opportunities and incentives; (2) engaging stakeholders; (3) integrating bottom-up and top-down approaches; and (4) developing flexible or unique regulatory mechanisms to cultivate the social culture of the place.

The cases presented in this section exemplify the different approaches to hybridity. Barcelona, a *formal-urban* district, boasts a unique collection of historic industrial buildings. In Medellín, a complex of buildings was constructed to house several large companies in a *central urban* district. Portland's *diffused-urban district* used a light rail line (PMLR) to accommodate the growth of existing businesses or attract new industries and employment to the district. Pedestrian and bicycle infrastructures have also been developed into a route dubbed the "Green Loop" that connects existing attractions, open space, recreational amenities, and Central City districts. Shenzhen, an *organic-urban district*, used a strategy of piecemeal renovation in the residential areas and old factory spaces by creating a denser street network that allows for more commerce and retail.

Hybrid districts that focus on knowledge-based economies and creative economies often contribute to a high standard of living and economic prosperity (OECD, 1996). Two big challenges arise in developing hybrid innovation districts: first, protecting manufacturing uses; and second, integrating and protecting existing social communities. To protect manufacturing uses, planning policy is needed, as this approach challenges the classical land use zoning system and the separation of uses between residential, industrial, and employment. Accordingly, an inevitable tension arises between the need for housing and the need for employment and industry. A free market approach to hybridity may lead to residential dominance and may create hurdles (in the form of "NIMBY" not in my back yard opposition) for businesses and industries. Thus, policy is required to preserve the variety of users; artisans, and artists in particular need ample space and reasonably priced locations that can be found (almost) only in old industrial buildings. Second, in protecting and integrating existing social communities, designated programs are essential. Many hybrid innovation districts are criticized for being no less than gentrification programs (Morisson and Bevilacqua, 2019), a process that involves the transition of inner-city neighborhoods from a status of relative poverty and limited property investment to a state of commodification and reinvestment. Therefore, the challenge is to develop programs and plans in combination with multiple actors, in which both government and private stakeholders work together with communities to improve social welfare, particularly for those in need and left behind by the digital divide (Irazábal and Jirón, 2020).

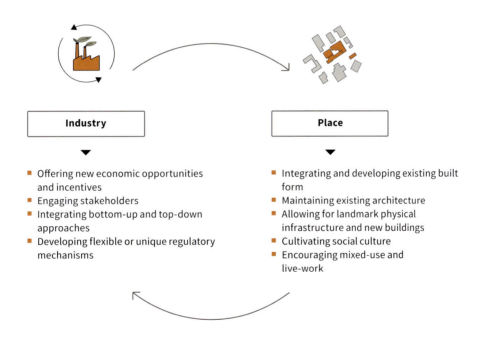

▪ Industry–Place Nexus in Forming Hybrid Districts

7

Industry and Place

7

Industry and Place

Clustering, reinventing, and hybridity are three contemporary approaches to developing industrial areas. Industrial clustering is a concept defined as a socio-spatial assemblage of people, buildings, and activities without any necessary center, boundary, or scale, where the production processes of some service-sector firms depend on infrastructure in a fixed, physical location. Industrial regeneration is a concept that refers to processes that boost existing industrial uses and reverse possible decline by improving the physical infrastructure, protecting and enhancing current land use, and building on the urban characteristics of the place. Hybridity is a relatively new concept that offers a spatial framework of mixed-use industrial zoning to preserve industrial districts in cities. Using the principle of densification, this framework proposes to construct hybrid buildings and districts based on the principles of walkability, alternative transportation, and neighborhood retail.

Although from the perspective of economic development these approaches differ from one another, they are all based on two related premises. The first is that industry has been and still is a central mechanism for economic growth for contemporary cities and regions; and the second that economic growth relies on different institutions collaborating and on various stakeholders forming a network. The three approaches to industrial development are based on an updated conception of the role of industry in cities, but also on the need to develop new frameworks of stakeholder participation. Thus, the foundational principles of 20th-century urban planning such as top-down policy, hierarchical decision-making, and limited stakeholder involvement cede their place to principles of integration, top-down and bottom-up initiatives, the creation of new coalitions, and encouragement of stakeholder involvement.

These new economic policy premises also manifest in the physical strategies. Generally, all the three approaches lean on two planning principles: compactness and connectivity. Compactness substitutes the distance and separation in zoning practices with new proximities among uses. This principle accompanies the need for collaboration and gives it physical expression. Connectivity is about defining new uses, paths, and mobility modes as a means of supporting the new proximities. Connectivity is often manifested in design as a means of updating a place's image as a whole.

Still, these approaches differ in their scale and initial concept. In terms of scale, clustering is an elastic approach of an undefined scale. It can be used for a region or a district; clustering can take place in rural, urban, or suburban environments. Furthermore, clustering growth is unlimited and its physicality is not always juxtaposed to its actual size or physical place. Distant sub clusters that produce products similar to

Contemporary Approaches to Industry and Place

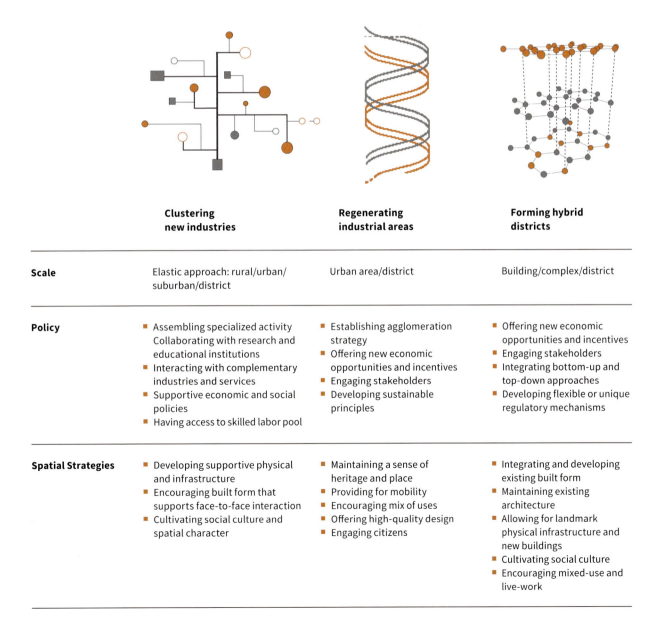

	Clustering new industries	Regenerating industrial areas	Forming hybrid districts
Scale	Elastic approach: rural/urban/suburban/district	Urban area/district	Building/complex/district
Policy	■ Assembling specialized activity Collaborating with research and educational institutions ■ Interacting with complementary industries and services ■ Supportive economic and social policies ■ Having access to skilled labor pool	■ Establishing agglomeration strategy ■ Offering new economic opportunities and incentives ■ Engaging stakeholders ■ Developing sustainable principles	■ Offering new economic opportunities and incentives ■ Engaging stakeholders ■ Integrating bottom-up and top-down approaches ■ Developing flexible or unique regulatory mechanisms
Spatial Strategies	■ Developing supportive physical and infrastructure ■ Encouraging built form that supports face-to-face interaction ■ Cultivating social culture and spatial character	■ Maintaining a sense of heritage and place ■ Providing for mobility ■ Encouraging mix of uses ■ Offering high-quality design ■ Engaging citizens	■ Integrating and developing existing built form ■ Maintaining existing architecture ■ Allowing for landmark physical infrastructure and new buildings ■ Cultivating social culture ■ Encouraging mixed-use and live-work

those of the main cluster can still be part of a single cluster. Regeneration focuses on the urban fabric and is often implemented at district scale. The point of departure for intervening when regenerating an area is the existing uses and people actually in the place. Lastly, hybridity is an urban approach that starts from the object, the single building, or a complex of buildings, to the level of the district. Its growth is cumulative: from the single to the many without necessarily following an overall strategic plan for the industrial area in the city as a whole. The various scales associated with these different approaches also express the key idea of each approach. Clustering fosters the specialization of existing or new industries; regeneration encourages sustainability, building on the past to construct a new future; and hybridity advocates flexibility, offering a new adaptable lifestyle model for the future.

Nevertheless, these approaches and cases teach us three important lessons. First, industrial development is about bridging the gap between industrial needs and zoning, which requires conceptualizing the city in a way that situates it within its broader regional social and economic context. Second, industrial development is about creating a manufacturing continuum, by identifying and developing sites that are appropriate for manufacturers at various stages (e.g. the maker stage, the start-up stage, the scale-up stage, the small and medium-sized enterprise stage, and heavy industry) based on regional strategic objectives (e.g. the growth of a particular sector) that could encourage the return of clean industry to the city (Reynolds, 2017). Third, industrial development in the 21st century is an ongoing search for strategies and concepts responding to the Fourth Industrial Revolution and its dynamic. All of the cases presented are characterized by a dynamic approach to policy and planning, an approach that implies a constant reassessing of strategies implemented, as well as initiating new, responsive, contextual strategies.

Finally, these cases show that societies are beginning to consider how industry can create place, sustain jobs, and promote environmental sustainability, all within the urban fabric. They suggest that manufacturing is not just the means but also the theme by which the future urbanism can and should be explored and developed.

PART II | PLACES OF MAKING

DIFFUSION | CENTRAL EASTSIDE, Portland, Oregon, USA.

DIFFUSION | BROOKLYN Navy Yard, New York City, New York, USA.

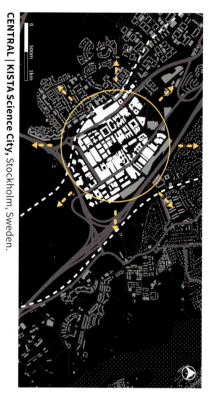
CENTRAL | KISTA Science City, Stockholm, Sweden.

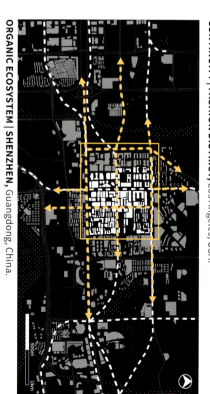
ORGANIC ECOSYSTEM | SHENZHEN, Guangdong, China.

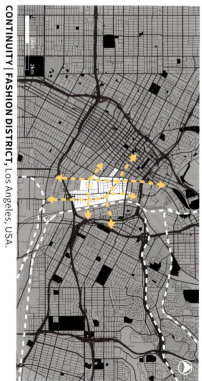
CONTINUITY | FASHION DISTRICT, Los Angeles, USA.

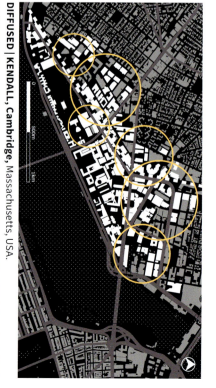
DIFFUSED | KENDALL, Cambridge, Massachusetts, USA.

164

7 | INDUSTRY AND PLACE

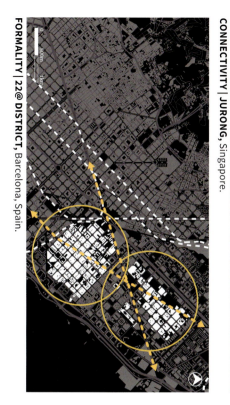

FORMALITY | 22@ DISTRICT, Barcelona, Spain.

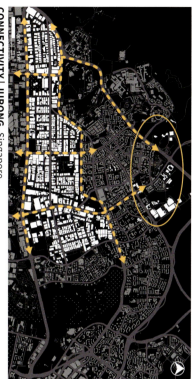

CONNECTIVITY | JURONG, Singapore.

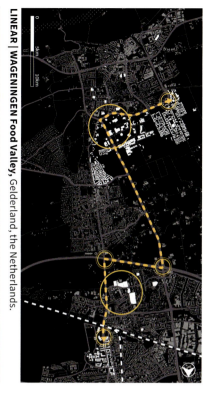

LINEAR | WAGENINGEN Food Valley, Gelderland, the Netherlands.

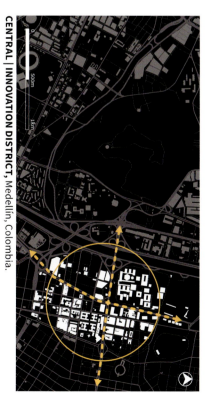

CENTRAL | INNOVATION DISTRICT, Medellín, Colombia.

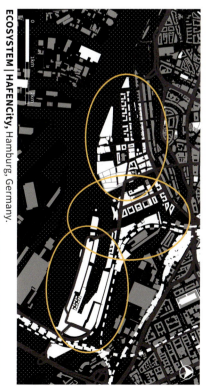

ECOSYSTEM | HAFENCity, Hamburg, Germany.

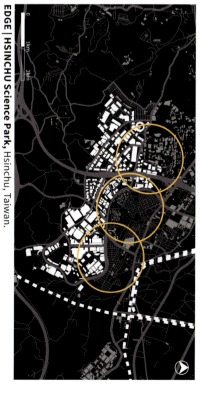

EDGE | HSINCHU Science Park, Hsinchu, Taiwan.

165

References

Abbot, Carl. 2004. "Centers and Edges: Reshaping Downtown Portland." In *The Portland Edge: Challenges and Successes in Growing Communities*, edited by Connie Ozawa, 164–183. Washington, DC: Island Press.

Abbott, Carl, Gerhard Pagenstecher, and Britt Parrott. 1998. From Downtown Plan to Central City Summit Trends in Portland's Central City 1970–1998: A Report to Association for Portland Progress City of Portland Metro Multnomah County. Portland, OR: Portland State University and State of Oregon.

Agarwal, Sucheta, Vivek Agarwal, and Jitendra Kumar Dixit. 2020. "Green Manufacturing: A MCDM Approach." *Materials Today: Proceedings* 26, no. 2: 2869–2874.

Anderson, C. 2012. *Makers: The New Industrial Revolution*. New York: Random House.

Arenas, Lehyton, Miguel Atienza, and José Francisco Vergara Perucich. 2020. "Ruta N, An Island of Innovation in Medellín's Downtown." *Local Economy* 35, no. 5: 419–439.

Auschner, Eika, Liliana Lotero Álvarez, and Laura Álvarez Pérez. 2020. "Paradiplomacy and City Branding: The Case of Medellín, Colombia (2004–2019)." In *City Diplomacy*, edited by Sohaela Amiri and Efe Sevin, 279–303. London: Palgrave Macmillan.

Barnhoorn, Ruben. 2016. "From the Region to The World: Becoming a Top Region in the Field of Agro & Food through the Implementation of Smart Specialization Strategies: A Critical Exploration of the State-of-the-Art, the Inception, Implementation and Effectiveness of RIS3 Oost Policy in The Foodvalley Region." Bachelor's Thesis, Radboud University. https://theses.ubn.ru.nl/bitstream/handle/123456789/1916/Barnhoorn%2C_Ruben_1.pdf?sequence=1

Bevilacqua, Carmelina, and Pasquale Pizzimenti. 2019. "Urban Planning and Innovation: The Strength Role of the Urban Transformation Demand. The Case of Kendall Square in Cambridge." In *New Metropolitan Perspectives*, Vol. 100 of Smart Innovation, Systems and Technologies, edited by Francesco Calabrò, Licia Della Spina, and Carmelina Bevilacqua, 272–281. New York: Springer. https://doi.org/10.1007/978-3-319-92099-3_32

Bozzuto, Paolo, and Chiara Geroldi. 2020. "The Former Mining Area of Santa Barbara in Tuscany and a Spatial Strategy for Its Regeneration." *The Extractive Industries and Society* 8, no. 1: 147–158. https://doi.org/10.1016/j.exis.2020.09.007

Brown, Julie, and Micha Mczyski. 2009. "Complexcities: Locational Choices of Creative Knowledge Workers." *Built Environment* 35, no. 2: 238–252. https://doi.org/10.2148/benv.35.2.238

Brown, Sarah. 2019. "Hybrid-Industrial Zoning: A Case Study in Downtown Los Angeles." Master's thesis, DSpace@MIT, Massachusetts Institute of Technology. https://dspace.mit.edu/handle/1721.1/122271

Bruns-Berentelg, Jürgen, Luise Noring, and Adam Grydehøj. 2020. "Developing Urban Growth and Urban Quality: Entrepreneurial Governance and Urban Redevelopment Projects in Copenhagen and Hamburg." *Urban Studies*. https://doi.org/10.1177/0042098020951438

Budden, Phil, and Fiona Murray. 2015. "Kendall Square & MIT: Innovation Ecosystems and the University." MIT Lab for Innovation Science and Policy. https://innovation.mit.edu/assets/MIT-Kendall-Sq.-Case_10.22.15.pdf

Cambridge Redevelopment Authority. n.d. "Kendall Square Urban Renewal Plan." www.cambridgeredevelopment.org/kendall-square-1

Castells, Manuel, and Peter Hall. 1994. *Technopoles of the World: The Making of Twenty-First-Century Industrial Complexes*. London: Routledge.

Celata, Filippo, and Raffaella Coletti. 2014. "Place-Based Strategies or Territorial Cooperation? Regional Development in Transnational Perspective in Italy." *Local Economy* 29, no. 4–5: 394–411. https://doi.org/10.1177/0269094214533903

Chan, Hung Hing, Tai-Shan Hu, and Peilei Fan. 2019. "Social Sustainability of Urban Regeneration Led by Industrial Land Redevelopment in Taiwan." *European Planning Studies* 27, no. 7: 1245–1269. http://doi:10.1080/09654313.2019.1577803

Chapple, K. 2014. "The Highest and Best Use? Urban Industrial Land and Job Creation." *Economic Development Quarterly* 28, no. 4: 300–313. https://doi.org/10.1177/0891242413517134

Charles, D. R. 2015. "From Technopoles to Science Cities." In *Making 21st Century Knowledge Complexes*. 1st edition. Julie Tian Miao, Paul Benneworth, and Nicholas A. Phelps, 82–102. London: Routledge.

Chen, Ching-Pu. 2013. "Cluster Policies and Industry Development in the Hsinchu Science Park: A Retrospective Review after 30 Years." *Innovation: Management, Policy & Practice* 15, no. 4: 416–436.

Chen, Stephen, and Chong Ju Choi. 2004. "Creating a Knowledge-Based City: The Example of Hsinchu Science Park." *Journal of Knowledge Management* 8, no. 5: 73–82. https://doi.org/10.1108/13673270410558792

Chen, Ting. 2017. *A State Beyond the State: Shenzhen and the Transformation of Urban China*. Rotterdam: NAI Publishers.

Chilson, John. 2017. "Lost Oregon: Walking around Portland's Central Eastside Industrial District." https://lostoregon.org/2017/05/26/walking-around-portlands-central-eastside-industrial-district/

Chou, Tsu-Lung. 2007. "The Science Park and the Governance Challenge of the Movement of the High-Tech Urban Region towards Polycentricity: The Hsinchu Science-Based Industrial Park." *Environment and Planning A: Economy and Space* 39, no. 6: 1382–1402. https://doi.org/10.1068/a38200

Cicerone, Gloria, Philip McCann, and Viktor A. Venhorst. 2020. "Promoting Regional Growth and Innovation: Relatedness, Revealed Comparative Advantage and the Product Space." *Journal of Economic Geography* 20, no. 1: 293–316. https://doi.org/10.1093/jeg/lbz001

Comunian, Roberta, Caroline Chapain, and Nick Clifton. 2010. "Location, Location, Location: Exploring the Complex Relationship between Creative Industries and Place." *Creative Industries Journal* 3, no. 1: 5–10.

Crombach, Charles, Joep Koene, and Wim Heijman. 2008. "From 'Wageningen City of Life Sciences' to 'Food Valley'." In *Pathways to High-Tech Valleys and Research Triangles: Innovative Entrepreneurship, Knowledge Transfer and Cluster Formation in Europe and the United States*, edited by Willem Hulsink and Hans Dons, 295–311. The Hague: Springer.

Curran, Winifred. 2007. "'From the Frying Pan to the Oven:' Gentrification and the Experience of Industrial Displacement in Williamsburg, Brooklyn." *Urban Studies* 44, no. 8: 1427–1440. https://doi.org/10.1080/00420980701373438

Cutting Edge Planning & Design. 2015. "Does Live/Work? Problems and Issues Concerning Live/Work Development in London? A Report for the London Borough of Hammersmith & Fulham." Hammersmith & Fulham. https://www.lbhf.gov.uk/sites/default/files/section_attachments/livework_final_lowres_tcm21-51146.pdf

Darchen, Sébastien. 2017. "Regeneration and Networks in the Arts District (Los Angeles): Rethinking Governance Models in the Production of Urbanity." *Urban Studies* 54, no. 15: 3615–3635.

Davis, Jenna, and Henry Renski. 2020. "Do Industrial Preservation Policies Protect and Promote Urban Industrial Activity?" *Journal of the American Planning Association* 86, no. 4: 431–442. https://doi.org/10.1080/01944363.2020.1753563

Donaldson, Sam, Christian Stow, and Jonathan Hobson. 2018. "UK Cyber Security Sectoral Analysis and Deep-Dive Review." UK Department for Digital, Culture, Media and Sport, RSM. https://assets.publishing.service.gov.uk/government/uploads/system/uploads/attachment_data/file/751406/UK_Cyber_Sector_Report_-__June_2018.pdf

Dougherty, Dale. 2012. "The Maker Movement." *Innovations* 7, no. 3: 11–14. https://doi.org/10.1162/INOV_a_00135

Duarte, Fábio, and Joaquín Sabaté. 2013. "22@ Barcelona: Creative Economy and Industrial Heritage – A Critical Perspective." *Theoretical and Empirical Researches in Urban Management* 8, no. 2: 5–21. www.jstor.org/stable/24873346

Etzkowitz, Henry. 2012 "Triple Helix Clusters: Boundary Permeability at University–Industry–Government Interfaces as a Regional Innovation Strategy." *Environment and Planning C: Government and Policy* 30, no. 5: 766–779. https://doi.org/10.1068/c1182

Etzkowitz, Henry, and Loet Leydesdorff. 1995. "The Triple Helix – University–Industry–Government Relations: A Laboratory for Knowledge Based Economic Development." *EASST Review* 14, no. 1: 14–19.

Ferm, Jessica, and Edward Jones. 2016. "Mixed-Use 'Regeneration' of Employment Land in the Post-Industrial City: Challenges and Realities in London." European Planning Studies 24, no. 10: 1913–1936. https://doi.org/10.1080/09654313.2016.1209465

Foord, Jo. 2009. "Strategies for Creative Industries: An International Review." *Creative Industries Journal* 1, no. 2: 91–113. https://doi.org/10.1386/cij.1.2.91_1

Franz, Tobais. 2017. "Urban Governance and Economic Development in Medellín: An 'Urban Miracle?'" *Latin American Perspectives* 44, no. 2: 52–70.

Garbade, Philipp J.P., Frances T.J.M. Fortuin, and Onno Omta. 2013. "Coordinating Clusters: A Cross Sectoral Study of Cluster Organization Functions in the Netherlands." *International Journal on Food System Dynamics* 3, no. 3, 243–257.

Gianoli, Alberto, and Riccardo Palazzolo Henkes. 2020. "The Evolution and Adaptive Governance of the 22@ Innovation District in Barcelona." *Urban Science* 4, no. 2: 16. https://doi.org/10.3390/urbansci4020016

Giloth, Robert, and John Betancur. 1988. "Where Downtown Meets Neighborhood: Industrial Displacement in Chicago, 1978–1987." *American Planning Association* 54, no. 3: 279–290.

Goodling, Erin, Jamaal Green, and Nathan McClintock. 2015. "Uneven Development of the Sustainable City: Shifting Capital in Portland, Oregon." *Urban Geography* 36, no. 4: 504–527.

Gorgoń, Justyna. 2017. "Regeneration of Urban and Post-Industrial Areas within the Context of Adaptation to Climate Change – the Polish Perspective." *Urban Development Issues* 53, no. 1: 21–26. https://doi.org/10.1515/udi-2017-0002

HafenCity Hamburg GmbH. 2006. "HafenCity Hamburg: The Masterplan." www.hafencity.com/upload/files/files/z_en_broschueren_19_Masterplan_end.pdf

Hall, Thomas, and Sonja Vidén. 2005. "The Million Homes Programme: A Review of the Great Swedish Planning Project." *Planning Perspectives* 20, no. 3: 301–328. https://doi.org/10.1080/02665430500130233

Hallam, Stevens. 2019. "The Quotidian Labour of High Tech: Innovation and Ordinary Work in Shenzhen." *Science, Technology and Society* 24, no. 2: 218–236. https://doi.org/10.1177/0971721819841997

Hansen, Teis, and Lars Winther. 2011. "Innovation, Regional Development and Relations between High- and Low-Tech Industries." *European Urban and Regional Studies* 18, no. 3: 321–339. https://doi.org/10.1177/0969776411403990

Hatch, Mark. 2013. *The Maker Movement Manifesto: Rules for Innovation in the New World of Crafters, Hackers, and Tinkerers*. New York: McGraw-Hill.

Hatuka, Tali, Eran Ben-Joseph, and Sunny Menozzi. 2017. "Facing Forward: Trends and Challenges in the Development of Industry in Cities." *Built Environment* 43, no. 1: 145–155.

Hatuka, Tali, and Erran Carmel. 2020. *The Dynamics of the Largest Cybersecurity Industrial Clusters: San Francisco Bay Area, Washington D.C., and Israel*. Tel Aviv: The Blavatnik Interdisciplinary Cyber Research Center (ICRC) at Tel Aviv University.

Hatuka, Tali, Issachar Rosen-Zvi, Michael Birnhack, Eran Toch, and Hadas Zur. 2018. "The Political Premises of Contemporary Urban Concepts: The Global City, the Sustainable City, the Resilient City, the Creative City, and the Smart City." *Planning Theory & Practice* 19, no. 2: 160–179. https://doi.org/10.1080/14649357.2018.1455216

Hatuka, Tali, and Yoav Weinberg. 2016. "Guidelines for Planning Industrial Sites." Israeli Ministry of Economy. https://lcud.tau.ac.il/wp-content/uploads/2016/10/industry_section3.pdf

Howland, Marie. 2010. "Planning for Industry in a Post-Industrial World." *Journal of the American Planning Association* 77, no. 1: 39–53. https://doi.org/10.1080/01944363.2011.531233

Hutton, Thomas A. 2006. "Spatiality, Built Form, and Creative Industry Development in the Inner City." *Environment and Planning A: Economy and Space* 38, no. 10: 1819–1841. https://doi.org/10.1068/a37285

Hwang, Bon-Gang, Lei Zhu, and Joanne Siow Hwei Tan. 2017. "Green Business Park Project Management: Barriers and Solutions for Sustainable Development." *Journal of Cleaner Production*, 153: 209–219.

Irazábal, C., and P. Jirón. 2020. "Latin American Smart Cities: Between Worlding Infatuation and Crawling Provincializing." *Urban Studies* 58, no. 3: 507–534.

Katz, Michael L., and Carl Shapiro. 1985. "Network Externalities, Competition, and Compatibility." *American Economic Review* 75, no. 3: 424.

Kimball, A.H., and D. Romano. 2012. "Reinventing the Brooklyn Navy Yard: A National Model for Sustainable Urban Industrial Job Creation." *WIT Transactions on the Built Environment*, 123: 199–206.

Kitheka, Bernard M., Elizabeth D. Baldwin, and Robert B. Powell. 2021. "Grey to Green: Tracing the Path to Environmental Transformation and Regeneration of a Major Industrial City." *Cities* 108. https://doi.org/10.1016/j.cities.2020.102987

Kourtit, Karima, Peter Nijkamp, Steef Lowik, Frans van Vught, and Paul Vulto. 2011. "From Islands of Innovation to Creative Hotspots." *Regional Science Policy & Practice* 3: 145–161. https://doi.org/10.1111/j.1757-7802.2011.01035.x

LA Fashion District: Urban Place Consulting Group. 2018. "Fashion District Business Improvement District Management District Plan." https://ctycms.com/ca-fashion-district/docs/fashion-district-bid-management-plan-2019-2026.pdf

La Porte, Kimberly. 2020. "The Brooklyn Navy Yard: A Mission-Oriented Model of Industrial Heritage Reuse." Master's Thesis, University of Pennsylvania. https://repository.upenn.edu/hp_theses/691

Leigh, Nancey Green, and Nathanael Z. Hoelzel. 2012. "Smart Growth's Blind Side." *Journal of the American Planning Association* 78, no. 1: 87–103.

Lepore, Daniela, Alessandro Sgobbo, and Fredica Vingelli. 2017. "The Strategic Approach in Urban Regeneration: The Hamburg Model." *UPLanD Journal of Urban Planning, Landscape & Environmental Design* 2, no. 3: 185–218. https://doi.org/10.6092/2531-9906/5415

Lester, Thomas W., and David A. Hartley. 2014. "The Long Term Employment Impacts of Gentrification in the 1990s." *Regional Science and Urban Economics* 45: 80–89. https://doi.org/10.1016/j.regsciurbeco.2014.01.003

Lester, Thomas W., Nikhil Kaza, and Sarah Kirk. 2013. "Making Room for Manufacturing: Understanding Industrial Land Conversion in Cities." *Journal of the American Planning Association* 79, no. 4: 295–313. https://doi.org/10.1080/01944363.2014.915369

Lindtner, Silvia, Anna Greenspan, and David Li. 2015. "Designed in Shenzhen: Shanzhai Manufacturing and Maker Entrepreneurs." *Aarhus Series on Human Centered Computing* 1, no. 1. https://doi.org/10.7146/aahcc.v1i1.21265

Los Angeles Mayor's Office of Economic Development. 2004. "Industrial Development Policy Initiative for the City of Los Angeles: Phase 1 Report." https://planning.lacity.org/code_studies/landuseproj/Resources/IDPI_Phase_1.pdf

Loures, Luís. 2015. "Post-Industrial Landscapes as Drivers for Urban Redevelopment: Public versus Expert Perspectives towards the Benefits and Barriers of the Reuse of Post-Industrial sites in Urban Areas." *Habitat International* 45: 72–81.

Love, Tim. 2017. "A New Model of Hybrid Building as a Catalyst for the Redevelopment of Urban Industrial Districts." *Built Environment* 43, no. 1: 44–57.

Malmberg, Anders. 2009. "Agglomeration." In *International Encyclopedia of Human Geography*, edited by Rob Kitchin and Nigel Thrift, 48–53. Oxford: Elsevier. https://doi.org/10.1016/B978-008044910-4.00131-0

Minner, Jenni. 2007. The Central Eastside Industrial District: Contested Visions of Revitalization. Portland, OR: School of Urban Studies and Planning, Portland State University.

Mistry, Nisha, and Joan Byron. 2011. "The Federal Role in Supporting Urban Manufacturing." www.brookings.edu/research/papers/2011/04/urban-manufacturing-mistry-

Morisson, Arnault, and Carmelina Bevilacqua. 2019. "Beyond Innovation Districts: The Case of Medellínnovation District." In *New Metropolitan Perspectives*, edited by F. Calabrò, L. Della Spina, and C. Bevilacqua, 3–11. Springer: Cham. https://doi.org/10.1007/978-3-319-92099-3_1

O'Connor, Justin, and Xin Gu. 2010. "Developing a Creative Cluster in a Postindustrial City: CIDS and Manchester." *The Information Society* 26, no. 2: 124–136. https://doi.org/10.1080/01972240903562787

Oden, Michael, Laura Wolf-Powers, and Ann Markusen. 2003. "Post-Cold War Conversion: Gains, Losses and Hidden Changes in the US Economy." In *From Defense to Development? Military Industrial Conversion in the Developing World*, edited by Sean DiGiovanna, Ann Markusen, and Yong-Sook Lee, 15–42. London: Routledge.

OECD. 1996. *The Knowledge-Based Economy*. Paris: OECD Publishing.

Owuor, Sophy. 2019. "Which US City Has the 'Most Innovative Square Mile on the Planet?" *World Atlas*. www.worldatlas.com/articles/which-us-city-has-the-most-innovative-square-mile-on-the-planet.html

Peterson, Sunny Menozzi. 2017. "Historic Heavy Industrial Sites: Obstacles and Opportunities." *Built Environment* 43, no. 1: 87–106.

Portland. 2021. "Metro 2040 Growth Concept." www.portlandonline.com/portlandplan/index.cfm?print=1&a=288082&c=52250

Portland Bureau of Planning & Sustainability. 2014. "Southeast Quadrant Plan Urban Design Proposals." www.portlandoregon.gov/bps/

Portland Bureau of Planning & Sustainability. 2017. "Central City 2035: Vol. 1 – Goals and Policy." www.portlandoregon.gov/bps/

Praticò, Alessio. 2015. "The Analysis of the New Strategic Area of Hamburg: The Redevelopment Project of the Hafencity's Waterfront." *Politecnico Milano* 7. DOI: 10.13140/RG.2.2.36784.56322.

Rantisi, Norma M., Deborah Leslie, and Susan Christopherson. 2006. "Placing the Creative Economy: Scale, Politics, and the Material." *Environment and Planning A: Economy and Space* 38, no. 10: 1789–1797. https://doi.org/10.1068/a39210

Rappaport, Nina. 2015. *Vertical Urban Factory*. New York: Actar.

Rappaport, Nina. 2017. "Hybrid Factory | Hybrid City." *Built Environment* 43, no. 1: 72–86.

Ratti, Carlo Associati. 2014. "Medellínnovation District." https://carloratti.com/project/Medellínnovation-district/

Reynolds, Elizabeth. 2017. "Innovation and Production: Advanced Manufacturing Technologies, Trends and Implications for U.S. Cities and Regions." *Built Environment Journal* 43, no. 1: 25–43.

Røe, Per Gunner, and Bengt Andersen. 2016. "The Social Context and Politics of Large Scale Urban Architecture: Investigating the Design of Barcode Oslo." *European Urban and Regional Studies* 24, no. 3: 305–314.

Rowe, Peter. 2006. *Building Barcelona*: A Second Renaixença. Barcelona: Actar.

Saxenian, AnneLee. 2004. "Taiwan's Hsinchu Region." In *Building High-Tech Clusters: Silicon Valley and Beyond*, edited by Alfonso Gambardella and Timothy Bresnahan, 190–228. Cambridge: Cambridge University Press. https://doi.org/10.1017/CBO9780511802911.009

Saxenian, AnneLee, and Hsu Jinn-Yuh. 2001. "The Silicon Valley–Hsinchu Connection: Technical Communities and Industrial Upgrading." *Industrial and Corporate Change* 10, no. 4: 893–920.

Scott, Allen J. 2000. *The Cultural Economy of Cities: Essays on the Geography of Image-Producing Industries*. Thousand Oaks, CA: Sage.

Sepe, Marichela. 2013. "Urban History and Cultural Resources in Urban Regeneration: A Case of Creative Waterfront Renewal." *Planning Perspectives* 28, no. 4: 595–613.

State Council Information Office. 2015. "Opinions of the State Council on Several Policies and Measures for Promoting Mass Entrepreneurship and Innovation." The People's Republic of China. www.gov.cn/zhengce/content/2015-06/16/content_9855.htm

Stevens, Hallam. 2019. "The Quotidian Labour of High Tech: Innovation and Ordinary Work in Shenzhen." *Science, Technology & Society* 24: 218–236.

Stouffs, Rudi, and Patrick Janssen. 2016. Rethinking Urban Practices: Designing for Jurong Vision 2050. Singapore: CASA Centre for Advanced Studies in Architecture, National University of Singapore.

Sun, Wenyong. 2018. "Huaqiangbei: Hundun Zhong de Diedai [Huaqiangbei: Cycles of Change in Chaos]." City PLUS / 城PLUS. http://mp.weixin.qq.com/s?__biz=MzA5MDUwOTI5MQ==&mid=2650043356&idx=1&sn=1e8b8fcfe1dc1535cecd4e4a93e8cafc&chksm=880a4958bf7dc04ef308a070ec54717c92d3acfff5a51753c6f2a2dc1ef3379fc52142142ed8#rd

TSMC. 2020. "Company Info: Taiwan Semiconductor Manufacturing Company Limited." www.tsmc.com/english/aboutTSMC/company_profile.htm

Van Winden, Willem, Erik Braun, Alexander Otgaar, and Jan-Jelle Witt. 2012. "The Innovative Performance of Regions: Concepts and Cases." www.urbaniq.nl/wp-content/uploads/2017/08/The-Innovation-Performance-of-Regions-Summary_0.pdf

Viladecans-Marsal, Elisabet, and Josep-Maria Arauzo-Carod. 2012. "Can a Knowledge-Based Cluster Be Created? The Case of the Barcelona 22@ District." *Papers in Regional Science*, 91, no. 2: 377–400.

Wial, Howard, Susan Helper, and Timothy Krueger. 2012. "Locating American Manufacturing: Trends in the Geography of Production." www.brookings.edu/research/locating-american-manufacturing-trends-in-the-geography-of-production/

Wolf-Powers, Laura, Marc Doussard, Greg Schrock, Charles Heying, Max Eisenburger, and Stephen Marotta. 2017. "The Maker Movement and Urban Economic Development." *Journal of the American Planning Association* 83, no. 4: 365–376. https://doi.org/10.1080/01944363.2017.1360787

Wolman, Harold, and Diana Hincapie. 2015. "Clusters and Cluster-Based Development Policy." Economic Development Quarterly 29, no. 2: 135–149. https://doi.org/10.1177/0891242413517136

Wood, Stephen, and Kim Dovey. 2015. "Creative Multiplicities: Urban Morphologies of Creative Clustering." *Journal of Urban Design* 20, no. 1: 52–74. https://doi.org/10.1080/13574809.2014.972346

Yang, Perry Pei-Ju, and Ong Boon Lay. 2004. "Applying Ecosystem Concepts to the Planning of Industrial Areas: A Case Study of Singapore's Jurong Island. *Journal of Cleaner Production* 12, no. 8, 1011–1023.

Yigitcanlar, Tan, and Tommi Inkinen. 2019. *Geographies of Disruption: Place Making for Innovation in the Age of Knowledge Economy.* Cahm, Switzerland: Springer.

Zhang, Jun. 2017. Chengshi Yunyu Chaungxin, Chuangxin Gaibian Chengshi–Shenzhen de Kongjian Kongji Zhuanxing [The City Incubates Innovation, Innovation Transforms the City–Spatial Transformation of Shenzhen]. City PLUS / 城PLUS. http://mp.weixin.qq.com/s?__biz=MzA5MDUwOTI5MQ==&mid=2650041868&idx=2&sn=498b90f3be3b48cbb7e84adf6a975966&chksm=880a5488bf7ddd9e42be62a6e089d1ba06b683083cd0fa32c64c86437701ab337e6311074e42#rd

Bottrop, Germany industrial mining reclamation including an indoor ski slope. Photo by Guy Gorek (CC BY 2.0).

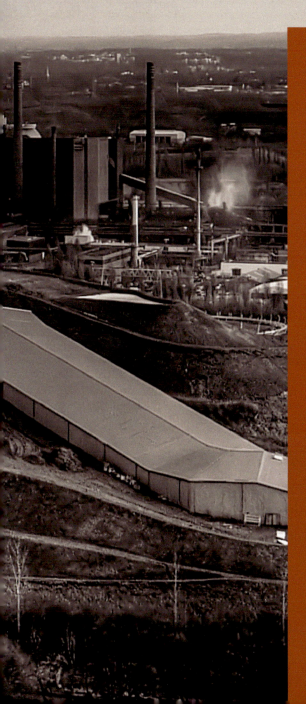

PART III

OPEN MANUFACTURING

PART III

Open Manufacturing

Work is a fundamental element in our life. People – whether working in a large factory far from home, a small business along a commercial street, an office in a tower, or a study at home – spend many hours in their workplace. As technology progresses and more attention is paid to sustainability and smart growth, the time has come to question the spatial solutions being used to support industry. What design and physical planning criteria should guide the contemporary development of urban industrial development? What parameters should be used to decide where manufacturing is located? What will manufacturing look like in the city of tomorrow? These are some of the challenges and questions that the planning profession must address.

Part III, "Open Manufacturing," offers thoughts on the future of industry in cities and ideas for harnessing the potential of today's innovations in manufacturing to develop centers of urban industry. It argues that city and regional governments, private developers, and planners should encourage the convergence of users and activities to create vibrant manufacturing and mixed-use economic clusters. Embracing this approach will help support the "New Industrial Urbanism" as the next phase in the city-industry evolution. New Industrial Urbanism is both a manifesto and a set of ideas and tools that calls for professionals to focus on the rather neglected issue of industry. It is the be-

ginning of a conversation about what seems likely to change dramatically in the near future, bringing our societies with it – advanced technology.

Challenges are multiple. In particular, it is clear that technological advances do not necessarily benefit everyone, let alone all workers. "The majority of adults in industrialized countries are currently able to escape poverty by working in paid employment. But this state of affairs is exceptional and should not be taken for granted" (Autor et al., 2020: 8). Indeed, there is a fear that automation will eventually mean that there are fewer jobs in which humans' productivity exceeds that of machines, causing mass unemployment. Moreover, a minority of workers with highly specialized skills would likely earn larger salaries while the majority lose ground (ibid.).

From this point of departure, inspired by the past, and learning from the present, the concepts and ideas in this section are organized by scale: the region, the city, the building, and how each is affected by contemporary changes to industry. This organizational structure is derived from the various new manifestations of industry in space and place, which influence and are influenced by type of industry, regulation, infrastructure, and target audience. Although scale was chosen as the organizing principle, the discussion is not meant to suggest a hierarchical approach but rather a relational one. Relational thinking "gives license for critical geographers to conceive of development processes and territorial politics in capitalism as operating both in a 'vertical' or 'upwards' dimension (e.g. from local-to-regional-to-national-to-global scales) and also 'horizontally' (place-to-place relations, including global connections, and differences)" (Jonas, 2012: 265). In that sense, tools and policies that are presented at each scale can also apply to other scales.

In what follows, Section 8, "Advancing Regions," summarizes key regional strategies and concepts designed and implemented to develop industrial ecosystems. Section 9, "Integrating Urban-Industrial Systems," focuses on the city scale, and discusses the processes of coding and regulation piloted in cities that have re-invented their industrial areas. Section 10, "Working, Living, and Innovating," presents new building typologies that integrate industry and manufacturing with other uses – especially housing and public amenities. Finally, the part ends with Section 11, offers a vision for "New Industrial Urbanism," a socio-spatial concept in which manufacturing is integrated into the fabric of cities and regions. New Industrial Urbanism offers a framework that unifies the economic sphere (technological trends and related economic development initiatives), the political-social sphere (policies that support human health, well-being, and growth), and the spatial sphere (physical planning). Above all, New Industrial Urbanism calls for developing new concepts that supports urban manufacturing and urban forms that are compatible with city life.

■ Open Manufacturing and Urban Life

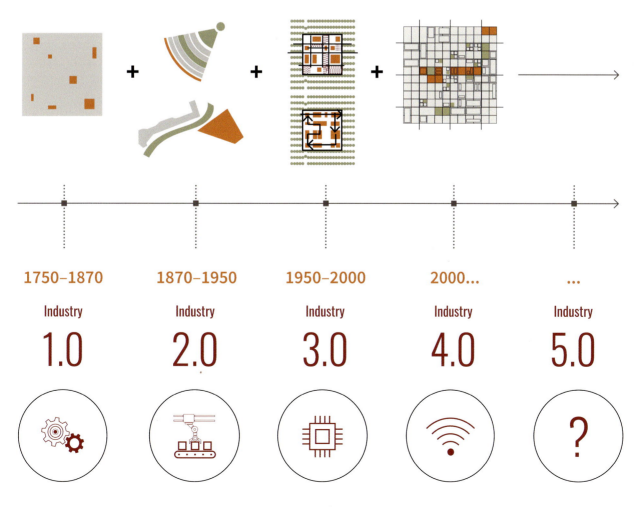

8

Advancing Regions

PART III | OPEN MANUFACTURING

8

Advancing Regions

Changes in manufacturing are reshaping both cities and regions. Since the start of the 21st century, cities and urban-edge locations have increasingly become specialized in particular industries and manufacturing lines (Helper et al., 2012, 12–13). In the United States, production in about two-thirds of the metropolitan areas is clustered around "anchor" industries (e.g. chemicals, machinery). The process of clustering is also connected to the fact that innovative companies operate at the intersection of software on one hand, and hardware and fabrication on the other (e.g. software in Silicon Valley, biopharmaceuticals in Boston, robotics in Pittsburgh). In this process of industrial specialization, developing a regional planning approach becomes critical for economic growth (Storper, 1997). This approach also reflects the spatial shift from the "metropolis" concept, viewed as a central, dense area which expands into adjacent and less dense "streetcar suburbs," to the "new regionalism" concept describing a spatial, economic, and a-hierarchical synthesis of varied urban forms. As described by political geographer and urban theorist Edward Soja, "the urban and the regional, formerly quite distinct from one another, are blending together to define something new and different, an evolving regional–urban synthesis that demands new modes of understanding" (Soja, 2015, 376).

This new approach to regionalism differs from the traditional one. Traditional regionalism advocated a harmonious yet hierarchical relationship between cities and regions. It addresses the ecological components of environmental protection, demographic aspects of population dispersal, and above all the control of urban growth. The new regionalism sees districts as important and vital, independent social units, capable of exerting combined forces to generate major economic development, technological innovation, and cultural creativity (Pastor, 2000; Weaver, 1984). This perception is associated with the strengthening of localism and the creation of a non-hierarchical and decentralized society (MacLeod, 2001; Swyngedouw, 1997). Thus, since the 1990s, glocal regions – not global or local ones but a hybrid configuration of both (Healey, 2006; Swyngedouw, 1997) – have received special consideration from policymakers as entities with distinct status and increasing autonomy (Allmendinger and Haughton, 2009; Gellynck and Vermeire, 2009). This relational perception of regionalism "decouple(s) regions and regional development processes from bounded notions of state and territory" and correspondingly, connect regions and regionalism to wider flows, networks, and processes of economic globalization and neoliberalism (Jonas, 2012: 270). This approach influences regional development and is evident on three levels:

- Economic: initiating and managing a clear economic and productive agenda in various fields, including industry and tourism for the region as a whole.

- Social: developing a collective consciousness and identity unique to the area, defined by individuals, groups, and organizations.

- Governance: establishing structure that supports shaping public policy and its implementation in the region, in negotiation with the central government.

It is important to note that changes in systems of governance enabled the strengthening of regional thinking around the world by empowering and delegating political powers from centralized hierarchical systems to spatially distributed systems (Soja, 2000). Thus, pursuing new regionalism, and thinking of a regional area as a subnational space, is not just a planning strategy but a political project that includes reshaping symbols, public policy, and institutional development, as a means for reinventing the area. Nevertheless, contemporary regional development often integrates economic and political interests that are expressed in a territorial fashion, and resiliency in the face of the uncertain global economics associated with relational thinking. This integration between the territorial and relational approaches to regional development is apparent in contemporary regional coordination strategies.

Regional Industrial Coordination

Economic interest is often a key trigger for developing a regional plan of action (Searle, 2020). The recognition of the region as an economic-spatial system also contributes to collaborative regional-level frameworks that are based on connecting associated social actors, cooperation, and equality among stakeholders. As the following examples illustrate, places that have succeeded in formulating such a common agenda may differ from one another geographically, politically, and culturally, yet economic benefits are always the common key driving their regional coordination strategies.

Research Triangle Regional Partnership (RTRP), Durham, North Carolina, USA

RTRP is an organization representing a ten-county geographic area with a population of 1.9 million. The organization is named for the region's three major universities (Duke University in Durham, NC; University of North Carolina at Chapel Hill, NC; and North Carolina State University in Raleigh, NC); it is also home to seven additional institutions of higher education. These universities facilitate knowledge-sharing with industry, which includes advanced manufacturing, life sciences, technology, agricultural technology, and clean energy. The RTRP is primarily engaged in marketing the region to international companies, with the goal of getting them to establish US branches or headquarters in the region.

In addition to having access to top universities and a wide range of job opportunities, residents benefit from a low cost of living, and businesses gain from low real estate prices, the lowest corporate tax rate in the US, as well as tax incentives for locating in Opportunity Zones (economically distressed areas) within the region (Research Triangle Regional Partnership, 2020). Yet, in spite of the wealth of universities and colleges in the region, there are still sharp racial gaps in educational attainment and economic well-being. In its pursuit of economic growth, the region is challenged to ensure that the region's social growth is inclusive and that the benefits of growth accrue to all of its residents regardless of race. Educational institutions and businesses need to do all they can to ensure job readiness for all residents, particularly minorities (Policy Link and Pere, 2015).

The uniqueness in this regional collaboration is its dynamic evolution and adaptive growth. The RTRP was originally established by the State of North Carolina as one of a number of regional partnerships to promote regional economic development. In 2010, the state cut funding to these partnerships and many of them dissolved. Still, the RTRP was able to secure new sources of funding, and is now primarily involved in marketing,

PART III | OPEN MANUFACTURING

Regional Coordination: Strategies and Activities

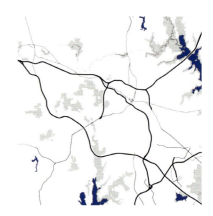

A persistent partnership

DURHAM, USA

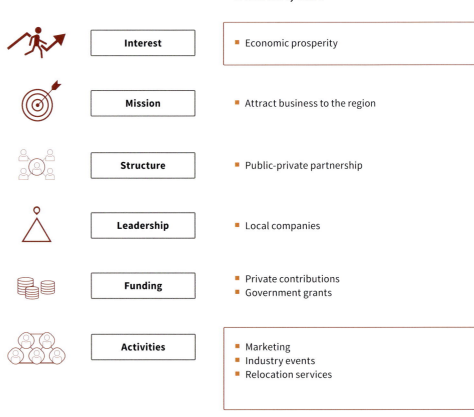

Interest	Economic prosperity
Mission	Attract business to the region
Structure	Public-private partnership
Leadership	Local companies
Funding	Private contributions Government grants
Activities	Marketing Industry events Relocation services

8 | ADVANCING REGIONS

A regional advisory council for cooperation and collaboration
SF BAY AREA, USA

Cooperation based on common interests
RUHRGEBIET, GE

A regional coordination platform
MEETJESLAND, BE

- Economic equity, climate change
- Economic prosperity
- Economic prosperity

- Facilitate regional collaboration
- Coordinate across interest areas
- Facilitate economic cooperation

- Regional advisory council
- Supra-local government body
- Regional advisory group

- Member governments
- Parliament
- Subcommittees
- Regional actors

- Member contributions
- Government grants
- Contracts for services
- Member contributions
- Government grants
- Member contributions
- Government grants

- Collaboration
- Research
- Policy advocacy
- Funding distribution

- Collaboration
- Research
- Funding distribution
- Planning

- Collaboration
- Marketing
- Policy advocacy
- Planning

181

The Association of Bay Area Governments (ABAG), San Francisco, California, USA

The San Francisco Bay Area (Bay Area) is made up of nine counties encompassing 101 cities and towns, and a population of more than 7 million people. The region comprises large cities, suburbs, and some rural towns. Since the late 20th century, the region has experienced development in the technology sector and rapid population growth. Unfortunately, the pace of new housing construction has not kept up with demand. Housing prices have skyrocketed, meaning that many people are unable to afford housing and are forced to move away. The region's transportation infrastructure is also struggling to keep up, and the region has run out of space to build additional infrastructure.

Historically, the Association of Bay Area Governments (ABAG) was established in 1961 in response to state legislation that threatened to take away local control over regional transportation assets (ABAG, 2020). Today, its mission is primarily to enhance cooperation and collaboration between area governments regarding a variety of region-wide challenges. Its work includes land use planning, housing, transportation, climate change, disaster resilience, and economic equity (Palm and Niemeier, 2017).

ABAG receives small contributions from member towns, cities, and counties, but its major source of revenue is grants for implementing regional programs such as the distribution of energy, efficiency incentives, and regional water management projects. ABAG also does some project implementation, such as creating a regional trail system and the aforementioned regional water management projects. While ABAG works with cities and towns to develop regional plans to manage this growth, the body has no legal authority to enforce the provisions of the regional plan.

Nonetheless, ABAG and its parent organization (the Metropolitan Transportation Commission) recently convened a broad group of stakeholders to develop a policy package to address the industrial, housing, and transportation crises (Roach and Chapple, 2018). Despite ABAG's lack of enforcement powers, the policy package has been taken up by state lawmakers, and may get passed into law. This example demonstrates the power of convening and collaborating, even when it is unclear how or whether informal agreements will be upheld.

The Regionalverband Ruhr, Ruhrgebiet, Germany

The Regionalverband Ruhr consists of 11 cities and four regional districts that are home to more than 5 million inhabitants. The Ruhr parliament is the overarching decision-making body consisting of representatives from all cities and districts as well as the relevant mayors. In the early 20th century, during the period of industrialization in Germany, the Ruhr area was one of the most economically prosperous regions in the country. As a coal and steel powerhouse, the area boasted many of the country's largest industrial companies and enjoyed international prominence. The Regionalverband Ruhr (originally, "Siedlungsverband Ruhrkohlenbezirk") was founded in 1920 as a "special purpose regional association" in order to help regulate the development and management of coal – one of the country's most valuable resources at the time (Keil and Wetterau, 2013). In addition to economic coordination, this first iteration of the association was responsible for local zoning and land use planning; significantly, it regulated the open space within and between cities and districts in order to preserve green space for recreational purposes. With the decline of coal mining after the two world wars, the Ruhr region was forced to reexamine its economic strategy. In the late 20th century, under the leadership of the Regionalverband Ruhr in collaboration with local industries, the region started pivoting toward clean energy technology. As early as 1984, the State of Nordrhein-Westfalen introduced a shift in industrial policy, from a coal-oriented to a more environmentally friendly one. The strategy has begun to pay off: the Ruhr area boasts over 100,000 jobs in the field of environmental technology and has a competitive advantage in energy supplies and waste disposal. Notably, this economic pivot plays to the region's strengths: many clean energy technologies originate from mining technology. In order to attract international attention to the region and encourage private involvement in its development, the Ruhr hosted the International Building Exhibition (IBA) in the region from 1989 to 1999. The public–private project resulted in the world-renowned Emscher Park, developed on land that had suffered from industrial use. As a result of the IBA's ecological and social reconstruction of the area, the park is now a tourist attraction with numerous art and architectural installations.

The year 2004 marked a major turning point for the Regionalverband Ruhr. The state government in Nordrhein-Westfalen reformed the Regional Planning Act and endowed the Regionalverband Ruhr with regional planning responsibilities. It was now tasked with developing regional master plans, promoting the development of the Emscher Landscape Park, and managing economic development planning (Gruehn, 2017).

One of the greatest challenges to the region was its persistent negative image (Berger, 2019). The Ruhr is still considered a region that is suffering economically, with low wages and poor housing conditions. Yet with significant contributions from the Regionalverband Ruhr, the area has gone a long way towards redefining its image, attracting industry and offering concrete paths forward for the region and its citizens. One reason why the organization has been so effective lies in its structure. All local players have a voice in the parliament and the entity's suborganizations serve as vehicles to implement the decisions it makes.

Plattelandscentrum Meetjesland, Regional Network, Meetjesland, Belgium

Located in Flanders on the northwest border of Belgium on the North Sea coast, Meetjesland consists of 13 municipalities varying in size from 6,000 to 32,000 inhabitants. In the 2000s, like other rural areas in Europe, Meetjesland faced the challenges caused by monotype agriculture and imbalanced regional development. Compared to other regions in Belgium, Meetjesland has struggled with economic development and employment. Nonetheless, it enjoys natural advantages, including adequate farm land, open space, and numerous tourism destinations. To make better use of these assets and address the aforementioned problems, the regional leadership created the Regional Network Meetjesland along with several other regional organizations, including Meetjeslandse Bouwmaatschappij and Regionaal Landschap Meetjesland (Brunell et al., 2008).

Although the European Union (EU) and the United Nations (UN) have been advocating for multifunctional agriculture in the region since the 1990s, the region itself was slow in adopting such initiatives. The absence of a strong regional organization ensured that each municipality continued to act in its own self-interest instead of acting for the benefit of the region by diversifying its economic engines. The region's infrastructure had started to show the wear and tear of old age; in some cases, the infrastructure was over a century old and could hardly meet the requirements of modern agriculture and the tourism industry. This resulted in an untenable situation that kept Meetjesland from larger business opportunities, and hindered regional collaboration. Competition within the region created an additional challenge for municipalities in Flanders. The existing regional bodies in charge of coordination were not able to effectively negotiate between all 13 municipalities in order to enforce initiatives towards more cohesive (and effective) economic development.

The regional network proposed by the Meetjesland 2020: Future Plan is considered one of the first pilot cases of regional governance in Europe. In addition, under the leadership of Plattelandscentrum Meetjesland, a wide array of regional organizations and the 13 municipalities work closely with each other to create a more inclusive and prosperous region. Plattelandscentrum Meetjesland set up various processes to address economic, cultural, social, and community challenges in the countryside through its signature Plattelandslab, which helps cultivate regional innovation efforts. Most importantly, it supports efforts to promote the region's agriculture and horticulture sectors through a wide variety of activities, including product showcases for agricultural products and international marketing efforts (Arnaut et al., 2007; Brunell et al., 2008).

Organizations like Toerisme Meetjesland, meanwhile, help to strengthen tourism in the region by managing visitor centers in Boekhoute, Eeklo, and Ursel, and championing museums and monuments. They created a region-wide website for tourism as well as cycling routes for visitors to explore the region. Landschap Meetjesland and other regional associations ensure an ongoing commitment to environmental preservation in this region. Through a wide variety of efforts, Landschap promotes regional character, recreation, recreational co-use, nature education, support for nature, as well as integrated and area-specific management. It also offers support to municipalities and heritage actors working on landscape heritage (Chen et al., 2012).

All the cases presented above faced considerable economic challenges. Moreover, historical competition and spatial development make regional coordination difficult, but using an integrated approach of both territorial and relational regional development has made cooperation easier and helped the regions to prosper. These examples have the following elements in common: a shared vision, an agreed-upon working model, and a regional action body.

- A shared (social and economic) vision. The basis for a regional vision is an agreement on economic interests and the identification of industrial and commercial anchors that act as engines of growth.

These interests and anchors orient the definition, frameworks, and scope of the region's production vision. This process makes it possible to clarify common interests, and subsequently to agree on a common strategic plan and implementation tools.

- Agreed-upon working model. The shift towards glocalization popularized the adoption of the "triple helix" as a working model for regional collaboration (Etzkowitz, 2012). This model marks the transition from the "statist model," in which government is the dominant actor driving the interactions between industry and academia from top to bottom, to an integrated model, where the different actors such as academia, industry, and government play equal roles. The triple helix model for regional collaboration blurs the boundaries of the traditional roles played by the various stakeholders while allowing each entity to maintain a leadership role in its unique area of expertise. For example, academic institutions remain the primary source of knowledge production while industry plays a key role in the production and commercialization of knowledge, and governments assert their regulatory function.

- Regional action body. Regional bodies establish actionable mechanisms, programs, and groups whose functions often include, but are not limited to, framing shared interests around a common theme, and defining vision and tasks. In pursuing the vision, these bodies are also responsible for strengthening regional economic cooperation with the private and public sector by, for example, defining a set of actions and cooperation in the field of policy, planning, research, and branding, and recruiting funding, usually a combination of public and private monies.

This regional dynamic clarifies that space or spatial forms are not the sole factor needed for actionable success. Rather, there is also a need for social actors who are embedded and actually use these multidimensional spatial settings (Mayer, 2008).

■ Working Models: Academia, Government and Industry

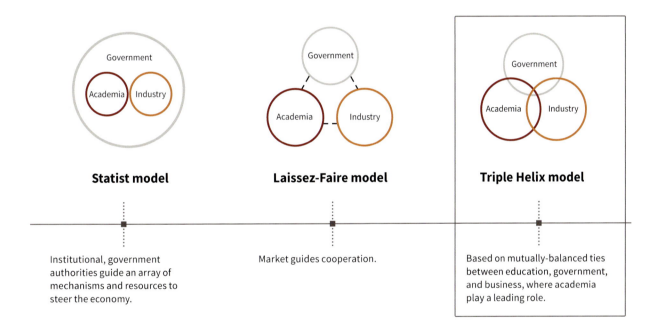

Towards Developing a Regional Ecosystem: The Case of Kiryat Shmona

A more recent example of an effort to define a regional vision is the Eastern Galilee region in Israel (Hatuka et al., 2019). The vision put forward by Tel Aviv University Laboratory for Contemporary Urban Design (LCUD) focuses on developing an industrial economic unit of expertise (cluster), which places the local residents at the center and seeks to promote a regional ecosystem with reference to three key themes:

- Education and industry, with an emphasis on agro tech and food tech. Eastern Galilee, surrounded by agricultural lands, is in a unique position to be a global center for technological innovation in the fields of agriculture and food. There is already a network of knowledge and research organizations that serve as a strong anchor for future growth.

- Tourism and agritourism, which includes a wide range of activities, including the purchase of produce directly from the growers, pick-your-own farms, and rural hospitality. This service industry has been established as a strategic way to revive agricultural areas, address the migration from rural to urban areas, protect the natural environment, and preserve cultural heritage.

- Lifestyle and well-being. Slow food and the slower living associated with rural locations are offered as alternatives to the city life that is often described as materialistic, fast-paced, and stressful. The term "slow" expresses a trend towards living life at a leisurely pace and is part of an ideological agenda that the Slow Movement emphasizes: sustainability, localism, organic, small batch, and unprocessed goods and – above all – slowing life's pace.

Based on these themes, four regional goals have been defined: first, developing a regional awareness concerning a slow lifestyle and sustainability; Second, consolidating resources and strengthening systemic, regional thinking around food tech and agro tech;

third, maximizing agglomeration in the field of tourism and industry. Integrating separate urban activities, such as commerce and industrial production, into concentrated anchors. Fourth, establishing a regional coordination body.

These themes and associated goals evolved from the growth engines in the region: unique industry that relies on diverse agriculture; natural and scenic assets; and academic and research institutions. The goals and assets outlined in the strategic plan guided the establishment of new boundaries for the economic cluster, boundaries that cross jurisdictional borders and do not depend on the organizational and political structure of the cities in the region. Rather they seek to form new regional coalitions around the main growth engines. The cluster itself includes two subregions: the southern subregion with many points of interest and tourism related to viniculture – vineyards, wineries, visitor centers, and shops; and the northern subregion, where there are tourist centers at the sources of the Jordan River and in the northern Hula Valley, agricultural tourism and industry. Structurally, the area is re-developed around a regional transportation ring that connects the centers of economic activity – wineries and tourism, academic institutions, and major industrial areas. These ideas formed the basis for detailed physical plans for industrial development.

EASTERN GALILEE AS AN INDUSTRIAL ECOSYSTEM
Israel

The Eastern Galilee project, envisioned as an industrial ecosystem, is based on analysis of development patterns in the region, and the need for a paradigm shift and transition from the "old regionalism," focusing on a territorial-administrative hierarchical structure, to "new regionalism," which includes complex horizontal networks, and multiple partnerships in a competitive economy.

Promoters of this a regional vision propose considering the Eastern Galilee region and the Golan Heights a single cluster. This socio-economic approach places the resident in the center, and seeks to promote a regional ecosystem by addressing three key, interlinked dimensions: education and industry (emphasizing agritech and food technology), tourism and consumption (emphasizing agritourism), and lifestyle and residents (emphasizing well-being and slow living).

Kiryat Shmona, Eastern Galilee Region, Israel . Photo courtesy of Moshe Kakon.

PART III | OPEN MANUFACTURING

The Region as an Industrial Ecosystem | Conceptual and structural diagram

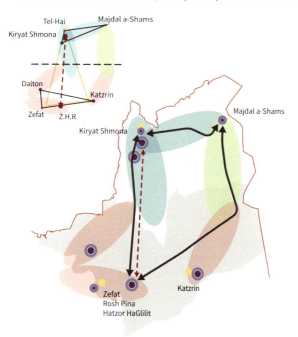

- Jordan River Drainage Basin
- Agritourism
- Vineyards and wineries
- Industrial area
- Academic institution

The Regional Ecosystem | Anchors, cities and places

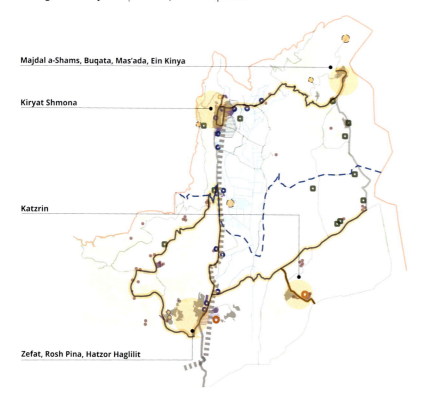

A two anchor scenario is recommended for Eastern Galilee, because it may make an optimal contribution to the following planning principles:

Compactization versus sprawl. Thematic identity for each core in the region; strengthening the regional industrial ecosystem; concentrating the industrial areas, based on partnerships between municipalities. Reinforcing the links between housing and industry / employment / tourism through new development typologies.

8 | ADVANCING REGIONS

Kiryat Shmona Strategic Plan | Design principles

Planning | Planning the city to the south, as part of the regional ecosystem

Existing situation | Developing the city without a clear vision or structure

Economy | Developing economic activity in a ring

Structure | Re-structuring the city around four related but distinct districts

Kiryat Shmona Strategic Plan | Holistic perspective

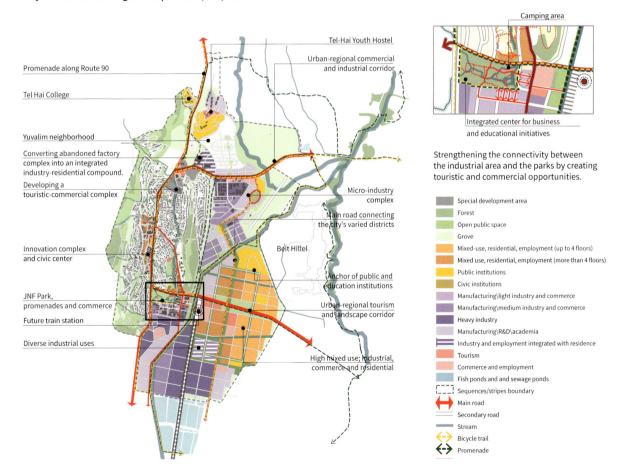

Strengthening the connectivity between the industrial area and the parks by creating touristic and commercial opportunities.

Maps and Diagrams by LCUD

PART III | OPEN MANUFACTURING

Production Models and Urban Change

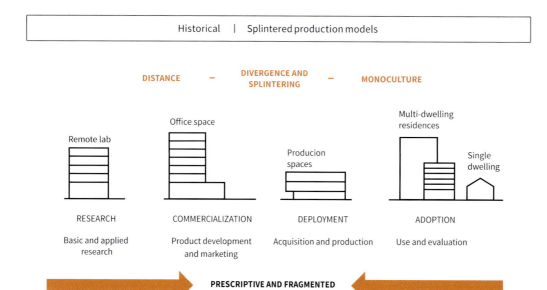

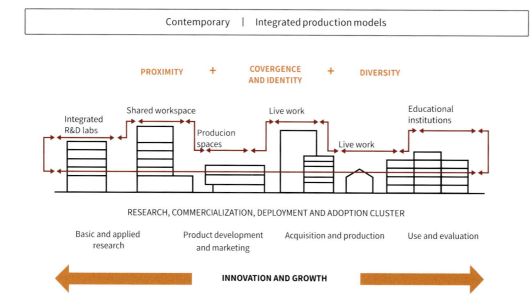

Summary: Regional Socio-Economic Visioning

New regionalism outlines a spatial logic associated with efficiency and agglomeration economics with a focus on infrastructure systems. It demonstrates that understanding and planning regions through infrastructure – whether capital-intensive or more mundane projects – provides an important vehicle for approaching a regional industrial framework (Harrison, 2020). The regional framework for infrastructure and industry is not limited to traditional infrastructure such as roads, pipes, or power sources, but also encompasses academic institutions, start-ups, and manufacturers capable of making prototypes and producing small volumes. In return, the latter can expedite the innovation process by creating opportunities for knowledge transfer between workers. This approach marks a shift from the approach that separates production levels (i.e. research, commercialization, deployment, and adoption) to one that emphasizes connections among production levels and supports spatial integration. To achieve production agglomeration and spatial integration, existing regulatory frameworks need to be amended and rethought, as well as traditional attitudes to mobility, water, and energy-related infrastructure systems. Scale matters. Some contemporary regions and city-regions are equivalent in size to a small country. "City-regions are now materializing at a rapid pace on all five continents, and all the more so as their growth is to a large extent powered by expanding global networks of trade and interaction" (Scott, 2019: 574). Yet city-regions are also replete with severe social and economic problems, including class divisions that threaten to break out into open social disturbances. Economic and political factors have a critical influence on the genesis and internal organization of the regions and on strategic planning as a whole.

The strategies and actions presented in this chapter highlight three important changes in regional industrial development: first, acknowledging the codependency between all components in the chain of production, especially between academia and industry; second, the shift from an approach based on production separation that reinforces physical distance, splintering, and industrial monoculturalism, to one based on integration at all levels with emphasis on proximity, convergence, and diversity; third, integrating an overarching regional economic agenda and physical planning. These shifts in the conceptualization of space, economy, society, and politics push cities to reassess their urban-industrial systems.

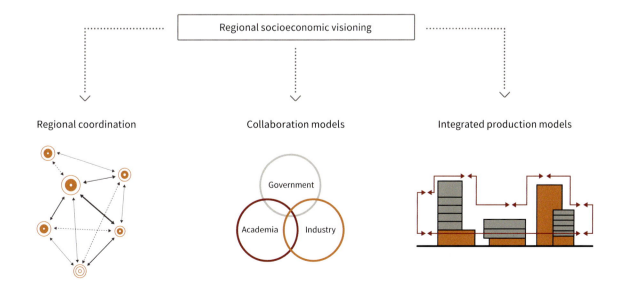

▬ Regions: Key Concepts in Industrial Development

9

Integrating Urban-Industrial Systems

9

Integrating Urban-Industrial Systems

In the coming decades, the question will not be whether growth in manufacturing is going to occur but where it will occur. A major factor in manufacturers' site selection decisions is the speed of delivery of goods to customers, and an increasingly important factor in choosing locations is access to transportation, which influences the speed of delivery. Regulatory issues are at the core of this dynamic and the need to develop mixed-use zones that permit diverse usage including industry.

Regulation is a central factor in the design of cities. Professional and governmental bodies have developed standards for the built environment that dictate all aspects of urban form and thereby shape communities. Furthermore, the methodical administration of public works, centralized supervision over land development, and the influential rise of the engineering and urban planning professions have made many of these standards into absolutes. Local governments automatically adopt and legitimize these development standards to shield themselves from taking responsibility for decision-making. Modifications are discouraged. Because higher governmental agencies do not allow flexibility, lesser agencies are similarly reluctant. Financial institutions and lenders have also been hesitant to support development proposals outside the mainstream, particularly when they do not conform to established design practices (Ben-Joseph,

2005). Standards not only shape and affect physical space; they are also an important aspect of planning practice. Furthermore, planning professionals spend most of their time writing and enforcing these rules. Architects and urban designers, even though they often complain about the constraints imposed by the multitude of codes, actively pursue their formulation – but with growing acknowledgment that much of the current regulatory mechanism is ineffective and exclusionary.

This going-along with the status quo, the static nature of regulations, and the failure to respond to changes and alter standards is particularly acute in the case of industrial development in cities. Land use categories, zoning regulations, and building codes, although defined differently worldwide, often do not keep up with the new industrial necessities and often hinder manufacturers from building factories in cities. This claim also applies to standardized storage and distribution practices, which often make ex-urban sites more affordable, but the need for warehouse space that supports the efficient distribution of products specifically created for inner city markets is growing. Moreover, industrial firms differ and some produce products that can be transported on smaller trucks (due to small size or small volumes) and thus use inner-city warehouse space (Leigh and Hoelzel, 2012: 88).

Bridging this gap between needs and regulations requires conceptualizing the city within its broader regional economy. It calls for viewing the center and the periphery, or the metropolitan area, as an innovation-production ecosystem that cultivates production along an "advanced manufacturing continuum" through a regional strategy (Reynolds, 2017). Each stage of industrial development requires a particular policy response that speaks to the urban landscape. Identifying and developing sites that are appropriate for manufacturers at various stages could encourage the return of industry to the city, along with updating the land use planning approach, which currently encourages the conversion of underutilized urban industrial land into other uses.

Updated planning regulations advocate an inclusive approach to smart growth, a term that currently refers to a set of urban design and planning standards, and policies that support the building of compact, mixed-use neighborhoods connected to the wider region. Although smart growth policies seek to encourage and diversify local economies, the related standards and policies often fail to protect industrial land from encroachment, and do not tend to call for urban land to be reserved for industry. Cities should not have to choose between supporting compact, mixed-use development or encouraging "urban industrial development." Instead, they need "approaches that explicitly safeguard productive urban industrial land and discourage industrial sprawl" (Leigh and Hoelzel, 2012: 87). To build livable cities with robust economies, policymakers must integrate their economic development, industrial policies, and environmental policies (Mistry and Byron, 2011: 6). Moreover, policymakers ought to "develop a new narrative about manufacturing and metropolitan economies," and "urban, industrial land use strategies should be linked to wider economic development and workforce objectives and should minimize mismatches among workforce, community revitalization, and city-wide economic development goals" (ibid.: 4).

Regulating Variability: From Separation to Consolidation

Given that traditional regulatory systems tend to view manufacturing as detrimental to residential uses, and with many cities losing their industrially zoned land to other uses including housing, the need to reform zoning codes is critical. Two issues need to be taken into account. First, the term "industrial" and "manufacturing" in the context of land use planning needs clarification. With manufacturing going through major technological changes, expanding and including more types of industrial activity, industrially zoned land now accommodates a broad range of uses that are often unrelated to traditional manufacturing activities. Second, digital transformation processes are occurring in industrial firms. Although firms differ greatly in adjusting to new technologies and determining how automation will influence labor, i.e. which new tasks are assigned to which occupations, and what incentives and decision rights people in those roles will have, their focus is the process of production. While labor replacement may have been a primary stated goal motivating previous waves of automation, the goal of this newer wave of automation is not so much to replace workers but rather to increase precision, safety, and product quality (Helper et al., 2021). Thus, if industry was formerly defined by its impact on the environment and by its scale and intensity (such as heavy and light industry), the shift in production models has created the need to provide a more refined set of categories. Light (sometimes also referred to as "general") industry is usually less capital intensive. Most light industry products are produced for end users rather being utilized in other industries. Facilities normally have less environmental impact than those associated with heavy industry. Heavy industry typically involves complex processes requiring large machine tools, massive buildings, and large-scale infrastructure. These industries often sell their products to other industries rather than to end users. They are very capital-intensive and often incompatible with other uses as they can cause significant pollution or risk of contamination, e.g. oil,

PART III | OPEN MANUFACTURING

◼ Integrated Environments: From Separation to Consolidation

Are segregated industrial areas still relevant given improved environmental regulations, new modes of production and the need to be integrated with other uses?

SEPARATION

CONSOLIDATION

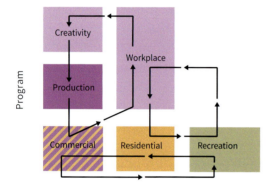

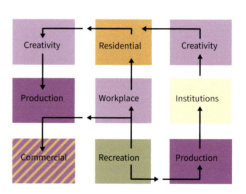

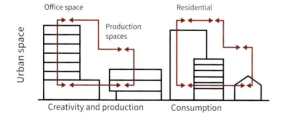

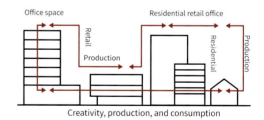

mining, steel, chemicals, machinery production etc. Yet, today, many newer industries, such as high-tech, biotech, and foodtech are much safer, and most do not cause nuisances to adjacent properties.

Beyond specific uses and manufacturing process, common distinctions between light, general, and heavy industry do not necessarily align with the scale and nature of contemporary manufacturing businesses. A large factory could be a heavy manufacturer, such as a chemical plant, or it could be a light one, such as semiconductor fabrication plants. Yet, the scale of operation has important locational and spatial implications. For instance, contrary to the conventional knowledge that cheap land is the single most important factor for site selection, small to medium-size enterprises value access to skilled labor the most. Acknowledging the scales of manufacturing businesses when planning land use will better position local governments to determine which and how much land should be reserved for specific types of manufacturing establishments (Kim and Ben-Joseph, 2014). It is also important to note that existing regulations and codes often label R&D with a separate use designation and prohibit its co-location in the same space or in close proximity to manufacturing and industrial facilities. However, such proximity is essential for advancing innovation, transforming the manufacturing process, diversifying the labor pool and creating more varied spatial forms.

Industrial land can be valuable for accommodating a wide range of businesses. Nonetheless, given that the residential use is still the least permitted use near manufacturing establishments, a broader district or city-wide approach is needed to create urban areas where the manufacturing workforce can live and work in close proximity, and where industrial activities are protected. In strong real estate markets, this will require a full array of interventions including new zoning, financial incentives and disincentives, and establishing close working relationships with local businesses to understand their future needs (Becker and Friedman, 2020). Indeed, some cities such as San Francisco, Chicago, Barcelona, and Shenzhen have all taken their

own unique district-wide approach by either expanding the uses included in the "manufacturing" and "industrial" categories, allowing for greater integration of other uses such as retail, office, and housing, or by becoming more specific about protecting the existing industrial legacy and operation.

These cities' efforts to define a more refined set of land use categories provide a basis that can be used to guide change. It also provides insights into developing strategies to achieve various objectives, including: protecting industrial land by preserving and encouraging productive activity and employment; incentivizing innovation by encouraging new industry and manufacturing activities; co-locating industry in the city by introducing new compatible uses (e.g. live/work); developing industrial land use conversion policies; and modifying regulatory tools (such as zoning). The maps of Barcelona, Medellín, Shenzhen, and Portland (see also Part II) exemplify various strategies for refining zoning categories by which these places reconsidered and applied unique industrial regulatory mechanisms to specific districts within their cities.

An example of such a case is San Francisco's use of the land use category PDR – Production, Distribution, and Repair. In the late 1990s, San Francisco saw a rapid transformation in the real estate market due to the "dot-com bubble" and growth of the high-tech sector. The limited land area in the city led to competition over space for development of new homes, businesses, and other uses. The eastern neighborhoods of the city, including areas where industrial uses were concentrated, experienced the brunt of this competition for space (San Francisco Planning Department, 2002). Due to a loophole in the zoning code, which allowed the construction or conversion of live/work lofts in industrial areas, developers began building large live/work buildings, and offices often displaced small manufacturers, changing the character of the neighborhoods. Over time, new residential projects in industrial areas resulted in conflicts between new residents and existing industrial users. Concerned that such conflicts would continue and the city might eventually lose most of its industrial land, the city embarked on a major rezoning of its eastern neighborhoods using a district-wide city approach that will continue to protect and support industrial operations while allowing some mixing of other uses.

As part of the effort, the city planning department suggested a new land use category entitled Production, Distribution, and Repair (PDR). In its recommendation for the change it stated that "the term PDR is used instead of 'industrial' to avoid conjuring images of heavy, 'smoke-stack' industry, such as large manufacturing plants, smelting operations, and refineries" (San Francisco Planning Department, 2002: 4). Given the widespread demand for more housing in the city, the Planning Department had two main objectives: stabilizing industrial land in order to protect PDR businesses, while also encouraging the development of housing affordable to low- and middle-income households. After many years of community planning processes, the city officially created the PDR districts in 2009 to help to protect the existing uses, especially industry and production.

The balance of providing for existing uses versus the economy and jobs is particularly challenging given that the real estate market is still pushing for higher-end returns from housing and commercial development. To keep the right balance and assure a mix of uses, the city needs not only a clear design and physical development plan but also incentives for developers to offset their impacts and/or build hybrid mix-used buildings. In 2014, for example, San Francisco passed a cross-subsidy program that allowed developers to build new office space at select PDR sites if they offset their impacts through the development of new industrial space. In 2016, city residents voted in favor of requiring developers to provide space "to build replacement space if they remove production, distribution, and repair (PDR) uses of 5,000 square feet or more, institutional community (IC) uses of 2,500 square feet or more, or arts activities uses of any size" (Proposition X). In subsequent years, the city continued its assessment of the districts, including a 2018 mixed-use PDR study and a current assessment which is trying to address such issues as conflicts between uses, especially residential and PDR, updating design standards and amending the "cross-subsidy" to encourage PDR on sites currently without PDR uses (San Francisco, 2020).

The San Francisco case clearly shows that creating a sustainable mixed-use district requires constant updating, strong community and business engagement, and most importantly a dedicated overseeing agency. This organization, whether public or private or a combination of the two, needs to continuously find new ways to maintain the right balance of mixed uses in an area to truly create a long-lasting hybrid district where a variety of uses can co-exist.

Barcelona, Spain

The Barcelona case showcases the transformation of the Poblenou district, a former industrial area, where the former "22a" zoning code, which reserved productive space exclusively for industrial purposes, was replaced with a new urban classification called "22@" (Gianoli and Palazzolo Henkes, 2020). The new classification permits mixed uses of complementary activities to encourage innovation in production processes including the integration of housing and public areas to allow people to live close to their places of work (Rota, 2005). The 22@ zoning code alters the traditional zoning model of separating manufacturing by introducing a model of mixed production activities as well as R&D, commerce, housing, and green areas. Coding categories include: industrial activities (storage and logistics), industrial, employment, and institutional, as well as residential and urban parks. The result is a fabric of diverse blocks, each offering a different array of uses and mix. In addition, the code encourages and allows higher density, rather than the low density that characterized the older industrial area, and permits mixed uses in existing and new buildings. The new regulatory framework also supports flexibility in terms of codifying use and architecture typologies. It does not define detailed or precise rules, allowing instead for different kinds of initiatives that vary in magnitude and building typologies, while respecting the typological and morphological diversity of previous industrial designs. The result is a gradual renovation of industrial spaces that created a district with a high standard of living in the center of Barcelona (Rota, 2005). To promote open and public spaces, the 22@ zoning code is also linked to a system of incentives that requires every development project to contribute to financing of public spaces including streetscapes (Rota, 2005). Given the complexity and extent of the old industrial makeup in Poblenou, gradual and flexible renewal was prioritized and the plan is periodically reviewed and adjusted.

Medellín, Colombia

In 2014, Medellín adopted a municipal ordinance with revision and long-term adjustments of the city's Territorial Organization Plan. This ordinance provided a legal instrument for directing real estate development and allowing the city to intervene in development decisions. The plan is rooted in an earlier effort when the city joined forces with a public telecommunications company (EPM-UNE) to transform Medellín into an innovation hub. As part of the plan, Medellín's Innovation District was defined and incorporated into the city's overall Development Plan, which is based on multi-stakeholder participation and inclusive development – the social aspect of integrated urban intervention. In this context, members of the community actively identify the problems and opportunities associated with their present condition. This is done by establishing the mechanisms for participation and creating spaces for information and dialogue. These measures enacted by the city empower residents to take part in community efforts and decision-making (Tholons, 2011). The city also established an economic inclusion strategy aimed at promoting the local economy and fostering opportunities for experimenting, promoting social enterprises, and strengthening local businesses. As part of the effort, an economic strategy – the Soft Landings program – was introduced to

attract innovative national and international actors to the district. Coding categories include low mixed-use (mainly residential with a low amount of commerce), medium mixed-use (residential mixed with commerce), high mixed-use (industrial, commerce, and residential), single use (institutional) and urban parks. The result is an integrated but diverse area. As a catalyst for the district, the city developed and built – in collaboration with public utility companies – an "anchor" complex (Ruta N) that serves as a center and agent of innovation and business for the area (EU University Business Cooperation, 2019). The complex represents the coding vision and includes three buildings, gardens, and access to key transportation nodes. The buildings house several large companies, public entities such as EPM-UNE, branches of Medellín's universities, as well as space for incubators and start-up programs. It is important to note that the emergence of Ruta N as a successful anchor in the district is due to the strong part played by the local government acting as a change agent. This included not only direct involvement, direct planning, and continued oversight, but also a strong partnership with the public and private sectors, and strong community engagement.

Portland, Oregon, USA

In the late 20th century Portland's Central Eastside Industrial District faced pressure from commercial, office, and housing development. Due to community involvement and the city's planning strategies, the traditional industrial area has evolved into a diverse mixed-use district that continues to maintain a strong industrial identity. During the 1970s, concern over the loss of Portland's industrial job base and pressures from commercial and office development spurred efforts to protect the district's industrial base. These concerns brought about community involvement including that of 1000 Friends of Oregon, a non-profit organization devoted to working on issues of land use and planning in the state. In the 1980s, the organization published a report titled "Central Eastside Industrial District: Benefactor of Portland's Economy" which was instrumental in changing the zoning of the district. The report suggested six subdistricts which were perceived as having distinct development patterns and needs. It also supported an industrial sanctuary designation to protect existing uses (Minner, 2007). About a decade later, the city adopted an Industrial Sanctuary Policy, which required non-industrial uses in the district to seek special conditional use review. The policy acknowledged that the industrial land in the Central Eastside was in danger of being repurposed. It also aimed to keep land prices lower by limiting speculative pressures and protecting older industrial buildings to ensure that there is a supply of affordable space for start-ups and small businesses (Jones, 2014).

With the growing changes in industrial production and pressure for new types of development, support for protecting the industrial sanctuary declined. In 2003, Portland modified the zoning within the area to accommodate what was referred to as a "new urban economy," or the creative class. This allowed the city to relax the industrial requirements, creating more flexibility by allowing businesses in digital production, retail, and office uses to move in (City of Portland Bureau of Planning, 2003). Coding categories include general industrial, heavy industrial, employment, commercial mixed-use with employment, and/or residential and urban parks. While still referred to loosely as an industrial sanctuary, the flexible zoning designation enacted in the early 2000s allows for integration of uses. As a result, the area saw an increase in restaurants, high-end retail, and knowledge-based businesses as well as artists' studios and the renovation of industrial buildings for multiple uses. This change illustrates the need to continuously amend restrictions and allow for the changing nature of some industries, while providing a policy framework that will protect and maintain those legacy industrial spaces that are still viable and thriving.

Shenzhen, China

Shenzhen was established as a special economic zone in the 1970s, and is considered an important experiment in industrial policy as part of China's reform era economy. At that time, industrial development relied on cheap land and labor, with industrial zones concentrated within adjacent transportation hubs and in close proximity to Hong Kong. Today, these areas are located in the older core part of the city. Formerly, major industries included electronics, textiles, and construction material production. Shangbu Industrial Park (established in 1982, and current site of the Huaqiangbei Electronics Market) was the earliest zone that specialized in electronics assembly in China. With the growth of the city and the growing demand for high-end commercial and residential development space, intensive and high-polluting industries moved towards other parts of the Pearl River Delta and to designated industrial parks on the outskirts of the city. Shangbu Industrial Park began to shift its use to accommodate the need for other uses and started to resemble a mixed commercial-production district. It is interesting to note that development policy at the time did not specify many types of industry and did not provide a clear separation between commercial activity and production. This created a mix of uses – especially commercial, retail, and production in the predominantly older industrial districts, which were in close proximity to older residential areas. Coding categories included mixed-use/manufacturing, government institutions, municipal and public utilities, sidewalks, plazas and urban parks.

This coding approach is associated with the changing dynamics of China's economic strategies and the shift from a top-down approach to urban development towards a more regional and local decision-making process. These changes were achieved through new, reformed sets of strategic schemes, regional plans down to the level of detailed municipal plans. Typically in China's urban planning process, once decisions have been made with regard to the urban functions, a detailed zoning plan is prepared, in which each block is allocated a single function, whether residential, shopping, cultural and educational, administrative, green space, or industrial zones, etc. Details of development are specifically defined for each block or parcel in an area. Besides usage, density, height, and volume of buildings, they also include the proportion of green spaces and the amount of public and essential services (Curien, 2014). If not administered uniformly across a large tract, this type of detailed parcel-level planning also allows for a matrix of uses and building types to exist within each block. Though highly regulated, the de facto results are more accommodating to existing and new uses, making for an urban form that is often varied, mixed, and organic.

In the early 2000s, efforts by China to support mass entrepreneurship and innovation through preferential tax policies resulted in the proliferation of creative spaces, innovation districts, and incubator spaces. The Shangbu and Huaqiangbei areas benefited from these incentives and their mixed-use architectural typologies accommodating commercial, residential, and industry catered to and excel at such local innovation.

The above examples share similar outlooks in accommodating changes to industrial regulatory frameworks, including:

- Developing an updated set of coding categories by assessing the existing coding, understanding its limitations and adopting a more nuanced set of categories. The updated categories are culturally and spatially based and therefore differ from one place to another.

- Supporting mixed, flexible use-based zoning by integrating commercial uses and office space with small- and medium-scale industrial uses; allowing certain compatible uses within the manufacturing industry to be in the same location (for example R&D and production lines); maintaining existing uses; incentivizing investors; attracting a diversity of workers; developing a more nuanced and detailed classification of industry and manufacturing typologies (e.g. introducing new classifications

for biotechnology and pharmaceuticals); defining manufacturing zones based on a nuanced, detailed classification of industry; distinguishing between artisans, small and medium-sized enterprises (SMEs), and large factories.

- Developing industrial protection measures by maintaining the viability of the zoning for industrial uses, introducing an industrial sanctuary designation (Portland), or defining special Planned Manufacturing or Industrial Unit Developments or districts such as Chicago's Planned Manufacturing Districts (PMDs).

- Setting special requirements to support manufacturing by requiring that a minimum floor area in all new developments be reserved for production and light industrial uses; and providing industrial businesses with certainty about their ability to remain or expand in current locations.

- Defining updated performance standards by guaranteeing that industrial uses do not cause negative impacts, while ensuring that permitted non-industrial uses remain compatible with the existing industrial base.

- Maintaining a flexible approach by using case-by-case projections to plan a district and allow for flexibility in use; utilizing a special overlay zoning or Planned Unit Development (PUD) that are not subject to the standard zoning requirements, but rather adhere to local criteria and guidelines to determine use, form, and design.

These regulatory mechanisms are often supported by economic policies and incentives mechanisms such as tax credits and cross-subsidized industrial rent (especially in mixed-use buildings). Additional actions are sometimes initiated by industrial organizations that leverage public and private funds to convert disused industrial buildings into space for small and medium-sized manufacturing businesses. This is the case of Greenpoint Manufacturing and Design Center (GMDC), a non-profit industrial developer in New York City that is dedicated to the creation and preserva-

PART III | OPEN MANUFACTURING

22@DISTRICT
Barcelona, Spain

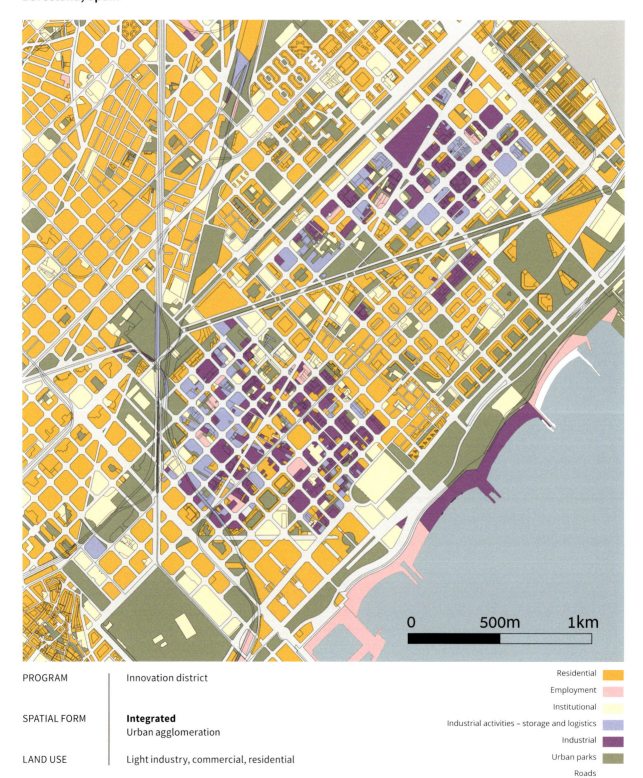

PROGRAM	Innovation district
SPATIAL FORM	**Integrated** Urban agglomeration
LAND USE	Light industry, commercial, residential

Legend:
- Residential
- Employment
- Institutional
- Industrial activities – storage and logistics
- Industrial
- Urban parks
- Roads

INNOVATION DISTRICT
Medellín, Colombia

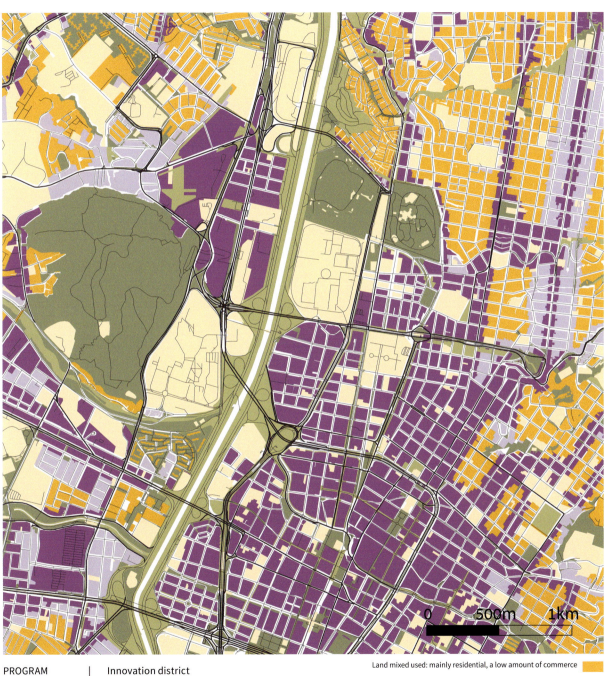

PROGRAM	Innovation district
SPATIAL FORM	**Integrated** Urban agglomeration
LAND USE	Light industry, commercial, residential

PART III | OPEN MANUFACTURING

CENTRAL EASTSIDE
Portland, Oregon, USA

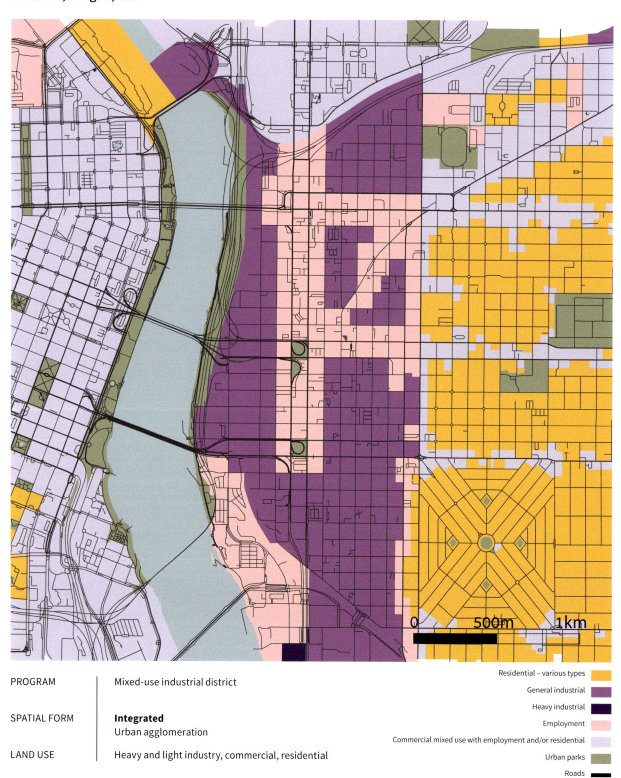

PROGRAM	Mixed-use industrial district
SPATIAL FORM	**Integrated** Urban agglomeration
LAND USE	Heavy and light industry, commercial, residential

Legend:
- Residential – various types
- General industrial
- Heavy industrial
- Employment
- Commercial mixed use with employment and/or residential
- Urban parks
- Roads

9 | INTEGRATING URBAN-INDUSTRIAL SYSTEMS

SHENZHEN
Guangdong, China

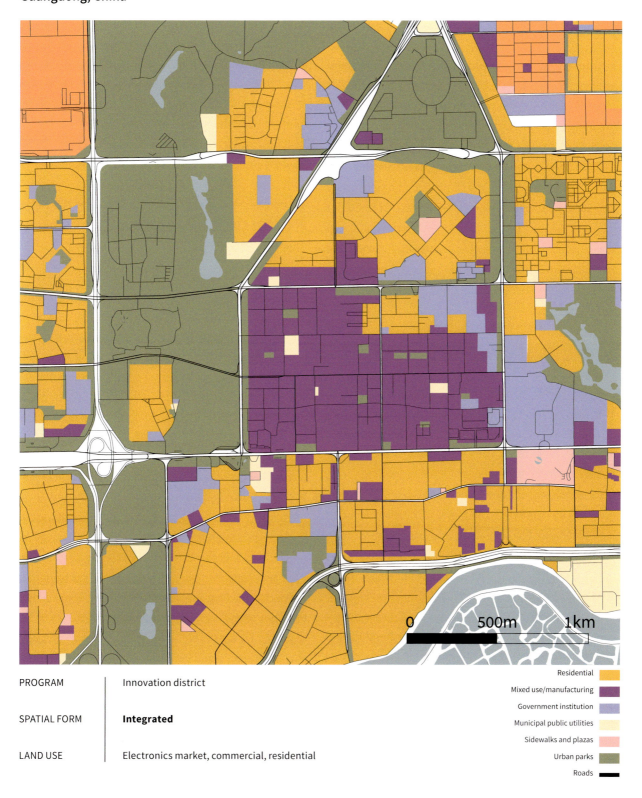

PROGRAM	Innovation district
SPATIAL FORM	**Integrated**
LAND USE	Electronics market, commercial, residential

Residential
Mixed use/manufacturing
Government institution
Municipal public utilities
Sidewalks and plazas
Urban parks
Roads

205

tion of permanent, affordable manufacturing space for small and medium-sized industrial firms. The organization aims to sustain manufacturing sectors in urban neighborhoods through planning, developing, and managing real estate, as well as offering related services. GMDC acquires and rehabilitates industrial buildings in Brooklyn, New York and rents them out to small manufacturing enterprises, artisans, and artists. In addition to the space, tenants are also provided with job training and a communal environment. This unique approach relies on local organizations and strong community associations and in the case of strong real estate markets, such as New York City, it has to fend off many challenges. These include pressure to convert underutilized industrial buildings to up-scale housing, gentrification, and regulations that may prohibit mixing of uses, especially living and working on a single premise.

Towards an Integrated System: Eastern Market Neighborhood, Detroit

The Eastern Market Neighborhood plan in Detroit, USA is a recent example of consolidating industrial functions with other uses, especially with housing. Eastern Market has been an active center for food wholesale and a cultural icon for the Detroit metropolitan area for more than 120 years, yet its historic buildings constrain the upgrading and expansion of food production and the growth of the current businesses they house (Planning and Development Department City of Detroit, 2019; Utile, 2021). The new plan for the area aimed to provide a vision for a development that would chart an implementation strategy for the growth and integration of food-business-centered production and distribution, housing, and the use of vacant land while integrating ecological and sustainable strategies. Led by Utile Inc. in collaboration with Detroit city government and the Nature Conservancy (a non-profit organization), the Eastern Market Neighborhood Framework and Stormwater Management

Network Plan published in 2019 guides both the expansion of the local industry and the redevelopment of its current core through the phased implementation of regulatory revisions, new building construction, vacant lot usage, streetscape improvements, and the integration of stormwater management landscape features. The plan suggests an integration of the existing cluster economy of production, distribution, and retail businesses through the expansion of the existing market while minimizing the displacement of existing businesses and residents, and protecting the historic market's built heritage (Planning and Development Department City of Detroit, 2019). Due to the limitations of the existing early 20th-century industrial buildings, businesses have been leaving the neighborhood as they seek adequate space to expand and modernize.

While the proposal provides the much necessary expansion, it would also present an additional challenge if typical development standards were implemented. According to common production and distribution facility requirements, staging and loading areas with their accompanying space for semitrailers to maneuver occupy large empty lots. In the case of Eastern Market, most of these spaces would occupy existing lots that were once used for housing, which would not only harm the historic character of the neighborhood but also increase stormwater runoff into the already overburdened sewage infrastructure. To mitigate these negative effects, the expansion was designed around an interior staging area, carefully planned trucking routes, and a green ecological buffering system. The plan also calls for new businesses and food-oriented production to be interwoven with greenways that, together with live/work buildings at the edges of the expansion area, buffer any industrial operations from the adjacent homogeneous residential neighborhoods. Design guidelines shape the industrial facilities to ensure that each creates a human-scale, active street edge and provides opportunities for plantings and public art. The plan also allows for dense, mixed-use residential development to better take advantage of proximity to the greenway and relieve development

EASTERN MARKET

Detroit, USA

Eastern Market has been an active center of food wholesale for the Detroit metropolitan area for more than 120 years. Yet its historic buildings constrain upgrading and expanding of the food production and distribution businesses they house. The Eastern Market Neighborhood Framework and Stormwater Management Network Plan guides both the expansion of the market and the redevelopment of its current core through the phased implementation of regulatory revisions, new building construction, streetscape improvements, logistics and truck routes, and the integration of stormwater management landscape features.

The plan provides a phased roadmap to achieve its goals on multiple fronts and assures regular opportunities for public input before individual projects are implemented. Market-specific zoning revisions and design guidelines were two powerful design tools struck a balance between directing development toward the plan's vision and providing the flexibility necessary to adjust to future unpredictability.

Eastern Market Plan, Detroit, MI, USA. Maps and drawings courtesy of city of Detroit, Utile Inc. and Michael Van Valkenburgh Associates.

PART III | OPEN MANUFACTURING

Planning and Implementation Strategies

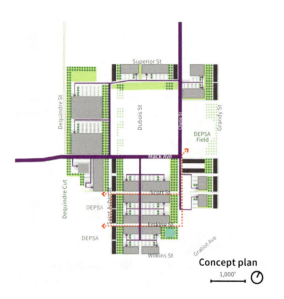

Concept plan

The concept plan for the expansion area lays out food facilities to minimize the visibility of parking and staging areas from the street, designates truck routes, and defines Safe Routes between an existing school and its track and field

Proposed market build-out

The first strategy, for the market expansion area, takes the form of a network of stormwater management landscape features that also function as public recreational greenways. These greenways are sized and located in conjunction with planned food facility parcels to capture and manage up to 100% of stormwater runoff from new development and keep it from entering the city's overburdened combined sewer system. This improves public health by preventing combined sewer overflows and street flooding in the area.

The second strategy, for the existing market area, encourages the sensitive and respectful reuse of existing buildings through zoning revisions and design guidelines, which are now being codified into law. New zoning limits the height of permitted development in the area of the market with the greatest concentration of heritage building stock to drive development toward their renovation and expansion, rather than demolition and replacement, while design guidelines sensitively shape the mass and material palette of any expansions.

Eastern Market Plan, Detroit, MI, USA. Diagrams courtesy of city of Detroit, Utile Inc. and Michael Van Valkenburgh Associates.

9 | INTEGRATING URBAN-INDUSTRIAL SYSTEMS

Expansion Area

The prototypical block development for the expansion area includes food production and distribution facilities – oriented to minimize the visibility of their parking and staging areas from public streets – and live-work buildings separated by stormwater management greenways.

Drawing created in collaboration with Michael Van Valkenburgh Associates.

Expansion Area

Design guidelines will further shape new food facilities to ensure their scale and organization of parking and staging areas does not negatively impact nearby residents. Facades will be required to incorporate glazed areas and active uses, as well as recessed areas to limit the length of continuous facades. Blank areas will provide future canvas space for Eastern Market's Murals in the Market program. Green and/or blue roofs and photovoltaic arrays are encouraged.

Existing Core

Design guidelines for new mixed-use buildings on the periphery of the market core encourage greater density, a mix of uses, and active street frontages. For those buildings located along the existing Dequindre Cut greenway, additional guidelines call for integrating active uses and additional public open space to make the greenway a place where visitors can spend time, rather than simply passing through.

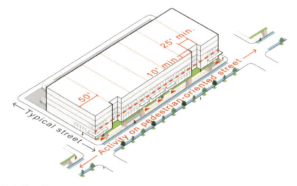

Existing Core

There are several opportunities for full-block and infill commercial development in the market core. Design guidelines for new commercial buildings encourage active street edges and articulated facades to continue the vitality of the existing market fabric.

Eastern Market Plan, Detroit, MI, USA. Diagrams courtesy of city of Detroit, Utile Inc. and Michael Van Valkenburgh Associates.

pressure to introduce new uses in old market buildings (Planning and Development Department City of Detroit, 2019).

The new neighborhood plan has succeeded in accommodating production and distribution facilities and their accompanying truck staging areas while maintaining the historic character of the place and integrating green stormwater infrastructure to mitigate the built area's runoff while providing recreational space. It also provided the city and the community with a clear, phased roadmap to achieve its goals on multiple fronts and with regular opportunities for public input before individual projects are implemented. Market-specific zoning revisions and design guidelines were two crucial tools that emerged from the planning process and that struck a balance between directing development toward the plan's vision and providing the flexibility necessary to adjust to future unpredictability. The community embraced these tools as a means to ensure that the working market remains vibrant and active, neither preserved as a museum piece nor pushed out by development pressures. Since adoption of the plan, multiple food-business developments have taken place in the expansion area, enabling the longstanding market businesses to expand, retain existing jobs, and create new ones. The plan has guided the proposed creation of a new zoning designation tailored to food-related businesses to ensure the market remains prosperous for future generations of Detroiters (Planning and Development Department City of Detroit, 2019).

Summary: Recoding the Industrial–Residential Nexus

Approaching industrial development through a flexible lens encourages complexity and promotes the development of heterogeneous places that include a variety of uses and activities. One of the planning strategies to achieve such diversity has been the development of industrial urban and urban-edge hybrid special districts. In these districts, varied operations such as office, retail, warehousing and light manufacturing, and, in some cases, residential and educational uses are mixed, which results in a diversity of functions and activities. To support such mixing, dimensional requirements such as minimum lot sizes, setbacks, building heights and overall density tend to vary and be more discretionary. Mixed uses in industrial areas increase the chances of public space becoming active, lively places where public spaces are used by a broader segment of the population, in addition to local inhabitants and users. Increased activity could bring about greater integration with social, cultural, and educational programs as well as greater access to jobs.

Three key approaches emerge from this process of recoding land uses: integration, transitioning, and anchoring, with the mixed-use district being the most integrated approach. Integration encourages hybrid urban development to include live/work and/or fully residential building complexes. Industrial use is a unified part of the city fabric, from the parcel level to the design of residential homes. Transitioning is often characterized by open space and landscape areas that serve as a buffer zone between non-compatible industrial uses and residential areas. Buffering allows proximity between different uses and relative flexibility within each area while assuring safety and mitigating for potential nuisances. This configuration often lacks a residential or housing component within the industrial zone. Finally, the anchoring approach is a centralized complex of production that acts as an industrial manufacturing center relatively independent from the surrounding neighborhoods in character and form. This layout supports residential development with compatible small–medium industrial uses typically of work/live types.

There is no doubt that public resistance to mixing of industrial and other uses will linger. However, it is also anticipated that communities will be more attuned to the benefits that a given industrial project will bring to their community. In other words, opposition to the integration of industrial uses could be addressed through good-faith and transparent negotiations among communities, industries, and governments.

Whether communities support or oppose integration between life and work, mixing is expected to continue, accelerating as a result of the twin forces of the Fourth Industrial Revolution, climate change concerns, and the global recession caused by COVID-19. Day-to-day digitalization progressed tremendously, with the expansion of e-commence and the wide-reaching shift to remote work. Conversely, it also presented a major challenge to workers' well-being as they struggled with adjusting to new work methods in a short period of time (World Economic Forum, 2020: 16).

PART III | OPEN MANUFACTURING

Industrial-Residential Nexus

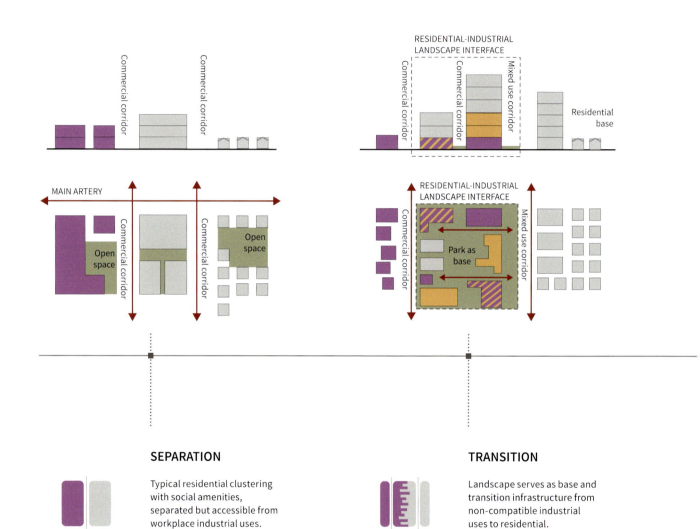

SEPARATION

Typical residential clustering with social amenities, separated but accessible from workplace industrial uses.

Program	Strict zoning.
Urban context	Industry plays a major role but not well integrated into the urban fabric

TRANSITION

Landscape serves as base and transition infrastructure from non-compatible industrial uses to residential.

Program	Residences and work-spaces with a mixed industrial-retail units.
Urban context	Industry plays major role in the mixed zone.

9 | INTEGRATING URBAN-INDUSTRIAL SYSTEMS

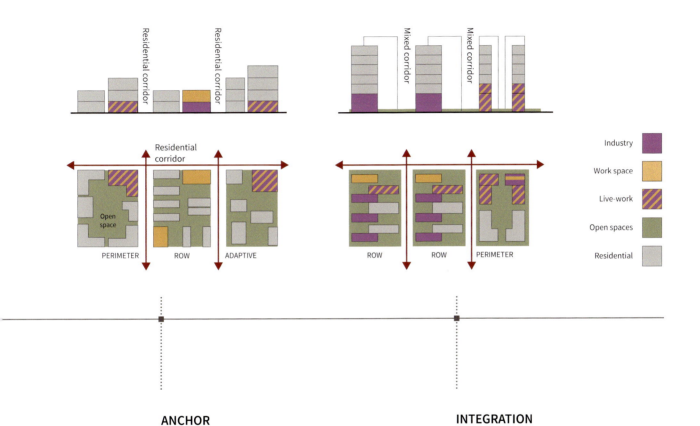

ANCHOR

Centralized and accessible industrial center of manufacturing, serves immediate blocks or neighborhoods.

Program	Residential with compatible small-medium industrial uses.
Urban context	Advanced industry is integral to the residential area.

INTEGRATION

Live-work + retail spaces, hybrid urban development.

Program	Small manufacturing unit extensions for urban and large-lot housing.
Urban context	Industry is integral to city fabric.

10

Working, Living, and Innovating

▬ Manufacturing in the City*

Urban services

Commercial cleaning, food preparation, event management, building services, specialist printing

Photo by Blaz Erzetic on Unsplash (CC).

Creative

Recording studio, stage/prop design, graphic design, glass blowing, fashion design

Photo by Evgenii Pliusnin on Unsplash (CC).

Production

3D printers, furniture restoration, shop/events display manufacture, medical prosthetics, VR Hardware and Software

Photo by Tom Claes on Unsplash (CC).

Utility

Car repairs, car rental, upcycling, kitchen installations, building supplies

Photo by Kiefer Likens on Unsplash (CC).

Distribution and Storage

Art storage, final mile logistics, parcel depot, food wholesalers, self-storage

Photo by Mark Timberlake on Unsplash (CC).

*This illustration is based on the New London Mix example activities (Beunderman, et al. 2018).

10

Working, Living, and Innovating

The demand from employers for remote-based work is increasing rapidly in many economies. Two trends are becoming clearly evident. First, the information technology and insurance industries are leading the field in offering opportunities for employees to work from home, with 74% of workers in those industries having access to remote work. But there are other industries, including finance, law, and business services, which could, in theory, do more of their work remotely. "Insights from the Glassdoor online platform show that access to working from home has nearly doubled since 2011, from 28% to 54% of workers mentioning that they had the opportunity to work from home" (World Economic Forum, 2020: 16). Second, global crises, such as the pandemic, accelerate new forms of work. The COVID-19 pandemic has shown that working from home is possible at a greater scale than previously imagined, yet business leaders remain uncertain about the productivity outcomes of the shift to remote or hybrid work. Although there is some skepticism regarding these processes and their effects on productivity, changes are already in progress.

Taking into account these dramatic changes, the social question is not to what extent automation and augmentation of human labor will affect current employment numbers, but rather under what conditions the global labor market can be supported towards a new equilibrium in the division of labor between human workers, robots, and algorithms (World Economic Forum, 2020: 49). The equivalent architectural question is: To what extent can the design of the built environment support these trends while also supporting the well-being and resilience of societies?

The architectural response to this question and to the growing demand for integrating industrial uses with other uses is developing a new type of project, known as synchronic typologies. This type of project simultaneously supports residential and industrial uses (Hatuka et al., 2020). Synchronization, unlike mixed-use, supports different operations existing and functioning in parallel, in the same built space, without interfering with each other and while optimally sharing resources. These include, but are not limited to, land utilization, service facilities, infrastructure systems, integrated living and office spaces, and diverse mobility options. The synchronic typology is based on several principles: optimal management and use of land resources, integration of housing and work (not necessarily by the same users), reducing the daily commute and dependence on private vehicles, and using the built area during all hours of the day. As a whole, synchronic typology is a new prototype that expresses the principle of integration.

The industrial uses in the synchronic typologies can range from light industry, designer-maker, storage space, logistics depots, or artists' work spaces, to commercial and community uses. Spatially, these projects may be structured around open or covered yards or be serviced from the street. Their size may range from multiple smaller maker units of 10 or 15 square meters to a single unit of c. 1,000 square meters or even more (Beunderman et al., 2018).

To be sure, integration between residential and work areas is not new. The novelty is the increasing trend towards encouraging employees to work from home for managerial reasons, saving operational and travel costs. This trend is supported by the accelerated use of digitization creating an unprecedented opportunity and demand for small home offices and businesses (Beunderman et al., 2018).

The Variety of Synchronic Architectural Typologies

Synchronic typology is an evolving concept with varied architectural and physical manifestations. Generally, there are two architectural approaches to developing synchronic architectural typologies: the centralized and decentralized, with differing attitudes towards the interface between housing and industry.

The centralized architectural approach refers to a range of projects in which industry is integrated within a building or architectural complex. Within this architectural approach, there are two key building types: the leveled and the wing. The leveled type refers to integrating industrial uses by using the lower stories, at street level or below ground, for industrial and commercial areas, with residential units built above them. The interface of this type of building with the urban environment includes industrial activity and/or commercial facades that pedestrians can engage with. These buildings allow for the integration of industrial activities and provide a response to the demand for storage and distribution space in city centers. There is a range of design interpretations. For example, in some instances industrial activity and use can be located at street level, creating an active, unique street-level ex-

perience where manufacturing activity is mixed with other uses. Another architectural option of this type places industry underground or on the top levels. The street front is then reserved mainly for commercial use.

Another centralized architectural type is the wing. This type refers to locating industry in a specific designated wing of a building or a complex. Residential and commercial activities are in other parts of the building, which often have integrated common areas as part of the overall plan. The wing layout provides physical separation of active industrial uses such as loading and unloading (apron space and truck turnaround) and thus has a street facade that is more pedestrian-oriented. The wing type also allows for varied ceiling heights and column spacing. The production-industrial area can be easily designed with higher floors and wider bays allowing for easy vertical stacking, wider flow with mechanized equipment, and the ability to integrate industrial grade air handling systems. The following cases illustrate these architectural types.

Strathcona Village, Vancouver, Canada

Strathcona Village, designed by GBL Architects in Vancouver, British Columbia, Canada is an example of the leveled architectural type. The project is a mixed-use industrial and residential development, located near the downtown core, on the southern edge of the Port of Vancouver. This site has historically been one of industry, a typology that is increasingly being converted to residential use due to the pressures of the ever-expanding inner city (GBL Architects, 2021). With the aim of providing more housing but also preserving existing industrial space, the project integrates industrial and residential uses that were formerly thought to be incompatible. The result is an innovative hybrid mixed-use typology, which offers cities a model for revitalization that meets economic and housing needs without sacrificing the existing urban fabric and character. The industrial, or production, distribution, and repair

(PDR) spaces, are interspersed with residential entrance lobbies (General Manager of Planning and Development Services, 2012). Strathcona Village includes 70 units of city-owned social housing, including 17 that are designed for families with young children and 23 that are rented at shelter rates, in compliance with the Downtown Eastside Housing Plan. The design is based on horizontal separation, with residential towers rising above a multi-story podium of mixed industrial, commercial, and office uses. On upper levels, near the apartments, the private landscape areas are removed from street level. Industrial logistics, such as delivery docks, are located in the alley behind the complex, which leaves the front clear for a pedestrian-friendly public streetscape. The impact of industrial activity on the residential units above them is minimized by the use of separate ventilation systems and capping the size of industrial units at 500 square meters. The public benefits from the project and its novel zoning because it expands the supply of both employment opportunities and housing (General Manager of Planning and Development Services, 2012: 12).

Iceland Wharf and Fish Island, East London, UK

An interpretation of the wing architectural type is the Iceland Wharf and Fish Island project in East London, designed by pH+ Architects (pH+ Architects, 2021). The site's industrial legacy includes rubber, plastics, petroleum, and sweets. Although not a true island, the area has an island-like feel because it is surrounded and crisscrossed by waterways, roads, and railroad tracks. According to the London Plan, it is designated as an "Other Industrial Location" (OIL), indicating that the site is meant to be developed for mixed uses, prioritizing employment, including warehouses, storage, and distribution, with additional potential for residential development (Ogundiya, 2018). Centrally located near London's Olympic park, public transport and other infrastructure is accessible, but increased connectivity within the neighborhood and to adjacent parts of the city are critical for its long-term vitality. The project's

mixed-use scheme includes 120 housing units, layered together with maker and retail spaces covering approximately 3,710 square meters of commercial space in flexible living and working environments (Duddy, 2018). The new standalone buildings are adjacent to the historic ammonia works that preserve the industrial feel of the area but now house maker spaces and offices. Old and new buildings are integrated and connected by courtyards and exterior walkways that allow light into interior spaces that would otherwise be dark. Industrial uses are concentrated near the main street, farther from the river. The five-story industrial building is designed to provide good access for large trucks receiving deliveries and loading outbound merchandise. The residential buildings are positioned at the rear of the lot, closer to the river. The common, public areas are open to all tenants for leisure use, and serve as a transitional space joining the project to the neighborhood. Permeable courtyards and entrances improve the complex's connection to its environs. Traditional zoning, density guidelines, and calls for "informality" are challenged not only by the mix of uses, but also by the variations in heights, frontages, massing, and materials.

Unlike the centralized approach, the decentralized architectural approach is applied by a multitude of projects in which industrial uses are spread throughout all parts of the building or land parcel. This approach represents a high degree of spatial integration and manufacturing activities are subject to strict environmental limitations and regulations. Within this approach, there are two key architectural types: the integrated and the entwined. The integrated type offers a wide range of layouts and configurations at the parcel/block level. Housing tends to be located both next to and above industrial operation, allowing for better connection and greater consolidation of uses. Industrial spaces are accessible for loading and unloading, and public passages connect to open areas within the block or the urban system of open spaces. The entwined type combines industry, product making, and housing by connecting to residential units in live/work or work/live layouts. This architectural configuration meets the increasing need to work from home and allows a non-separated commercial business and a residential use within the same space. In the case of live/work, space is typically defined as a residential occupancy and the commercial allocation can be no more than 50% of the unit. With work/live, however, the space is commercial in nature and the residential use does not exceed 50%. In both cases, the business owner both resides and operates a business within the same space. Unlike home occupancies, the business may have employees and customers just like any other type of commercial business. In the work/live category, manufacturing operations such as fabrication and materials handling, repairs, and processing operations are allowed as long as they do not create hazardous conditions. The following cases illustrate these architectural types.

Wick Lane, East London, UK

An example of the integrated type is Wick Lane, Hackney Wick, East London, designed by dRMM Architects. It is part of an extensive plan for continuing development of the area in East London that was renovated prior to the 2012 Olympic Games. Hackney Wick is known for the Victorian warehouses along the canal, which are home to a thriving artistic community. The Wick Lane project serves as a bridge joining the Fish Island conservation area that preserves Victorian warehouse buildings, described above, to its north and an industrial area with a Strategic Industrial Land (SIL) designation to its south (dRMM, 2020). The planners' vision was to renovate the district and transform its post-industrial landscape in a manner that improves the housing conditions and economic prospects of residents, while preserving the local heritage. Therefore, the project includes 175 affordable, good-quality residential units and about 2,500 square meters of employment space. The employment spaces are varied ranging from double-height industrial units to free-standing one, two, or three-story commercial units that enliven the main street. The scheme is composed of six distinct buildings, each with their own charac-

ter, shape, and material. They relate to the neighborhood's vibrant history and provide a transitional space between the adjacent industrial and conservation areas. Residential and industrial activities are integrated using varied buffer spaces to shield housing from industrial nuisances. For example, a buffer is used between the SIL to the south of Wick Lane, and homes are set back. This allows the SIL to be developed in the future without negatively affecting the Wick Lane residents.

Westferry Studios, London, UK

Westferry Studios, also in East London, exemplifies the entwined typology. This live/work project, designed by CZWG, was completed in 1999. Its development was facilitated by support from the public sector, which provided the land. The London Docklands Development Corporation (LDDC) and the Peabody Trust envisioned a project that would support small businesses in East London without specifying the type of business. Westferry serves as an "incubator" for new businesses, which benefit from subsidized rents and receive seed money. This has helped the project attract residents working in creative fields. The building's design declares its location between Westferry Road to the east and Docklands Light Railway to the north, with 9-meter-high, light-cream bricks set against a background of blue-grey bricks (CZWG, 2021). A four-story building built around an inner courtyard houses 29 live/work units. The project is unique because life-work integration takes place within each unit. There are some limits on the type of industrial activity permitted, and renting a unit solely for residential purposes is forbidden. Units on all floors are directly accessible through exterior passageways. Being built around a courtyard facilitates developing public amenities and commercial spaces on the ground level, while also allowing loading and unloading in the common space.

These timely projects also raise some planning and policy concerns. In some instances, these types of projects could change the local character of the area and increase real estate values, and in time, these districts may change to be predominantly residential, a process often referred to as "residential reversion" (Cutting Edge Planning & Design, 2018: 13–14). A free-market approach may well lead to residential dominance and may present challenges to business and industry in the form of NIMBY (not in my back yard) resistance to their presence in a residential area. Affordability is also a major concern. The paradox is that the potential users of synchronic typologies are artisans and artists who need reasonably priced space that can (almost) only be found in old industrial buildings. In areas where real estate markets are hot, the only way users (who are not owners) can maintain control of these spaces is through long-term rent subsidies or municipal programs that oversee long-term leases. These concerns and others are part of a larger debate, and emerging policy focuses on the solutions for industry in the contemporary city: protecting industrial land for activities that cannot be mixed, intensifying industrial and employment space, and mixing a much wider range of employment space with residential and other uses (Beunderman et al., 2018: 9).

PART III | OPEN MANUFACTURING

Synchronic Architectural Typologies

CENTRALIZED

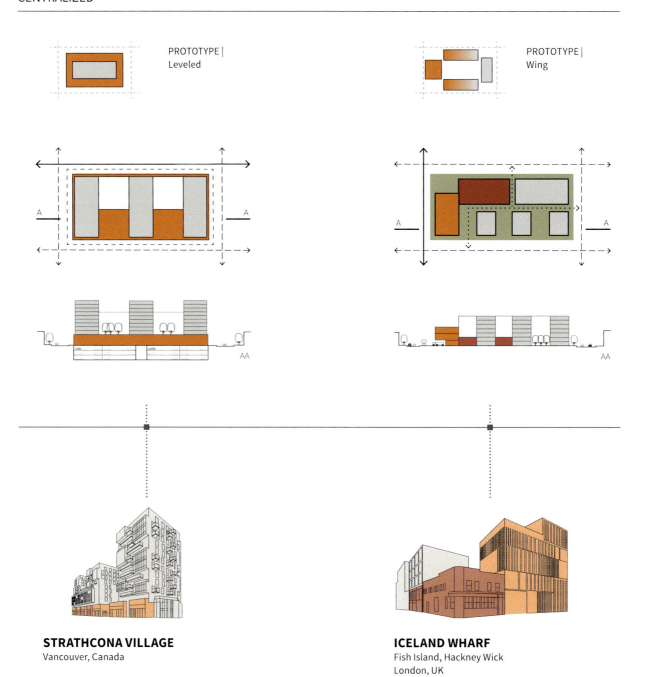

STRATHCONA VILLAGE
Vancouver, Canada

ICELAND WHARF
Fish Island, Hackney Wick
London, UK

10 | WORKING, LIVING, AND INNOVATING

DECENTRALIZED

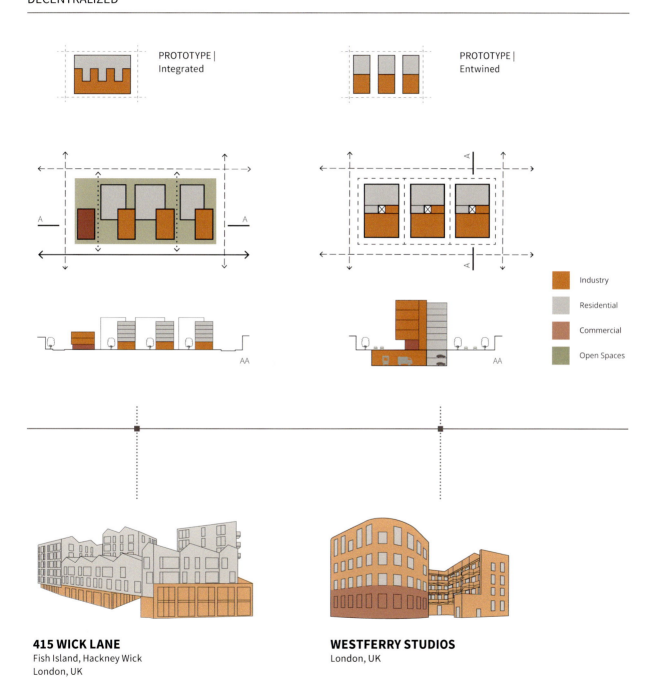

415 WICK LANE
Fish Island, Hackney Wick
London, UK

WESTFERRY STUDIOS
London, UK

223

PART III | OPEN MANUFACTURING

STRATHCONA VILLAGE
Vancouver, Canada

Office: GBL Architects

Concept: Preservation of existing industrial space while increasing the supply of local housing in the area using a sustainable community model. This renewal project provides affordable housing required in a neighborhood where about 30 percent of the population works locally.

Ground floor — Industrial uses are located along the street and provide access and connectivity to public space; commercial and factory outlets are exposed to pedestrians.

First floor — Measures to reduce the industrial impact on residential units including: separate ventilation systems, defined the size of an industrial unit.

Residential towers are built on top of a multi-story podium of mixed uses.

Industry
Residential
Commercial
Open spaces

224

10 | WORKING, LIVING, AND INNOVATING

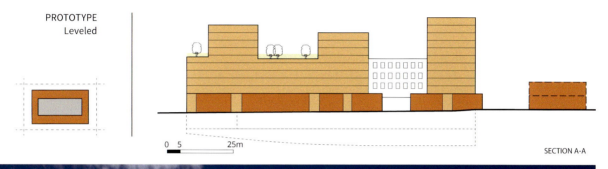

SECTION A-A

Strathcona Village, Vancouver, British Columbia, Canada. Photo courtesy of GBL Architects Inc. Photographer: Ema Peter.

225

PART III | OPEN MANUFACTURING

ICELAND WHARF
Fish Island, Hackney Wick
London, UK

Office: pH+ Architects

Concept: Integrating existing industrial area with residential buildings, and creating a high density living environment.

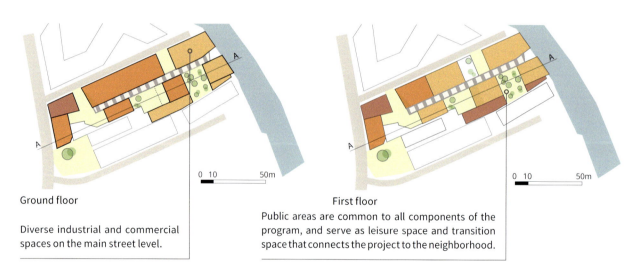

Ground floor

Diverse industrial and commercial spaces on the main street level.

First floor
Public areas are common to all components of the program, and serve as leisure space and transition space that connects the project to the neighborhood.

The place occupied by industry grows as it moves from the river towards the main street.

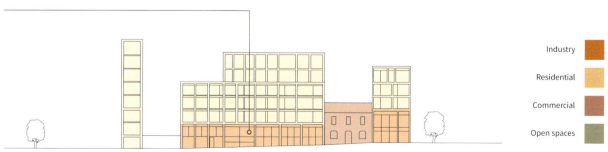

Industry
Residential
Commercial
Open spaces

226

10 | WORKING, LIVING, AND INNOVATING

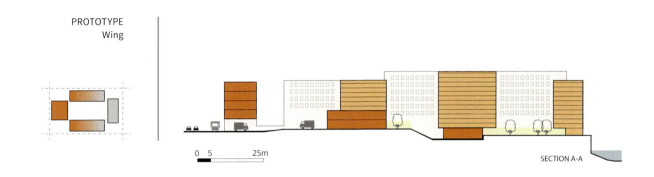

PROTOTYPE
Wing

0 5   25m

SECTION A-A

Iceland Wharf, Hackney Wick, East London, UK. Photo courtesy of Ph + Architects.

227

PART III | OPEN MANUFACTURING

415 WICK LANE
Fish Island, Hackney Wick
London, UK

Office: DRMM Architects

Concept: Regenerating post-industrial landscape while preserving the local heritage in order to improve the economic prospects and living conditions. Creating an employment-oriented complex that includes a mix of light industry, retail trade, office and residential areas, while relying on a nearby industrial area.

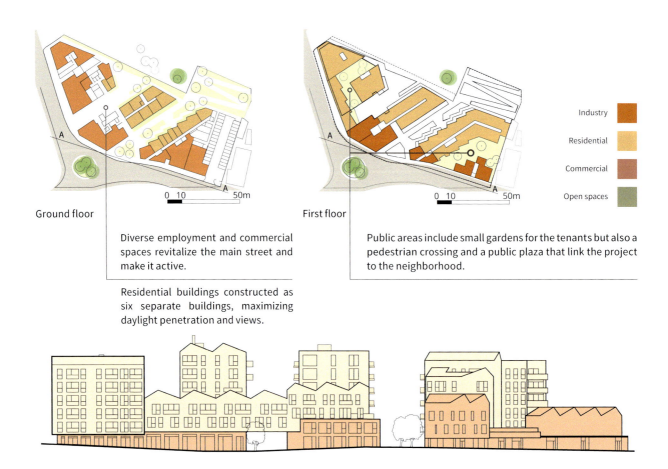

Ground floor

Diverse employment and commercial spaces revitalize the main street and make it active.

Residential buildings constructed as six separate buildings, maximizing daylight penetration and views.

First floor

Public areas include small gardens for the tenants but also a pedestrian crossing and a public plaza that link the project to the neighborhood.

10 | WORKING, LIVING, AND INNOVATING

PROTOTYPE
Integrated

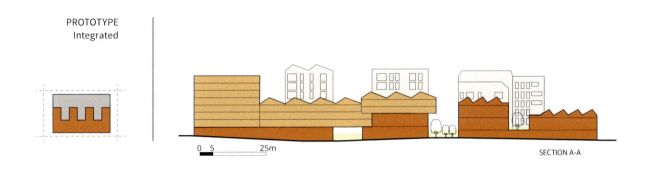

SECTION A-A

Wick Lane, Hackney Wick, London, UK. Photo courtesy of dRMM Architects.

229

PART III | OPEN MANUFACTURING

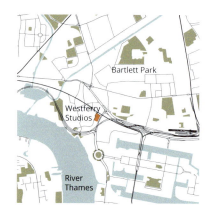

WESTFERRY STUDIOS
London, UK

Office: CZWG Architects

Concept: An "incubator" for small businesses operating in East London. Tenants receive support and subsidized rent.

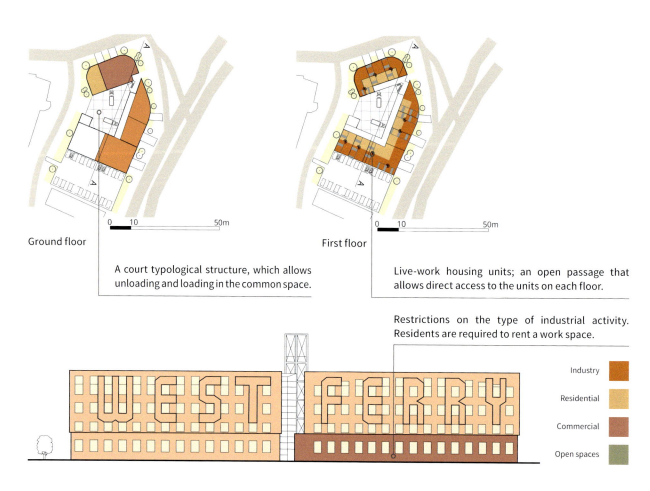

Ground floor

A court typological structure, which allows unloading and loading in the common space.

First floor

Live-work housing units; an open passage that allows direct access to the units on each floor.

Restrictions on the type of industrial activity. Residents are required to rent a work space.

Industry
Residential
Commercial
Open spaces

10 | WORKING, LIVING, AND INNOVATING

PROTOTYPE
Entwined

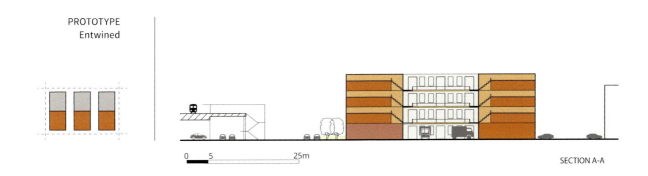

SECTION A-A

Westferry Studios, East London, UK. Photo by Google street view.

231

PART III | OPEN MANUFACTURING

THE BEDS ABOVE SHEDS CONCEPT, ICENI PROJECTS
Prototype, London

Office: Iceni Projects Ltd.

Concept: Constructing warehouses near customers' homes helps to improve and streamline the delivery rate. Pollutant emissions of vehicles can be reduced when distribution is carried out by smaller electric vehicles that travel shorter distances. The model allows the construction of apartments in the city center including affordable housing.

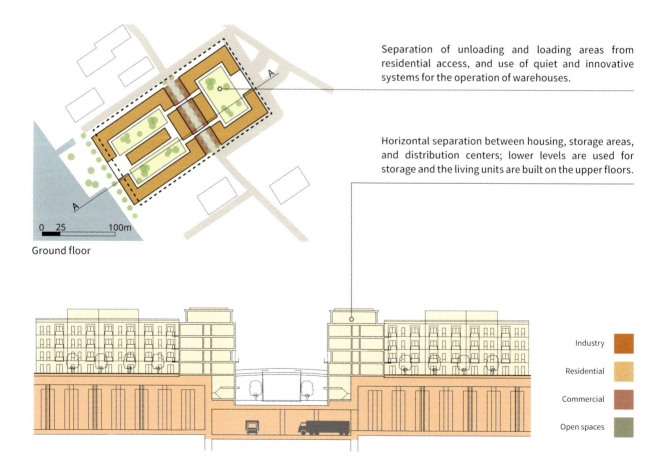

Separation of unloading and loading areas from residential access, and use of quiet and innovative systems for the operation of warehouses.

Horizontal separation between housing, storage areas, and distribution centers; lower levels are used for storage and the living units are built on the upper floors.

Ground floor

Industry
Residential
Commercial
Open spaces

10 | WORKING, LIVING, AND INNOVATING

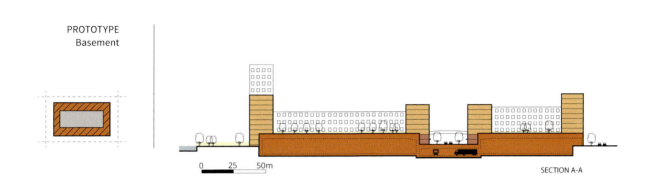

PROTOTYPE
Basement

SECTION A-A

'Beds and Sheds' mixed-used concept. Image courtesy of Paul Drew, Director of Design, Iceni Projects Ltd.

233

Summary: Locating Synchronic Architectural Typologies in the City

Synchronic typologies are an evolving, emerging form of development. They manifest the need for creating industrial and employment-based residential environments, adapted to the contemporary lifestyle and relying on new technologies. This trend is viewed as an inclusive and sustainable approach for solving the dual challenge of the 21st century city – that is, the provision of suitable housing and places to work across the city (Beunderman et al., 2018). Current policies include housing and tax credits, subsidized mortgages, and the construction of public housing as well as special land use laws and subdivision regulations to provide mixed-income and mixed-use housing development. What is missing in housing affordability is the link to labor market and economic development. Lack of affordable housing can negatively impact accessibility for workers and increase demands on transportation systems. Synchronic typologies are about bringing together an industrial/employment environment and a residential environment in a way that could not have been promoted before.

It is anticipated that this international trend will proliferate and include new conceptual ideas responding to new forms of consumption and habitation. Thus for example, one of the pressing issues is the growth of online purchasing. Many companies are seeking to relocate their distribution centers in close proximity to residential and office locations, but such spaces are at a premium or often unavailable in city centers dominated by non-industrial uses and without space for warehousing. A paper architectural project by Iceni Projects Consultants tries to address this increased demand for storage space and supply centers in central London. The challenge, says Paul Drew, Director of Design, Iceni was to see

> how we could make employment-led mixed-use schemes work; where the increased efficiency of land for various uses did not create a series of conflicts.

> We wanted to ensure that any business presence would not be inhibited by residential neighbours. Equally, the communities alongside businesses should be able to put up with potentially intrusive neighbours.

> (Drew, 2020)

The proposal offers an attempt to meet the needs of both trends by developing a building type that integrates storage and housing, beds above sheds. The vision is that constructing warehouses in close proximity to customers' homes helps improve and streamline schedules and delivery times. The main design principle is a horizontal separation, with storage spaces and distribution centers on the lower level and residential units on the floors above. Underground and rear-facing spaces can be utilized for storage, while street frontage is dedicated for commercial uses or light industry. The proposal also calls for separate loading zones and using innovative, quiet systems for operating the warehouses. Recently, Iceni has begun to engage with wider questions such as: Is it possible to move around less and still make the economy work? What form will distribution networks take? With increased home deliveries, how might haulage and delivery logistics operate in the future? How should "first mile" and "last mile" deliveries integrate into the urban fabric? Can these solutions contribute to society as it achieves zero carbon? (Drew, 2020).

These timely questions echo *Industry 4.0*, *industrial ecosystems*, and *industrial ecology* concepts, and the increasing need to develop sustainably. Reshaping the urban space in a variety of ways, this new approach to live and work is still in its infancy, and can be expected to develop. The question, therefore, is not whether additional synchronous typologies projects will be developed but to what extent and where in the city.

10 | WORKING, LIVING, AND INNOVATING

■ **Key Features of Synchronic Architectural Typologies**

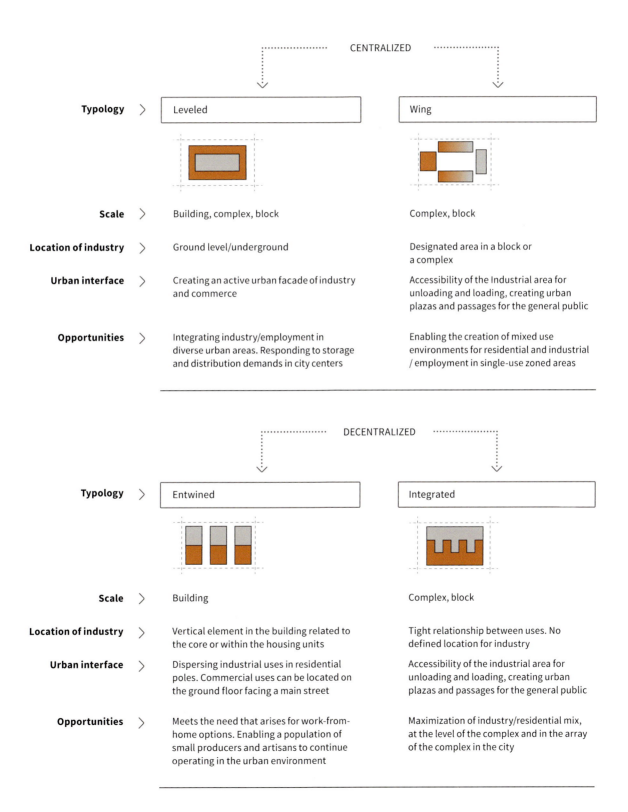

235

11 New Industrial Urbanism

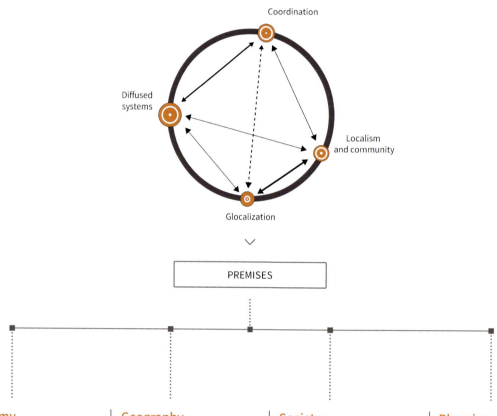

Economy	Geography	Society	Planning
Glocalization	**Coordination**	**Localism and Community**	**Diffused Systems**
Territorial attachment and proximity is a source of competitive advantage for industries that gets involved in the internationalization process.	An industrial ecosystem that encourages knowledge transfer and provides support, such as administrative services.	Community institutions (i.e. universities) that promote small businesses, start-ups, and innovation.	Mixed-use zones that permit industrial use, flexible building codes, and agreements that foster coexistence.

▬ New Industrial Urbanism: Premises

11

New Industrial Urbanism

New Industrial Urbanism is a socio-spatial concept which views manufacturing as part of city life. New Industrial Urbanism aims to shape a new approach to industrial planning through a renewed understanding that urban locations carry a competitive advantage due to access to skilled labor, educational institutions (centers of research and experimentation), and customers. New Industrial Urbanism emphasizes the local economy, and seeks to impact the social sphere by empowering small and medium-sized firms and individual entrepreneurs, as a means to buttress localism. Its goal is to adapt cities and prepare societies for the future world of work.

New Industrial Urbanism argues that urban manufacturing matters. It matters for production and job creation in cities lacking economic opportunity. When manufacturers began to move their operations from the core of the city to the outskirts, they separated factories from the city's workforce, adding to the "spatial mismatch" between class and income. Bringing manufacturing jobs back to the center of a city could mitigate the negative effects of industrial sprawl and increase opportunities for diversifying the labor market. In addition, urban manufacturing offers a chance to locate living-wage jobs in close proximity to urban residents. This potential adjacency will bring measurable environmental benefits associated with shortening commutes and reducing the delivery distances between firms. Proximity can also bolster economic clusters' strength, due to the positive effects of knowledge spillover and a robust labor market. Promoting urban manufacturing is also a good fiscal policy as cities can generate additional revenue by allowing industrial land to be used more efficiently. Finally, there is a visceral quality to urban manufacturing that is essential to place-making and civic pride in cities. The essence is about connecting to the means of production and tapping into the city's creative and constructive spirit. By building on industry, cities will be celebrating their past, present, and future as centers of production.

Four key premises form the basis of New Industrial Urbanism:

1. Glocalization (economy). Neither local nor global but viewing territorial attachment and geographical proximity as sources of competitive advantage for industries involved in the internationalization process.

2. Coordination (geography). Developing an industrial ecosystem that encourages knowledge transfer, collaborations, and provides shared support, such as administrative and community service.

3. Localism and community (society). Seeing the local community and its varied institutions

PART III | OPEN MANUFACTURING

such as schools, hospitals, and non-profits as the power engines for promoting innovation, start-ups, and small businesses.

4. Diffused systems (planning). Developing mixed-use zones that permit industrial activities through flexible building codes and agreements that foster coexistence.

These normative premises suggest that manufacturing, whether advanced or traditional, comprises much more than an economic convergence.

New Industrial Urbanism: Key Planning Concepts

New Industrial Urbanism offers a framework that unifies the economic sphere (technological trends and related economic development initiatives), the political-social sphere (policies that support human health, well-being, and growth), and the spatial sphere (physical planning). It is based on four key planning concepts: scalar strategies, integrative approaches, coding complexity, and synchronic typologies.

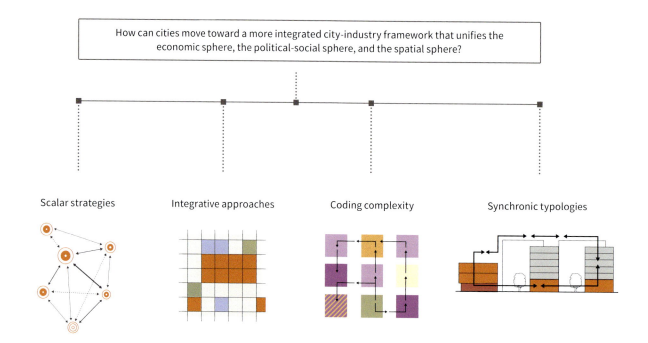

■ New Industrial Urbanism: Key Planning Concepts

Scalar Strategies

Caring for a city's social needs, planning regulations, and advanced manufacturing requires a different perception of the city. Such a conceptualization situates the city within its broader development by viewing the regional area as an innovation-production ecosystem that cultivates production and livability on a continuum from the local-urban scale to the peripheral-regional expanse. At the regional level, collaborative frameworks evolve over time and employ a range of interaction strategies among industrial actors and institutions. At the level of the urban, establishing a variety of use classifications and designing architectural typologies is key to attracting new manufacturers and ensuring multiple uses of space. Compatible uses need to be coupled with adjustable spatial building configurations to accommodate different scales of industry. Put together, these approaches should offer some flexibility in adapting the urban social and physical context to the dynamic and changing nature of industry.

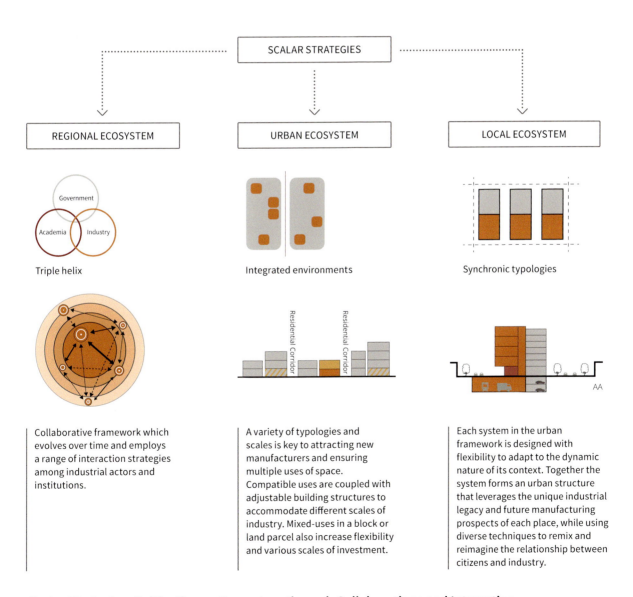

■ **Scalar Strategies: Cultivating an Ecosystem through Collaborations and Integration**

PART III | OPEN MANUFACTURING

Integrative Approaches

Bridging the gap between city and industry, with a basic desire to create livable, mixed-use integrated neighborhoods, requires that we also pay attention to concepts that go beyond determining lot sizes, building shapes, or their scales. Some of these concepts may include:

- Connectivity, encouraging urban design standards and planning policies that support the building of mixed-use industrial neighborhoods connected to the wider region by different types of transportation systems. Supporting and diversifying local economies. Conserving natural resources and farmland. Protecting existing industrial areas from encroachment and promoting urban land zoned for new industry.

- Complexity, creating symbiotic relationships through the diversification of industrial, business, and housing types. Integrating new forms and typologies of architectural design and sustainable ecological systems.

- Character, supporting outward-looking industrial development and buildings that address the public realm and are reflective of the manufacturing function and identity of the structures and the space they serve. Displaying and blending the distribution system associated with each industry as part of the overall district design.

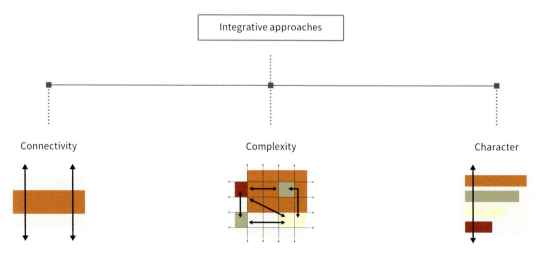

Integrative approaches

Connectivity

Encourages urban design standards and planning policies that support the building of mixed-use industrial neighborhoods connected to the wider region by different types of transportation systems, support and diversify local economies, conserve natural resources and farmland, protect industrial area from encroachment, and encourage urban land to be used and reserved for industry.

Complexity

Creates a symbiotic relationship through the diversification of industrial typologies, businesses, and housing types. Allow the reinterpretation of some areas, the integration of new forms of architecture, design and ecological systems, and provision for an evolving character to preserve the ever-necessary world of manufacturing.

Character

Support an outward looking industrial development and buildings that address the public realm and are reflective of the manufacturing function and identity of the structures and the space they serve (logistics). These characteristics have greater impact on the creation of livable, mixed neighborhoods than the size of the lot, the footprint of the structure, or the massing and scale of the building.

■ **Integrative Approaches: Developing New Standards for Industrial Environments**

Coding Complexity

New Industrial Urbanism is about integrating flexible zoning. This step requires the reevaluation of current permitted uses and the consideration of mixing housing with retail, research and development, food production, offices, services, etc., and any other form of production that does not cause negative impacts. It will also require the creation of new regulatory frameworks and zoning categories to adjust for the changing character of manufacturing. This flexibility also implies redefining the following:

REGULATING

Flexible zoning

- Reevaluating permitted use by right especially mixing of housing (live work, others)+ R&D, retail, food/restaurants, mixed-use buildings, office.
- Creating new zoning categories to adjust for changing character of manufacturing.

Environmental/ecological regulations

- Ensure industrial uses do not cause negative impacts, while permitted non-industrial uses are compatible with industrial base.
- Calculate ecological footprint and impact for each locale.
- Incorporate energy and waste use and mitigation.
- Develop low-cost ecological solutions. (eg. stormwater filtration).

Performance standards

- Regulate development "impacts" such as nuisance factors, impervious surface, landscape surface area, trip generation, etc.
- Regulate nuisance standards (odor, noise, vibration, glare, toxics, etc.).
- Develop performance criteria (floor area, impervious surface, trip generation, etc.) as an evaluation framework for development alternatives.

Compatible adjacency

- Regulate uses to ensure compatible adjacencies, a balance of activities, circulation, and access to green space, while still allowing flexibility in land use.
- Encourage incremental growth and adaptation to future changes.
- Assure no proximity conflicts between all factors above (e.g. environmental, form).
- Integrate the industrial area with residential life, social and cultural activities, leisure and recreation, and the surrounding neighborhoods.

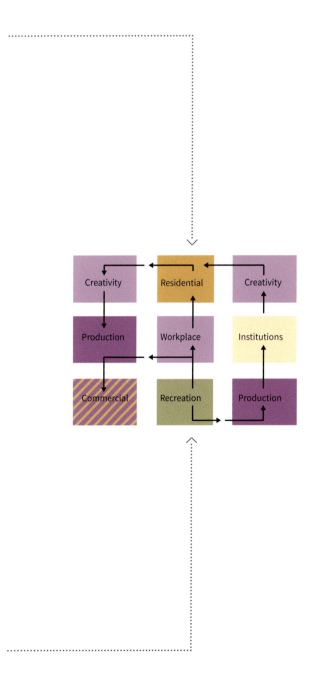

■ Coding Complexity: Creating New Regulatory Frameworks

Synchronic Architectural Typologies

Architectural synchronization is a conceptual approach that allows each use to exist and operate in parallel in the same building space. It assures that spaces are used without interfering with each other while utilizing and jointly managing resources. This approach is based on five key principles: optimal management and utilization of land resources; a combination of residence and work, not necessarily of the same users; reducing commuting and dependence on private vehicles; use of built space for 24/7 programmatic functions; and exposure of industry to the public. Implementing synchronic typologies requires an in-depth examination of the urban space including the following:

- Urban mapping and analysis: assessment of existing spatial layout of the production areas in the city, with a focus on production, distribution, and storage environments. Analysis of programmatic characterization and opportunities for the development.

- Complimentary policy: definition of the geographical distribution of typologies in the city. Formulation of economic criteria for prioritizing and promoting synchronous projects throughout the city.

These four key concepts – scalar strategies, integrative approaches, coding complexity, and synchronic typologies – are not all-inclusive but are the lenses through which it is suggested the future city should be developed with an aim of supporting and preparing society for enhanced digitization.

New Industrial Urbanism is a much-needed proactive planning and architectural effort. "In the absence of proactive efforts, inequality is likely to be exacerbated by the impact of technology. Jobs held by lower wage workers, women and younger workers were more deeply impacted in the first phase of the economic contraction" (World Economic Forum, 2020).

11 | NEW INDUSTRIAL URBANISM

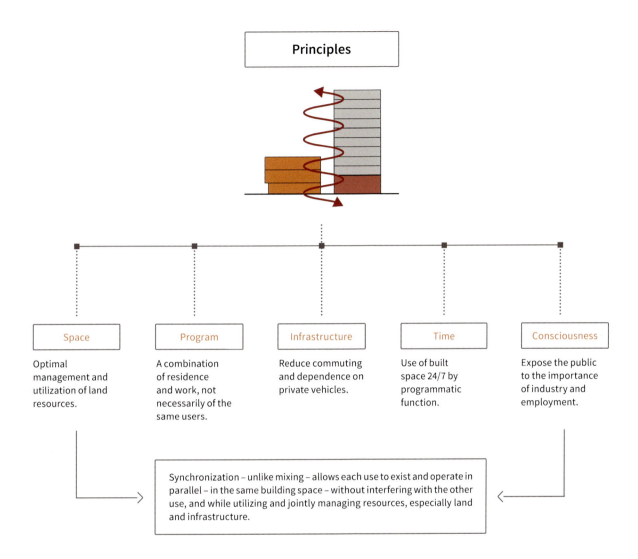

■ Synchronic Typologies: Space, Time and Program Compression

Experimenting and Developing a New Industrial Urbanism

Over the past century, countries around the world have experienced rapid urbanization around their edges and deindustrialization in their cores. Cities worldwide will have to continue adjusting to climate change, large-scale migration, shifts in family structure, rapid technological changes, public health crises, and other powerful social and political forces. As they do so, they will have to address acute social needs, identify the underlying trends, and re-assess patterns and systemic features of the built environment. Adjustments also bring new economic opportunities made possible by advanced technological changes, and social challenges as cities become ethnically diverse, persistently unequal, with ageing infrastructure. In responding to these challenges, regulatory flexibility and physical planning are key mechanisms. Through the design of physical spaces, as well as the policies and technologies that shape how those spaces are used, cities will be able to sustain and enhance the quality of the human environment including places of production.

Indeed, as described in this book, some cities around the world are experimenting with flexible regulatory and participatory frameworks in order to achieve more integrated city-industry areas that will accommodate their changing needs and future uses. At the level of the design and architecture, these districts also allow experimentation with new typologies of blended-style buildings.

Cities should see industrial planning as a purposeful intervention in the public arena aimed at improving the quality of life in place and spaces. In doing so, the economy, society, and the built environment must be addressed simultaneously, and without prioritizing one over another. This approach is based on a premise that the industrial sector is dependent on society and vice versa. This codependency should remind us that each plan for an industrial area or site is a complex, sociopolitical project that can, should, and often will shape the development of the future of a city. Accordingly, what is needed for industrial development to be extended is a concrete vision that addresses the social needs and the physical environment.

Visioning must not neglect education about manufacturing. Education is necessary if we are to dispel lingering misconceptions that industry is always unsafe and polluting and manufacturing should be presented as an appropriate and even desirable activity within the city. When industrial processes were most noxious, factories moved out of the city and into windowless big-box structures; the animosity was mutual: manufacturers were just as content to exclude the public as the public was to banish factories from the city.

New Industrial Urbanism is both a conceptual and methodological spatial challenge that demands careful reflection as to how we perceive and develop our cities and regions. Thus, it is only by systematically approaching the challenge of encouraging manufacturing and supporting its development, as well as by unifying planning with policy, that we will be able to develop resilient future cities. Regrettably, most industrial place-making today stands in poor relationship to civic processes and good design. It has often been shunted-off as a bureaucratic task of rule writing, standards formation, and code enforcement. Such roles rob the urban planning profession of its central goal: to foster democratic civic processes and outcomes whereby communities retain their local character, make the most of existing conditions of the built and natural environment, and create developments that are sensitive to their immediate surroundings. This attitude must be altered if industry is to be welcomed back, and reassume its role as a good, productive urban citizen. Transparency about the business and practice of industry and a clear, New Industrial Urbanism approach by planners and policymakers would enhance the marketability of our cities and restore industrial pride to all.

11 | NEW INDUSTRIAL URBANISM

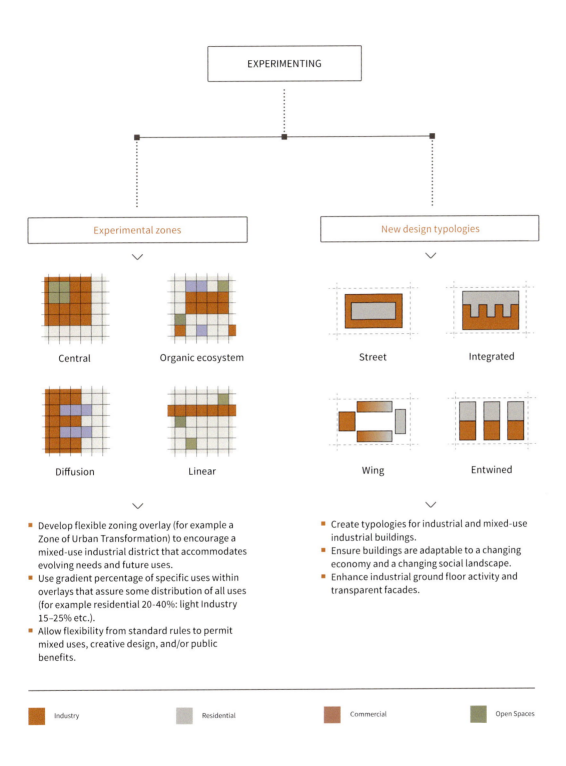

■ **Developing New Frameworks for Action**

PART III | OPEN MANUFACTURING

■ People and Making in the City

Photo by Science in HD on Unsplash (CC).

Photo by CDC on Unspla (CC).

Photo by Science in HD on Unsplash (CC).

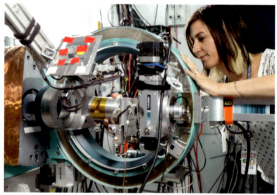
Photo by Science in HD on Unsplash (CC).

Photo by Mixabest (CC BY-SA 3.0).

Photo by Science in HD on Unsplash (CC).

248

11 | NEW INDUSTRIAL URBANISM

Photo by Malcolm Lightbody on Unsplash (CC).

Photo by Hosny Salal on Pixbay (CC).

Photo by This is Engineering RAEng on Unsplash (CC).

249

References

ABAG, Association of Bay Area Governments. 2020. About. https://abag.ca.gov/about-

Allmendinger, Phil, and Graham Haughton. 2009. "Soft Spaces, Fuzzy Boundaries, and Metagovernance: The New Spatial Planning in the Thames Gateway." *Environment and Planning A: Economy and Space* 41, no. 3: 617–633.

Arnaut, Mark, Freddy Bertin, and Bart Van Herck. 2007. "Meetjesland 2020: Toekomstplan. Eeklo: Streekplatform Meetjesland." https://lib.ugent.be/nl/catalog/rug01:001357351

Autor, David, David Mindell, and Elisabeth Reynolds. 2020. *The Work of the Future: Building Better Jobs in an Age of Intelligent Machines*. Cambridge, MA: MIT Press.

Becker, Jennifer, and Adam Friedman. 2020. "Mixed-Use Neighborhoods: A Challenging Strategy for Maintaining Industry." In *The Design of Urban Manufacturing*, edited by Robert N. Lane and Nina Rappaport, 212–219. New York: Routledge.

Ben-Joseph, Eran. 2005. *The Code of the City: Standards and the Hidden Language of Place Making. Urban and Industrial Environments*. Cambridge, MA: MIT Press.

Berger, Stefan. 2019. "Industrial Heritage and the Ambiguities of Nostalgia for an Industrial Past in the Ruhr Valley, Germany." *Labor* 16, no. 1: 37–64.

Beunderman, Joost, Alice Fung, Dan Hill, and Martyn Saunders. 2018. "Places that Work Delivering Productive Workspace and Homes in London's New Neighborhoods." www.centreforlondon.org/publication/places-that-work/

Brunell, Dieter, Filip De Rynck, Kristof Steyvers, and Herwig Reynaert. 2008. "The Impact of Local Governance on Local Government Leadership – Setting the Stage for a Pilot Case: Preliminary Hypotheses." Paper for the 58th Political Studies Association Annual Conference, Swansea, United Kingdom, April 1–3.

Chen Hua, Gao Ning, and Georges Albert. 2012. "From Village Construction to Regional Development: The Rural Cluster Development Model." *Journal of Zhejiang University (Humanities and Social Sciences)* 42, no. 3: 131–138.

City of Portland Bureau of Planning. 2003. "Central Eastside Industrial Zoning Study." https://scholarsbank.uoregon.edu/xmlui/bitstream/handle/1794/9213/Portland_Central_Eastside_Industrial_Zoning_Study_2003.pdf

Curien, Rémi. 2014. "Chinese Urban Planning: Environmentalizing a HYPER-functionalist machine?" *China Perspectives* 2014, no. 3: 23–31. https://doi.org/10.4000/chinaperspectives.6528

Cutting Edge Planning & Design. 2018. "Does Live/Work? Problems and Issues Concerning Live/Work Development in London: A Report for the London Borough of Hammersmith and Fulham." www.lbhf.gov.uk/sites/default/files/section_attachments/livework_final_lowres_tcm21-51146.pdf

CZWG Architects. 2021. "Westferry Studios." https://czwg.com/projects/workspace/westferry-studios/

Drew, Paul. 2021. Interview with authors.

dRMM Architects. 2021. "Wick Lane, Integration of Industrial and Residential Mixed Use." https://drmm.co.uk/project/wick-lane/

Duddy, Lindsay. 2018. "pH+ Architect's Iceland Wharf Creates a 'Flexible, Tethered, Living and Working Environment'." *ArchDaily*, November 3. www.archdaily.com/904762/ph-plus-architects-iceland-wharf-creates-a-flexible-tethered-living-and-working-environment

Etzkowitz, Henry. 2012. "Triple Helix Clusters: Boundary Permeability at University–Industry–Government Interfaces as a Regional Innovation Strategy." Environment and Planning C: Government and Policy. https://doi.org/10.1068/c1182

EU University Business Cooperation (UBC). 2019. *Ruta N Medellín: From Drug Capital to Innovation Hub*. https://ub-cooperation.eu/pdf/cases/I_Case_Study_RutaN.pdf

GBL Architects. 2021. "Strathcona Village." www.gblarchitects.com/projects/strathcona-village/

Gellynck, Xavier, and Bert Vermeire. 2009. "The Contribution of Regional Networks to Innovation and Challenges for Regional Policy." *International Journal of Urban and Regional Research* 33, no. 3: 719–737.

General Manager of Planning and Development Services. 2012. "CD-1 Rezoning: 955 East Hastings Street." Development and Building Policy Report, Vancouver Council City. https://council.vancouver.ca/20120918/documents/p5.pdf

Gianoli, Alberto, and Riccardo Palazzolo Henkes. 2020. "The Evolution and Adaptive Governance of the 22@ Innovation District in Barcelona." *Urban Science* 4, no. 16. DOI: 10.3390/urbansci4020016.

Gruehn, Dietwald. 2017. "Regional Planning and Projects in the Ruhr Region (Germany)." In *Sustainable Landscape Planning in Selected Urban Regions*, edited by Makoto Yokohari, Akinobu Murakami, Yuji Hara, and Kazuaki Tsuchiya, 215–225. Tokyo: Springer Japan.

Harrison, John. 2020. "Seeing Like a Business: Rethinking the Role of Business in Regional Development, Planning and Governance." *Territory, Politics, Governance*. https://doi.org/10.1080/21622671.2020.1743201

Hatuka, Tali, Gili Inbar, Coral Hemo-Goren, and David Kambo-Maina. 2019. "Strategic Plan: Eastern Galilee as an Industrial Ecosystem, Submitted to the Kiryat Shmona Municipality." [Hebrew]. https://drive.google.com/file/d/1Pu12GY0AvKmm3zl-5JrAtPSreHpAsKVfJ/view

Hatuka, Tali, Gili Inbar, and Zohar Tal. 2020. "Synchronic Typologies: Integrating Industry and Residential Environments in the City of the 21th Century." [Hebrew]. https://drive.google.com/file/d/15sebgmXVJHmjEAvydrNHnFeO7rOkNszY/view

Healey, Patsy. 2006. *Urban Complexity and Spatial Strategies: Towards a Relational Planning for Our Times*. London: Routledge.

Helper, Susan, Timothy Krueger, and Howard Wial. 2012. "Locating American Manufacturing: Trends in the Geography of Production." The Brookings Institution. www.brookings.edu/research/reports/2012/05/09-locating-american-

Helper, Susan, Elisabeth Reynolds, Daniel Traficonte, and Anuraag Singh. 2021. *Factories of the Future: Technology, Skills, and Digital Innovation at Large Manufacturing Firms*. Cambridge, MA: MIT.

Jonas, Andrew E. G. 2012. "Region and Place: Regionalism in Question." *Progress in Human Geography* 36, no. 2: 263–272. https://doi.org/10.1177/0309132510394118.

Jones, Allison. 2014. "Industrial Decline in an Industrial Sanctuary Portland's Central Eastside Industrial District, 1981–2014." Master's Research Paper, Portland State University. https://pdxscholar.library.pdx.edu/geog_masterpapers/2

Keil, Andreas, and Burkhard Wetterau. 2013. *Metropolis Ruhr: A Regional Study of the New Ruhr*. Essen: Regionalverband Ruhr.

Kim, Minjee, and Eran Ben-Joseph. 2014. "Matching Supply and Demand: A Prospect on the Spatial Needs of Manufacturing Activities and Land Use Policy Implications." Paper for the Association of Collegiate Schools of Planning Conference, Philadelphia, PA, October 30 November 2.

Leigh, Nancey Green, and Nathanael Z. Hoelzel. 2012. "Smart Growth's Blind Side." *Journal of the American Planning Association* 78, no. 1: 87–103.

MacLeod, Gordon. 2001. "New Regionalism Reconsidered: Globalization and the Remaking of Political Economic Space." *International Journal of Urban and Regional Research* 25, no. 4: 804–829.

Mayer, Margit. 2008. "To What End Do We Theorize Sociospatial Relations?" *Environment and Planning D: Society & Space* 26, no. 3: 414–419.

Minner, Jenni. 2007. *The Central Eastside Industrial District: Contested Visions of Revitalization*. Portland, OR: School of Urban Studies and Planning, Portland State University.

Mistry, Nisha, and Joan Byron. 2011. "The Federal Role in Supporting Urban Manufacturing." www.brookings.edu/research/papers/2011/04/urban-manufacturing-mistry-

Palm, Matthew, and Deb Niemeier. 2017. "Achieving Regional Housing Planning Objectives: Directing Affordable Housing to Jobs-Rich Neighborhoods in the San Francisco Bay Area." *Journal of the American Planning Association* 83, no. 4: 377–388.

Pastor, Manuel. 2000. *Regions That Work: How Cities and Suburbs Can Grow Together*. Vol. 6 of *Globalization and Community*. Minneapolis, MN: University of Minnesota Press.

pH+ Architects. 2021. "Iceland Wharf and Fish Island, East London." https://phplusarchitects.com/case-study/iceland-wharf/

Planning and Development Department City of Detroit. 2019. "Eastern Market: Neighborhood Framework and Stormwater Management Network Plan." https://issuu.com/utiledesign/docs/eastern_market_neighborhood_framework_and_stormwat

Policy Link and Pere. 2015. "Equitable Growth Profile of the Research Triangle Region." www.policylink.org/resources-tools/an-equity-profile-of-research-triangle-region.

Ogundiya, Anne. 2018. "Planning Permission Report: Iceland Wharf, Fish Island, London E9 5HJ – 18/00095/FUL." London Legacy Development Corporation. October 23. www.london.gov.uk/moderngovlldc/documents/s60391/06a%20Report%20of%20Iceland%20Wharf%2018-00095-FUL%2023102018.pdf

Research Triangle Regional Partnership. 2020. "Our Region." www.researchtriangle.org/our-region/

Reynolds, Elizabeth. 2017. "Innovation and Production: Advanced Manufacturing Technologies, Trends and Implications for U.S. Cities and Regions." *Built Environment Journal* 43, no. 1: 25–43.

Roach, Emily, and Karen Chapple. 2018. "Creating a Regional Program for Preserving Industrial Land: Perspectives from San Francisco Bay Area Cities, Institute of Transportation Studies, Research Reports." https://EconPapers.repec.org/RePEc:cdl:itsrrp:qt2sw9f2k6

Rota, Miguel Barceló. 2005. "22@ Barcelona: A New District for the Creative Economy." In *Making Spaces for the Creative Economy*, edited by Waikeen Ng and Judith Ryser, 390–399. The Hague: ISOCARP (International Society of City and Regional Planners).

San Francisco Planning Department. 2002. "Industrial Land in San Francisco: Understanding Production, Distribution, and Repair." http://sf-planning.org/sites/default/files/FileCenter/Documents/4893-CW_DPR_chapter5_2.pdf

Scott, Allen J. 2019. "City-Regions Reconsidered." *Environment and Planning A: Economy and Space* 51, no. 3: 554–580. https://doi.org/10.1177/0308518X19831591

Searle, Glen. 2020. "Metropolitan Strategic Planning after Modernism." *Planning Theory & Practice*. 21, no. 2: 325–329.

Soja, Edward. 2000. *Postmetropolis: Critical Studies of Cities and Regions*. Malden, MA: Blackwell.

Soja, Edward. 2015. "Accentuate The Regional." *International Journal of Urban and Regional Research* 39: 372–381. https://doi.org/10.1111/1468-2427.12176

Storper, Michael. 1997. *The Regional World: Territorial Development in a Global Economy*. New York: Guildford Press.

Swyngedouw, Eric. 1997. "Neither Global nor Local: 'Glocalization' and the Politics of Scale." In *Spaces of Globalization*, edited by K.R. Cox, 137–166. New York: Guildford Press.

Tholons. 2011. "Bridging Development: The Medellín Experience (Whitepaper)." www.slideshare.net/fgarde/tholonsMedellínwhitepaper2011

Utile. 2021. "Eastern Market: Neighborhood Framework and Stormwater Management Network Plan." www.utiledesign.com/work/detroit-eastern-market-neighborhood-framework-plan/

Weaver, Clyde. 1984. *Regional Development and the Local Community: Planning, Politics, and Social Context*. New York: Wiley.

World Economic Forum. 2020. "The Future of Jobs Report 2020." www3.weforum.org/docs/WEF_Future_of_Jobs_2020.pdf

INDEX

Figures indexed in italic page numbers. Photographs indexed in bold page numbers.

22@District, Barcelona, Spain 79, **137**, 138–140, 154–156, 197–199

ABAG *see* Association of Bay Area Governments, San Francisco, California

abandoned industrial sites 17

academia 63, 83, 85, 87, 104, 184–185, 191, 241; and government 63; and industry 63, 87, 93, 104, 184, 191

academic institutions 63–64, 66, 78, 84, 93, 104, 184, 186, 191

acoustic pollution 41, 115

active industrial sites 17

activities 41, 44, 78, 84, 131, 135, 139, 142, 174, 180, 184, 186, 210; arts 198; civic 114; complementary 198; diverse 135; innovative 88; knowledge-intensive 113; maritime 118; mining 112; mixed-use 117; nighttime 115; specialized 104; street-level 119; urban 186

adjacent industrial space 45

administration 91, 119, 144, 194

advanced production systems 26

AEG turbine plant 26

agglomeration 44, 78, 83, 86, 114, 130, 169; benefits 85; condensed central 104; dense 88; economy 117, 191; maximizing 186; processes 78; rural 86, 104; strategies 130; urban 86, 104, 202–204

agreements 115–117, 184, 238; bilateral 64; informal 182; mutual 90

agriculture 41, 87, 90, 138, 184, 186; diverse 186; land 46, 86, 88, 140, 186; modern 183; monotype 183; multifunctional 183

agritourism 186–187

Akalla 89

Alfeld 26

Allegheny Conference on Community Development, Pittsburg 67, 72

ALMMII *see* American Lightweight Materials Manufacturing Innovation Institute

Amazon 92

amenities 25, 34, 47, 130; local 84; minimal 35; providing varied 35; social 212

American Apparel Clothing Co. 119

American Lightweight Materials Manufacturing Innovation Institute 66

anchors 86–87, 199, 212–213, 241; commercial 184; concentrated 186; major 90; strong 186; successful 199

Andrew Christian Clothing Co. 119

animal husbandry 87

apartments 89, 109, 115, 219

Apple Park *30*

apprenticeships 69

approaches 17–18, 24, 26–27, 78–79, 83, 113–116, 136, 138, 156, 160, 162, 191, 219; centralized 219; city-wide 197; dynamic 162; economic 83; elastic 160–161; flexible 114, 201; free-market 221; hierarchical 174; hybrid 136; inclusive 139, 195; innovative 139; integrated 184, 210; mixed-use 104; new 36,

70, 178, 239; one-stop-shop 91; relational 179; surgical 130; top-down 156–157, 161, 200

architects 24–27, 34, 70, 136; Albert Kahn 26; and engineers 25; Peter Behrens 26, 72; pH+ Architects 219; and planners 136; Richard Rogers 27, 34, 75; Tim Love 41, 63–64, 136; Tony Garnier 41, 73; and urban designers 194

architectural approaches 218–219

architectural design 24–26, 242

architectural typologies 145, 198, 201, 218, 244

area 47, 92, 130, 186; commercial 44, 218; conservation 220; distressed 67, 179; geographical 36, 63, 179; mixed-use 115, 130, 136; open 25, 219; parking 36; planned 144; production-industrial 218; public 198, 219; redeveloped 117; regional 179; rural 84, 109, 183; urban 19, 61, 104, 109, 117, 169, 186, 197; zoned 78, 109–110, 142

ARM *see* Advanced Robotics for Manufacturing Institute

artificial intelligence 63, 66

artisans 156, 201, 206, 221

artists 109, 130, 156, 200, 206, 217, 220–221

assets 61, 104, 137, 167, 183, 186; aesthetic 118; agricultural 104; regional transportation 182; scenic 186

Association of Bay Area Governments, San Francisco, California 182

Atlanta 47, 52, 73; USA **53**

Austin Chamber of Commerce 67

automation 36, 43, 70, 174, 195, 217

Autonomous Industrial Space 46, *52*

Barcelona 79, 138–140, 146, 154–156, 168, 170–171, 197–199, 202, 240, 247; city center of 138, 199; City Council 138–139; government of 138; and the plan for the 22@District 138

barriers 17, 45, 169

Bauhaus school 26

Beds Above Sheds Concept, Iceni Products *232*, **233**

Behrens, Peter 26

benefits 36, 44, 78, 84, 87–88, 90, 169, 174, 179, 183, 210; economic 46, 112, 179; long-term 116; measurable environmental 56, 239; public 219

Bernhard, Karl 26

BIDs *see* Business Improvement Districts

Biogen Co. 92–93

biopharmaceuticals 178

biotech start-ups 92–93, 197

biotechnology 56, 63, 78, 104, 201

BMW Werk München 44, 49

BNYDC *see* Brooklyn Navy Yard Development Corporation

Boston's Red Line 93

Botanical Garden of Medellin 140

boundaries 84, 160, 184, 186; final 44; juridical 44, 112; new 186; physical 46

Broad Institute (MIT and Harvard) 92–93

Brooklyn Navy Yard **108**, 113, 116–118, *124*, *129*, 130, 169

Brooklyn Navy Yard Development Corporation 116–117

buffering 206, 210, 220

building types 35–36, 201; architecture 35; development of new architecture 35; new 36; primary 35; and programs 35–36; synchronic 36; unsuitable 141

buildings 24, 26–27, 34–36, 115–117, 119, 130, 136, 140, 160, 162, 195, 197, 199, 218–219, 242; codes 64, 70, 110, 194, 238; consensus 130; designed 130; existing 26, 130; factories 34, 64, 110, 141, 194; four-story 220; green 114, 117, 130; heights 119, 210; high-rise 145; historic 206–207; and infrastructure standards 116; mixed-use 201; multi-story 136; new 136, 157, 161, 198, 219; non-industrial 119; office 34, 115; preserving 142; technology 64, 136

Bukit Merah, Singapore **65**

Bus Rapid Transit, New York 117

Business Improvement Districts 118, 130, 169

businesses 44, 67, 86, 88, 92–93, 113, 117–119, 141–143, 179–180, 197, 199, 206, 218, 220–221, 242; clean tech 113; creative 143; existing 143, 156, 206; food-related 210; food tech 87; green 114; and industries 156; local 118, 139, 197, 199; small 47, 116–117, 174, 200, 220; strategies 74, 117

California 67, 79, 111, 118; agricultural and marketing heritage 34; and Apple's planned project in Cupertino 34; inspired suburban development model 91; and Silicon Valley 34, 89, 91, 170, 178

Cambridge, Massachusetts 63, 86, 92–93

Cambridge City Council 93

Cambridge Innovation Center 92

Cambridge Redevelopment Authority 104, 118–119, 166

Campus of Wageningen University & Research, Wageningen, Netherlands **82**

campuses 35–36, 44, 93; enclosed 46; high-tech 46; independent 47

capital 18, 25, 63, 66–67, 84, 87, 89–93, 140, 142, 145, 168, 191, 195; attracting overseas 90; intellectual 84; investments 67; private 90; venture 66, 90, 145

care centers 135

cars 27, 44, 71

Castells, Manuel 90, 167

categories 67, 114, 197–198, 220; new land use 198; refining zoning 197; traditional 113; updated 201

cell phones 145; *see also* mobile phones

Central Eastside Industrial District, Portland, Oregon 137, 141–143, *150*, 167, 170, 199–200, *204*

challenges 56, 64, 73, 118, 130, 139–140, 156, 166, 168, 174, 183; to business and industry 221; central 56; economic 184; primary 63; region-wide 182; social 17

changes in industry 18, 66, 142

Charles River, Boston 104

chemicals 178, 197

Chengdu Chipscreen Medicine Industry Production: Design and Use *31*

Chicago 44–45, 67, 69, 72, 75, 168, 197; development history 45; effort to protect manufacturing 45; planned manufacturing districts 201

China 79, 137–138, 143–145, 156, 171, 200–201; e-waste economy 145; electronics sales 144; industrial policy in reform era economy 143–145, 200

CIAM see *Congrès International d' Architecture Moderne*

circuit board manufacturing 145

cities 17–19, 34–36, 40–47, 56–57, 60–61, 63–64, 69–70, 73, 109–110, 112, 114–119, 130–131, 136, 138–142, 168–171, 174–175, 182, 194–195, 197–200, 239; central 112; contemporary 19, 160, 221; creative 112, 169; developing 78; and districts 182; industrial 111–112; and industrial areas 35; and industry 17, 40–41, 44, 70, 79, 242; livable 138, 195; maritime 46; mixed 138; planned 40; populous 44; and regions 18, 65, 75, 78, 170, 175, 178; resilient 112, 169; small 45; smart 112, 169; sustainable 136, 168–169; and towns 182

citizen engagement 112

citizens 113, 119, 183

city centers 36, 89, 115, 136, 138, 140–141, 143, 218; historic 46; renewal 118

city development 18, 35, 39–53, 57

city government 67, 88, 114, 137

city-industry dynamics 18, 78

city life 44, 175, 186, 239

City of Cambridge *see* Cambridge

City of Chicago *see* Chicago

City of Detroit *see* Detroit

City of Los Angeles *see* Los Angeles

classifications 64, 139, 201; creative 113; detailed 201; new 139, 198; urban 198

clean energy technologies 183

clean tech industries 114

CleanTech Park, Jurong 114

clustering 78–79, 86, 88, 93, 104–105, 130, 135, 160–162, 178; as an adaptive process 86; approach 84, 104; complementary 88; culture 139; development 105; economic 139; growth 160; industrial 160; ongoing political process 104; physical 90; and regenerating 135; residential 212

clustering industries 79, 83–103, 137, 161, 191, 240; Food Valley, Wageningen, Netherlands 86–88, 104, 167; Hsinchu Science Park, Taiwan **85**, 86, 90–92, *99*, 104, 167; Kendall Square, Cambridge, Massachusetts **85**, 86, 92–93, 104, 166; Kista Science City 78, **85**, 86, 88–90, *96*, 102–104, 128–129

INDEX

Clustering New Industries, Program, Spatiality and Catalysts *102, 103*

clusters 63, 66, 72, 74, 83–84, 86–90, 92–93, 104–105, 160, 162, 168, 186; automotive design 67; biotech 92; conceptualizations 86; developing 69, 104; development of 66, 68, 84, 87–88; economic 56, 83, 174, 186, 239; evolution of 84, 86; first 93, 104; food innovation 88; growing 118; growth 87; growth and identity 105; high-tech 144; of industries 83–84, 88, 113; initiatives 88; innovative 86; key knowledge 141; knowledge-intensive agri-food 86; largest ICT 89; single 162, 187; small 139; social networks 83; successful 84; vibrant 84; zoned 47

Coding Complexity: Creating New Regulatory Frameworks *243*

Common Industrial Type: Patterns, Order and Geography *54, 55,* 60

companies 18, 35–36, 45–46, 67, 75, 83–93, 114–116, 130, 139, 141; agriculture 86; early-stage startup 93; existing 87; food 86; foundry 112; with high capital turnover 46–47; high-profile 114; innovative 178; international 41, 47, 140, 179; large 88, 92, 140, 156, 199; oil 113; private limited liability 89; public telecommunications 199; real estate 89; recruiting 66, 84; semiconductor 90; single product distribution 143; steel manufacturing 46

company towns 41–42, 75

competition 46, 93, 119, 136, 138, 169, 183, 197; foreign 44; historical 184; local 92; public 104

competitive processes 118

components 63, 66, 86, 89, 145, 191; critical 84; ecological 178; entrepreneurial training 66; important 90; major 130; for success 86

computers 43, 66, 70, 89

concepts 34, 36, 63–64, 69, 109, 112, 135, 138, 160, 162, 171, 174–175, 242; contemporary 18; green 112; hybrid 114; metropolis 178; new 160; socio-spatial 18, 175, 239

conceptualizing 34, 191; the city 110, 162, 195; a new approach addressing urban land use strategies 70

conflicts 92, 139, 142–143, 197–198; intractable 44; neutralizing of 27; potential 143

congestion, reducing 93

conglomerates 87, 91

Congrès International d'Architecture Moderne 41

Consolidated Aircraft Corporation plant, Fort Worth, Texas, USA 1942 **71**

Contemporary Approaches to Industry and Place *161*

contemporary industrial development, overarching concepts of 63, 66

Contemporary Manufacturing as a Multifaceted Challenge *65*

Cornell Tech 66

Cornell University 66

CRA *see* Cambridge Redevelopment Authority

CTP *see* CleanTech Park

cultural entrepreneurs 130

culture 78–79, 84–89, 95, 97, 99, 101, 121, 123, 125, 127, 137–139, 145, 147, 149, 151; and identity 84; of innovation 86; internal 90; local 105; of research and reciprocation 87; social 105, 156–157, 161

Cupertino, California 34

customers 18, 63–64, 84, 90–91, 110, 194, 220, 239

cyber technology 78

DCP *see* Department of City Planning

decentralization 41, 43, 74; of manufacturing to rural areas and offshore locations 109; of the production process 36

densification 41, 56, 79, 113–114, 116, 136, 160; economic 139; residential 114

density 83–84, 93, 198, 201, 209–210; concentrated 83; guidelines 219; high 104; low 198; of organizations and firms 83

Department of City Planning, Chicago 45, 72, 118–119

departments 45, 109, 118–119, 136

design 17–18, 25–27, 34–36, 90–91, 113–115, 118–119, 121, 123, 125, 127, 139, 147, 149, 151, 153; building's 220; of a city-industry dynamic 56; of factories 25, 34–35; high-quality 113, 130–131, 161; of housing and industry 114; initiatives 143; innovation 115; interpretations 218; multifaceted 130; and physical planning criteria 174; requirements 116; of residential homes 210; strategies 60, 78, 143; of varied work spaces and factories 34 design guidelines 207, 210; for new mixed-use buildings 209; shaping the industrial facilities 206; urban 142

designation 67, 208, 220; dominant zone 142; flexible zoning 200; industrial zoning business 114; manufacturing zoning 45; new zoning 210; policies and strategies 87

Detroit 26, 66, 206–207, 209–210; city government 206; metropolitan area 206–207

developers 25, 34, 114–116, 119, 130, 139, 197–198; and architects 34; incentivizing to attract clean industry 114; industrial 201; master 104; private 116, 174; real estate 89, 136

developing 61, 63–66, 83–84, 90–91, 104–105, 138–139, 141–142, 156–157, 160–162, 170, 178–179, 186, 197, 201, 217–218; clusters 104; economies 61, 73; hierarchical relationships 83; hybrid innovation districts 156–157; industrial areas 64, 160; new frameworks for action *247*; a regional ecosystem 186; specialized complexes 135; supportive physical infrastructure 105

development 17, 24–25, 34–36, 61, 63–64, 66–70, 72, 86–90, 92–93, 104–105, 113–116, 119, 135–136, 140–142, 182–183, 197–198, 200–201, 206–207, 210, 220; accelerators 66; companies 86; of industry 18, 64, 78, 93; and management of coal 182; of manufacturing ecosystems 69; mixed-use 118, 136, 138, 142, 195, 204; patterns 42, 45, 187; policies 200; pressures 44, 113, 210; processes 116, 141, 175, 178; programs 93; projects 199; of science cities 90; standards 119, 194, 206; top-down approach 140; of urban areas in relation to industry 19

digital age 66

digitization 43, 61, 63, 218, 244

distribution 182, 198, 206, 219, 244; businesses 207; clusters 119; efficient 110, 194; facilities 41, 209–210; geographical 244; practices 110, 194; processes 63, 78; space 218; and storage 216; systems 242

districts 92–93, 115–119, 130, 133, 138–144, 156, 160–162, 170–171, 178, 182, 197–201, 220–221; industrial mixed-use 119, 130; *see also* industrial districts

diversifying 139, 142, 183, 197, 239, 242; production activities 135; by region 183

diversity 84–85, 113, 142, 191, 201, 210; of businesses 113; in company size and scope 85; manufacturer 63, 66; morphological 199; of workers 201

dock buildings 116

Dockland 115

Docklands Light Railway 220

duty-free imports 91

e-businesses 113

East London 219–220

Eastern Galilee Region 186–187

Eastern Market Neighborhood Framework and Stormwater Management Network Plan 207, 209

Eastern Market Neighborhood Plan, Detroit 206, *207*

eco-industrial parks 64, 67–68, 74

economic 84, 86, 111, 179; activities 41, 56, 79, 130, 139, 186; clusters 56, 83, 174, 186, 239; contraction 244; cooperation 181, 184; engines 183; globalization 61, 178; interest 118, 179, 184; opportunities 56, 111–113, 130–131, 156–157, 161, 239; and political factors 191; prosperity 114, 156, 180–181; recession 88; and social goals 116; strategies 116, 182, 199–200

economic development 72, 74–75, 89–90, 105, 112–113, 119, 138–139, 141, 168–169, 182–183, 195; activities 117; and employment 183; goals 70, 138, 195; initiatives 141, 175; issues 136; major 178; policies 67; regional 179; strategies 69, 83

economic growth 66, 84, 113, 140, 156, 160, 178–179; enhancing 130; generating 69; national 61; regional 66; urban 113–114

economists 18, 25, 56, 73–74

economy 36, 41, 45–47, 63–65, 67, 69, 72, 75, 110, 113, 167–170, 185, 238–239; advanced 17, 35, 41, 61; competitive 187; creative 156; developed 145; emerging 64; knowledge-based 156; metropolitan 138, 195; post-industrial 56; regional 67, 110, 143, 195

ecosystem 63–64, 130, 145, 186; formal manufacturing 145; innovation-production 110, 195

education 69, 89, 115, 135, 144, 179, 185–187; attainments 179; formal 110; and industry 186–187; institutions 18, 61, 63, 66, 90, 104–105, 161, 179, 239; programs 210; secondary 91; vocational 135

electronics 27, 44, 70, 88, 92, 144–145, 200; assembly 144, 200; center 88; factories 144; industry 27, 145

INDEX

employees 18, 24–25, 27, 35–36, 45–47, 91, 116, 118, 142, 217, 220; encouraging 218; plant's 47; potential 93; qualified 88; services 25, 46

employers 24, 27, 41, 46, 217

employment 56, 61, 135–136, 143, 156, 197–198, 200, 202, 204, 217–218, 220; based living environments 138; high-density 142; increased 92; industrial 110, 156; and industry 156; opportunities 136, 141, 143, 219; prioritizing 219; space 220–221

Employment Opportunity Subarea 142

Emscher Landscape Park 183

encroachment, protecting industrial land from 110, 195, 242

energy efficiency 63–64

energy production 64

energy technology 183

engaging citizens 111, 131, 161

engineers, and architects 25

entrepreneurs 25, 40, 63–64, 66, 87, 93, 130, 145, 239

entrepreneurship 68, 89, 91, 145, 167, 171, 201; and innovation programs 145; policy 145; supporting mass 145, 201

environment 24–25, 34–35, 65, 69, 73–74, 84, 86–88, 104–105, 135, 138, 166–170, 194–195; communal 206; dynamic 138; hazards 46; heterogeneous 135; human 36; impact 46, 195; industrial 36; living 27, 88; natural 186; physical 131; pollution 44; protection 178; residential 41, 44, 73; social 84; suburban 160; support 217

EOS *see* Employment Opportunity Subarea

Europe 25, 27, 87, 112, 167, 183–184

evolution 24, 40–44, 66–67, 69–70, 73–75, 79, 84, 86, 143, 145, 162, 166, 168; city-industry 174; development 35; programmatic 24; technological 69

expansion 34, 84, 87, 91, 113, 141, 206–207, 211; areas 206, 208–210; mobility infrastructure 143; projects 117; and success 87; supporting cluster 66

factories 17–18, 21, 24–27, 34–35, 40–41, 44–46, 56–57, 72–73, 136, 138, 145; building 34, 64, 110, 141, 194; common single-story 136; and companies leaving the area 46; decentralized 36; design 25–26; design and use: diachronic perspective *32, 33*; and

expanding industries 17; iconic 26–27, 35; industrial 25, 119; labor-intensive 35; large 35, 47, 174, 197, 201; management 35; mass-production 35; multi-story 136; prominent 26; structure 25, 27; underutilized 109

Fagus Factory *28, 29*

Fair-Haired Dumbbell Building, Central Eastside Portland OR, USA **137**

Fashion District, Los Angeles 113, 118–119, *126, 129,* 130, 169

Features of Clustering New Industries *85*

Features of Regenerating Industrial Areas 109, *111*

Ferm, Jessica 61

Fiat Lingotto Factory 26

firms 34–35, 41, 56, 61, 63–64, 83–84, 90, 110, 141, 195, 239; knowledge-based 139; large 63; medium-sized 63–64, 239; multinational 64; and organizations 83; private high-technology 90; service-sector 44, 160; transnational 91; venture capital 92; *see also* companies

Flanders 183

food 47, 86–87, 138, 143, 166, 168, 186, 206–207; and agriculture companies 86; business developments 208, 210

Food Innovation cluster 88

food technology 78, 88, 186–187

Food Valley, Wageningen, Netherlands 86–88, 104, 167

Forest Park 47

Forming Hybrid Districts: Program, Spatiality and Land Uses 79, *154, 155*

Fourth Industrial Revolution 41, 67, 69, 162, 211

funding 87, 90, 105, 179–180; distribution 181; government 61; new sources of 179; public 130; recruiting 184; stable streams of 87; structure 66

Futian District of Shenzhen 144

garden cities 40, 42

Garment District, Los Angeles **111**, 118–119

Garnier, Tony 41, 73

GBL Architects 218

gentrification 109, 118, 139, 141, 143, 157, 167, 169, 206; process 118; programs 157; residential 109

Germany 23, 41, 44, 49, 78, 113–114, 182; heavy industry in 114; industrialization in 182; and the North Duisburg Landscape Park in North Duisburg 112

globalization 178

glocalization 184, 238–239

GMDC *see* Greenpoint Manufacturing and Design Center

Goose Island, Chicago, USA **77**, **78**

government 63, 66, 69, 83, 85, 87–88, 90, 109, 113–114, 118–119, 184–185, 190–191, 241; agencies 63, 66, 88, 194; buildings 88; and business 185; central 87, 91, 144, 179; federal 67, 84; grants 180–181; and industry 63, 85, 185; institutions 200; investments 140; local 88, 92, 104, 194, 197, 199; municipal 105, 144; policies 69; and private stakeholders working together 157; progressive 104; research institutes 90

green 74, 94–103, 112, 114, 117–118, 120, 122, 130, 146–156, 168–169, 201, 206, 208–210, 240, 247; buildings 114, 117, 130; concepts in production and manufacturing organizations 112; ecological buffering system 206; stormwater infrastructure 210

Greenpoint Manufacturing and Design Center 201, 206

greenway 206, 208–209

Gropius, Walter 26, 73

growth 61, 63, 65–66, 83–84, 86–87, 110–112, 121, 123, 125, 127, 141–144, 147, 156, 162, 206; cluster's 105; endogenous 141; engines 44, 186; and integration of food-business-centered production 206; interlinked 112; rapid 56, 109; regional 87, 167; slow 109; social 139, 179; stimulating 68; urban 45, 178

Guangdong Provincial Level State-Owned Enterprise 144

Hackney Wick, East London 220

Hamburg 60, 78, 111, 114–116, 166, 170; "enterprise policy" 114; HafenCity 60, **111**, 113–116, *122*, *128*, 129–130, 168; waterfront 114

health 25, 87, 110, 135, 141; economic 109; home assistance 69; human 175

heavy industry 35, 112, 114, 144, 162, 195, 197

heritage 110–113, 130–131, 142, 161, 206; cultural 186; landscape 184; and place 113, 130–131, 161

high-tech industries 45, 90–91, 144–145; accelerating 144; recruiting 67; regional hub for innovation and 144; small 156

Hoelzel, Nathanael Z. 109

homes 44–46, 88–89, 92, 140, 143, 145, 174, 179, 182, 217–218, 220; in Huaqiangbei 145; new 197; occupancies 220; residential 210; in Shenzhen 145

horizontal sprawl (industrial areas) 44

housing 41, 44, 116, 118, 136, 138–139, 142–143, 156, 182, 195, 197–198, 206, 217–219; conditions 183, 220; developers 115; development 104, 199; diverse 130; and industry 114, 218; policy 89; prices 182; public 140; sites 141; social 219; types 242; units 219; up-scale 206

Howard, Ebenezer 40

Hsinchu City 78, 90–92

Hsinchu Science Park Administration, Taiwan **85**, 86, 90–92, *98*, *99*, 102–104, 167, 170

Huaqiangbei, Shenzhen, China 137, 143–145, 156, 171, 200–201

human capital 87, 89, 93, 105

human-computer interactions 66

hybrid buildings 41, 74, 136, 160, 169

hybrid districts 79, 85, 137, 139, 156, 161, 191, 240; 22@District, Barcelona, Spain 79, 137–140, 146, 154–156, 168, 170–171, 197–199, 202, 240, 247; Central Eastside Industrial District, Portland, Oregon 137, 141–143, 167, 170, 199–200, 204; features in generating 135; features of 137; forming 79, 135–145, 156–157; Huaqiangbei, Shenzhen, China 137, 143–145, 156, 171, 200–201; industry place nexus in forming 156–157; integrating diverse industrial activities 135; long-lasting 198; Medellinnovation District, Mendellin, Columbia 79, 134, 138, 140–141, 148, 154–156, 197, 199, 203, 240, 247; successful 143; supporting employment mix 135; urban-edge 210

hybrid management models 36

hybrid mix-use buildings 198

hybrid urban development 210

hybridity 36, 41, 78–79, 135–136, 138, 156, 160, 162; advocates of 138; development of 156; framework of

138; idea of 41; new 136; rejiggers 136; return to in the late 20th century 136

hybridization 156

IBM 67, 88–89; electronic data processing machine at NACA, Langley VA, USA 1957 **71**

IBZ *see* Industrial Business Zones

Iceland Wharf & Fish Island, East London, UK 219–220, *226*, **227**

iconic designs 26, 115, 139

ICRC *see* Interdisciplinary Cyber Research Center

ICT *see* Information and Communication Technologies

IDPI *see* Industrial Development Policy Initiative

ILUP *see* Industrial Land Use Policy Project

implementation 45, 112, 142, 166, 179; phased 206–207; by recycling models between plants 57; of synchronic typologies 244; tools 184

imports 91

incentives 46, 69, 104–105, 109, 130–131, 156–157, 161, 195, 198–199, 201; economic 27, 61; financial 68–69, 91, 197; floor area 119; government 45; mechanisms 201; tax 61, 75, 91, 179

incubators 84, 87, 89, 93, 110, 141, 199, 220

industrial 170, 195, 198, 210; activities 56, 78, 109–110, 117, 119, 138–139, 195, 197–198, 202, 218–220; anchors 105; assets 67; base 130, 141, 199, 201; businesses 45, 110, 119, 201; cities 17, 27, 40, 45, 70; clusters 83–84, 88, 113; companies 47, 115, 182; designers 145; designs 199; displacement 109; ecology 63–64, 68–69, 73–74, 95, 97, 99, 101, 105, 121, 123, 125, 127, 131, 147, 149; ecosystems 63–64, 69, 74, 79, 84, 143, 175, 187, 238–239; environments 19, 242; facilities 47, 68, 197, 206; firms 143, 194–195, 206; jobs 44, 47, 110; land use 118, 138, 195, 197; landscapes 35, 44; legacies 69, 219; mixed-use districts 119, 130; monoculturalism 191; production 41, 110, 144, 186, 200; projects 64; regeneration 160; regions 90; sanctuary 142–143, 200–201; sector 109, 114, 130; sprawl 56, 138, 195, 239; urban development 43, 69, 73, 79, 239; urbanism 18–19, 59, 61, 63–64, 69, 174–175, 238–239, 244, 249; waste 64, 67

industrial areas 41, 44–47, 78–79, 107, 109–110, 112, 114, 130–131, 135–136, 139, 143–144, 161–162, 197, 199; autonomous 47; in cities 131, 136; designing 135; dilapidated 138; existing 113, 242; flexible new 60; identifying 130; major 186; older 141, 198; urban 109

industrial buildings 25, 46, 156, 200, 206, 221; designing 25; disused 201; existing early 20th-century 206; historic 142, 156; planned 35; protecting older 200; underutilized 206

Industrial Business Zones 117

industrial development 61, 64, 66, 68, 144, 160, 162, 186, 191, 194–195, 200; changing 64; contemporary 63; outward-looking 242; regional 191; urban 138, 174, 195

Industrial Development Policy Initiative 118–119, 169

Industrial Disclosure Statement 142

industrial districts 47, 79, 136, 141, 160, 199; first 141; historic 141; hybrid 138; older 200; preserving 136

industrial land 40, 47, 63, 69, 73, 75, 109–110, 112–113, 118–119, 195, 197–198, 200; abandoned 131; allowing effective use of 56, 239; inventory 112; loss of 41, 119; productive urban 138, 195; protecting 197, 221; sustainability of 119, 130; underutilized urban 195; urban 109, 167

Industrial Land Use Policy Project 119

industrial parks 36, 41, 46, 90, 116, 144; autonomous 64; designated 200; new Southside 47; typology 47; walled-off 117

industrial policies 91, 138, 143–144, 183, 195, 200; local 109; regional 56

Industrial-Residential Nexus *212*, 213

Industrial Revolution 17, 40, 42–43, 69, *70*; and Development Patterns *42*, *43*; first 136; fourth 41, 67, 69, 75, 162, 211

industrial sites 43, 47, 138; abandoned 17; active 17

industrial spaces 40, 46, 119, 199–200, 219; adjacent 45; integrated 44; irregular 109; new 136, 198; preserving existing 218

Industrial Technology Research Institute 90–91

industrial zones 46–47, 51, 136, 144, 200–201, 210; integrated 44; older 144; special 67; successful mixed-use 117

industrialization 25–26, 41, 45, 113, 182

industry 17–19, 40–42, 44–46, 56, 63–64, 66–70, 72–74, 83–87, 90–105, 112–115, 141–144, 156–157, 159–162, 174–175, 184–187, 190–191, 194–195, 200–201,

217–219, 238–242; agri-food 87; biotechnology 92, 144; changes in 18, 66, 142; in cities 69, 112, 160, 174; clean 114, 162; co-locating 197; communications 144; complementary 84, 104–105, 161; construction material 144; craft 143; data-heavy 93; developing 18; diverse 138; economic 139; encouraging high-tech 90; expanding 17, 41; grassroots 145; green 117; high-polluting 200; incubator 142; insurance 217; knowledge-based 41; labor-intensive 144; local 92, 182, 206; major 144, 200; and manufacturing typologies 41, 175, 201; next-generation 114; non-polluting 113; petrochemical 113; polluting 114, 144; private 88; service 41, 186; skill-intensive 93, 115; smoke-stack 198; steel 114; and tourism 179; tourism 183; traditional 27, 139; trucking 110; urban 56, 174

Industry - Place Nexus in Forming Hybrid Districts *157*

Industry-Place Nexus in Regenerating Industrial Areas: *131*

Information and Communication Technologies 89–90, 139, 141

infrastructure 47, 84, 95, 97, 99, 101, 104–105, 114–117, 121, 123, 138, 143, 160–161, 182–183, 191; development 91, 115; national 91; network 45, 114, 139; and new buildings 157; pedestrian and bicycle 143, 156; region's 183; sustainable 117, 130; systems 191, 217

initiatives 66–67, 83, 88, 112, 160, 183, 199

innovation 17, 42–43, 61, 63, 66, 70, 72–75, 78, 84, 86, 89, 144–145, 166–171, 197–199, 201; cluster for fashion 118; commercial spaces 137; development 89; districts *148*; industrial 90; local 144, 201; place-based 105; process 88, 191; technological 178, 186

innovation districts *134*, 140–141, 145, *148*, 170, 201–203; developing hybrid 156–157; and industrial ecology 144; new 140; proliferation of 145

institutions 88, 90, 92, 95, 97, 99, 101, 121, 123, 125, 127, 147, 149, 151, 190; academic 63–64, 66, 78, 84, 93, 104, 184, 186, 191; community 238; economic 137; educational 18, 61, 63, 66, 90, 104–105, 161, 179, 239; foundational 86–87, 89; government 200; labor market 17; research 186

integrated 44, 190, 202–204; common areas 218; framework 69; urban intervention 199

Integrated Industrial Space *48*

integrating diverse industrial activities 135

integrating urban-industrial systems: Barcelona 79, 138–140, 146, 154–156, 168, 170–171, 197–199, 202, 240, 247; Medellinnovation District, Medellin, Columbia 79, 134, 138, 140–141, 148, 154–156, 197, 199, 203, 240, 247

integration 79, 113, 130, 136, 191, 197–198, 200, 206–207, 210–213, 217–218, 241–242; of food-business-centered production 206; of industrial activities 218

integrative approaches (concept) 244

Intel 45–46, 89

Interdisciplinary Cyber Research Center 168

internet-related digital media 56, 113

Israel 40, 45, 51, 168, 186–187

ITRI *see* Industrial Technology Research Institute

jobs 17, 56, 64, 67, 109–110, 114, 119, 143, 174, 183, 198; high paying 143; high-skilled 67; industrial 44, 47, 110; and industry 114; living-wage 56, 239; local 67, 116; service 56, 69

Jones, Edward 61

Jordan River 186

JTC *see* Jurong Town Corporation

Jurong, Singapore 78, **109**, 111, 113–114, *120*, *128*, 129–130, 242

Jurong Town Corporation 114, 130

Kahn, Albert 26

Kendall Square, Cambridge, Massachusetts **85**, 86, 92–93, *100*, 104, 166

Kendall Square Association 93

Kendall Square Urban Renewal Plan 102–104, 128–129, 166

Key Approaches in Industrial/Urban Development *79*

Kiryat Gat, Israel 45–46, **51**

Kiryat Shmona, Eastern Galilee Region, Israel **187**

Kiryat Shmona Strategic Plan *189*

Kista Science City 78, **85**, 86, 88–90, *96*, 102–104, 128–129; Kista and Akalla combined their business centers and forming 89; known as Sweden's Silicon Valley 88; and STING business incubator 89

Korean industries 91

KSURP *see* Kendall Square Urban Renewal Plan

labor 17, 35, 67, 69, 78, 114, 144, 200, 217; availability 64, 110; cost optimization 36; intensive activities 41; international 89; laws 35; low-wage 64; markets 56, 70, 217, 239; overseas 78; pools 40, 104–105, 161, 197; power 24, 27; productivity 17; replacement 195; specialized 104; unskilled 17

Laboratory for Contemporary Urban Design 186

land 41, 45–46, 63, 67–68, 74, 79, 110, 113–115, 119, 138–139, 143–144, 197, 203; allocations 66; area 47, 197; arid 45; cheap 144, 197, 200; commercial 45; contaminated 110; costs 64, 110; development 194; residential 118; rural 44; vacant 206; zoned 45, 195

LCUD *see* Laboratory for Contemporary Urban Design

LDDC *see* London Docklands Development Corporation

light industry 47, 113, 195, 202–204, 217

light manufacturing 136, 210

logistics 87, 91, 135, 198, 202, 207, 242; depots 217; industrial 219; and industrial areas 53

London Docklands Development Corporation 220

Lordstown, Ohio 47

Los Angeles 44, 67, 111, 113, 119, 130, 167, 169; economic drivers for 119; Fashion District 113, 119, 130, 169; Fashion District Business Improvement District 118; and New York City 44

Love, Tim 41, 63–64, 136

low-cost manufacturing 144

management 86, 95, 97, 99, 101, 111–112, 116–117, 121, 123, 125, 127, 130, 147, 149, 180; non-profit 117; optimal 217, 244; organizations 139; and revitalization efforts 117; scientific 27, 75; structures 116, 130; supply chain 56

manufacturers 46–47, 56, 61, 63–64, 66–67, 70, 110, 162, 191, 194–195, 239; displacing small 197; green 114, 118

manufacturing 17, 41, 44–47, 56, 60–61, 65–66, 73–75, 78, 90, 109–110, 135, 144–145, 174–175, 194–195, 197–198; activities 40, 45–46, 60, 78, 197, 218–219; advanced 44, 179; businesses 92, 113, 197, 201; firms 73, 110, 112, 141; high-tech 118, 144; industrial 46; industries 66, 201; and industry 17; jobs 56, 61, 239; processes 63, 112, 197; products 90, 136; regions 44; sector 17, 19, 61, 63, 69, 113; small-scale 45, 143; spaces 18, 144, 206; workforce 197; workshops 25

Manufacturing in the City **216**

Marco Polo Tower 115

mass production 35, 41–42, 70, 72, 136, 145

Massachusetts 78, 86, 93

masterplans 91, 104, 138–140, 168

Medellin, Colombia 140

media 56, 113, 118–119, 139, 167

Meyer, Adolf 26

mixed-use development 118, 136, 138, 142, 195, 204

Mobil Oil 113

mobile phones 145

model 27, 34, 36, 40–43, 45, 91, 116–119, 130, 139, 184, 198; of 21st-century manufacturing 118; of mixed production activities 198; for regional collaboration 184

Munich 44, **49**

municipalities 44, 47, 86, 88–89, 93, 119, 183–184

neighborhood 141–142, 197, 206, 219; mixed-use industrial 242; residential 45–46, 136, 206

new industrial urbanism 18–19, 59, 61, 63–64, 69, 174–175, 238–239, 244, 249; coding complexity 244; integrative approaches 242, 244; key planning concepts *240*; premises *238*; scalar strategies 244; synchronic architectural typologies 220, 230

new industries 27, 79, 115–116, 143, 156, 161–162, 242; clustering 79, 83–103, 137, 161, 191, 240; and employment 143, 156; encouraging 197

New Key Concepts in Industrial Development *62*

New York City 66, 117, 201, 206; and Los Angeles 44; post-industrial 117; purchase of the Brooklyn Navy Yard 116; steps in to assist the Brooklyn Navy Yard Development Corporation 117

North Carolina 63, 179, 182

OECD countries 64

offices 34, 41, 47, 109, 116, 130, 135, 140, 142, 197, 199–200, 219; commercial 142; development 141, 199; and housing sites 141; small home 218; space 89, 104, 118, 139, 190, 198, 201, 217

Olympic Games 1992 (Barcelona) 138

Olympic Games 2012 (London) 220

open manufacturing 174–175

Open Manufacturing and Urban Life *175*

open spaces 143, 156, 182–183, 210, 219

ordinances 119, 199

Oregon 79, 138, 142, 166, 168, 199, 204

organizations 24, 27, 34, 36, 83, 88, 114, 118, 139, 141, 179, 183–184, 198–199; collaborative 88; and companies 83, 114; external 67, 84; grassroots 145; industrial 27, 201; internal 191; land use planning watchdog 142; local 206; non-profit 89, 116, 199, 206; professional 66; public 140; regional 183–184; virtual 86

overarching concepts of contemporary industrial development 63, 66

parallel initiatives 69

parks 90–92, 104, 183; CleanTech Park, Jurong 114; eco-industrial 64, 67–68, 74; public 112; stand-alone industrial/business 47; urban 198–200, 202–204; world-renowned Emscher Landscape Park 183

partnerships 69, 85–87, 90, 105, 117, 179; private 66, 87, 116–117, 141; regional 179

PDR *see* production, distribution, and repair

Pearl River Delta 144, 200

People and Making in the City *248, 249*

perspectives 18, 61, 69, 84, 160; economic 86; people's 141; rational 24

photovoltaic arrays 209

physical infrastructure 86, 88–89, 109, 157, 160–161; *see also* infrastructure

physical planning 60–61, 78, 174–175, 191; *see also* planning

Place Nexus in Clustering Development *105*

Planned Manufacturing Districts 45, 47, 201

Planned Unit of Development 114, 130, 201

planning 60–61, 78, 174–175, 191; and architects 136; authorities 113; central 112; challenges 112; and design of factories 25; direct 199; efforts 109; and implementation strategies *208, 209*; industrial 239; policies 56, 135, 156, 242; process 200, 210; strategic 191; strategies 64, 66, 78, 179, 199, 210; top-down 64, 139; vision 115

plant 25–27, 34, 44, 47, 57, 61, 75; assembly 47, 49; chemical 197; modern 26; relocating 17; semiconductor fabrication 197

Plattelandscentrum Meetjesland, Regional Network, Meetjesland, Belgium 183–184

PMDs *see* Planned Manufacturing Districts

PMLR *see* Portland–Milwaukie Light Rail

Pohang Steel Company 46

policies 66–69, 72, 83, 86, 104–105, 110, 112–114, 118, 142, 145, 171, 175, 195; collaborative 66; common 67; to connect companies and individuals 104; designated 87; economic 201; environmental 138, 195; existing 67; fiscal 56, 239; national 104–105; new 67, 114; post-industrial 17; public 179; social 105, 161; state-led 145; urban 78

policy initiatives 19, 66

policymakers 17, 66–67, 91, 113–114, 135–136, 138, 178, 195

politics 69

pollution 17, 40–41, 44, 115, 195

population 89–90, 109, 140, 179, 182, 210; attracting new 114; growth 114, 182; local 109

population dispersal 178

Portland 138, 141–143, 150, 154–156, 166, 168, 170, 197, 199–201, 204, 240, 247; approach to urban revitalization 143; business core 142; Central City 143, 156, 170; Central City Plan 1988 142; Central Eastside Economic Development Policy 142; Central Eastside Industrial Council 142; Central Eastside Industrial District 137, 141–143, 167, 170, 199–200, 204

Portland–Milwaukie Light Rail 143, 156

POSCO *see* Pohang Steel Company

PPPs *see* public–private partnerships

practices, of reducing industrial waste 64

preferential tax policies 145, 201

preservation 118–119, 137; cultural heritage 117; environmental 184; family-based ownership models 45; industrial land 119, 130

press coverage 87; *see also* media

private cars 44; *see also* cars

producers 24, 63, 83, 86

production 17–18, 24–27, 34–36, 39–53, 56–57, 67, 72–73, 83–84, 94–103, 119–120, 146–155, 170–171, 190–191, 195, 198, 200–201, 239–240, 247; activities 198; advanced 45; agricultural 45; in cities and regions 18; and commercialization of knowledge 184; costs 17, 25, 41; digital 200; distribution, and repair 78, 197–198, 218–219; domestic 61, 78; environment 18; facilities 41; food 206–207, 209; hardware 89; levels 191; local 56; and manufacturing organizations 112; methods 35; models and urban change *190*; physical 36; problems 26; small-scale 35; spaces 34; steel 67; units 24; water 64

production processes 24–27, 34–36, 160, 198; innovation in 198; revolutionized 40; technology of 24

productivity 61, 84, 113, 174, 197, 217

products 18, 24–25, 27, 63–64, 67, 69, 89, 91, 110, 142, 145, 190, 194–195; agricultural 184; consumer 110; design 27, 145; designing 27; developers 86; food 64; local 69; marine 46; new 90; prices 25; quality 195; semi-finished 91; semiconductor 90; and successes 87

programs 34–36, 87, 91, 115, 117, 139, 141, 145, 199, 202–204, 212; absorption 141; and activities 139; company 139; cross-subsidy 198; designated 156; economic 116; educational 210; implementing regional 182; initiating 105; municipal 221; pilot 34; and plans 157; recycling 109; social urbanism 89, 140; strategic development 139

projects 65, 69, 75, 104–105, 112, 115–116, 118–119, 130, 207, 210, 217–221; mixed-use 104; political 179; private 183; revitalization 115; strategic 90; successful 112; synchronous 244

public amenities 139, 175, 220

public housing 140

public open spaces 104, 209

public–private partnerships 87, 137, 180

PUD *see* Planned Unit of Development

Pulau Ayer Chawan, Singapore 113

Pulau Merlimau, Singapore 113

Pulau Pesek, Singapore 113

qualified expenditures 67

questions 19, 73, 78, 84, 112, 174, 194, 217; architectural 217; concerning regulations 70; social 217

railroad cars 41

real estate 41, 92, 136

real estate developments 92, 199

recreational amenities 143, 156

redevelopment 115–116, 130–131, 139, 144, 156, 206–207; planned 116; post-industrial 118; process 112, 130; successful 113

regenerating 79, 109–110, 112, 135, 161–162; industrial areas 79, 85, 111, 131, 137, 161, 191, 240; processes 112

regeneration 78, 112–113, 136, 162, 166–169; economic 117; processes 112; social 117; strategies of 78; urban projects 139

regional collaboration 179, 181, 184

regional coordination strategies 179–180, 184, 191

Regional Coordination: Strategies and Activities *180, 181*

regional development 47, 68–69, 73, 178–179; approaches to 179; contemporary 179; imbalanced 183; partnerships 67, 84; processes 178; relational 184; strategies 69; in terms of infrastructure 47

regional ecosystems 79, 85, 137, 161, 186–187, 191, 240

Regional Ecosystems: Anchors, Cities and Places *188*

regional framework for industry 191

regional framework for infrastructure 191

regional governments 112, 174

regional strategies 175, 195

regional thinking 179, 186

regionalism 178–179, 187, 191

Regionalverband Ruhr, Ruhrgebiet, Germany 182–183

regions 18, 63, 65–67, 69, 78, 86–88, 91–92, 160, 170–171, 174–175, 177–180, 182–184, 186–187, 191, 242;

distressed industrial 112; marketing to international companies 179; prosperous 182, 184

regrowth of cities and metropolitan areas 70

reinventing industrial areas 78–79, 107–119, 130–131, 160, 169, 179; Brooklyn Navy Yard 108, 113, 116–118, *129*, 130, 169; Fashion District, Los Angeles 113, 118–119, 130, 169; HafenCity Hamburg 60, 111, 113–116, 128–130, 168; Jurong, Singapore 78, **109**, 111, 113–114, 128–130, 242

research 35, 72, 78, 86–89, 93, 104–105, 113–114, 116, 135, 139, 181, 184, 190–191; applied 190; biotech 93; centers 64, 84, 140; collaboration 87; competitive 87; and development companies 86; facilities 84; genetic 92; institutes 87–88; organizations 86–87, 186; programs 87; support 87; university 93

Research Triangle Regional Partnership 63, 167, *179*

residential 41, 46, 91, 135, 156, 210, 221; buildings 104, 210, 219; development 138–139, 200, 206, 210, 218–219; dominance 156, 221; enclaves 46; and industrial activities 220; projects 197; reversion 136, 221; units 114, 218–219; use 197, 218, 220

residents 44–45, 112, 114, 116, 118, 140–141, 179, 187, 199, 206, 209, 220; and industry 45; local 131, 186

Rhodes Manufacturing Co., Lincolnton, NC, USA 1908 **71**

robotic technologies 36, 66

robotics 36, 61, 178

Rogers, Richard 27, 34, 75

RTRP *see* Research Triangle Regional Partnership

Ruhr area 182–183

Ruta N & Innovation District, Medellin, Colombia **73**, 134, 140–141, 166, 183, 199

San Francisco Bay Area 69, 168, 182, 198

San Francisco Planning Department 69, 75, 197–198

San Martí 138

Santa Barbara 112, 166

scalar strategies (concept) 244

Scalar Strategies: Cultivating an Ecosystem through Collaborations and Integration *241*

science cities 89–90, 167

Semiconductor Manufacturing Corporation 90–91, 171

service jobs 56, 69

services 34–36, 41, 44, 46–47, 61, 73, 78, 83–84, 87, 91, 104–105, 201, 206; administrative 238; business 217; commercial 114; consulting/computer 89; creative 143; ecosystem-related 131; employees 25, 46; financial 91; industrial 143; and infrastructure 78; innovative 44; public 139; repair 110; residential 91

Shangbu Industrial Park 144, 200–201

Shanzhai Manufacturing and Maker Entrepreneurs 145

Shenzhen, China 79, 138, 143–145, *152*, 156, 167–169, 171, 197, 200, *205*

Shenzhen Chipscreen Biosciences Company 34

Shenzhen Municipality High-Tech Industrial Belt Development Plan 2001 144, 156

SID *see* Southside Industrial District

SIL *see* Strategic Industrial Land

Silicon Valley 34, 89, 91, 170, 178

skilled labor 18, 61, 63, 78, 84, 197, 239

social fracture, accelerating 69

social housing 219

software production 89, 178

Southside Industrial District 47

spaces 24–25, 34–36, 116–117, 119, 156, 167, 169–170, 182, 190–191, 197–201, 206, 212–213, 219–221, 241–242, 244; apron 218; architectural 78; common 220; creative 145, 201; flexible 35; floor 115; green 139, 182, 201; incubator 142, 145, 201; living 136; low-cost 110; public 34, 84, 128, 199, 210; replacement 198; residential 115; transitional 219–220; work 109

Spain 79, 137–138, 198, 202

spatial 40, 44, 47, 56, 75, 86, 135, 178; approaches 18, 79; connectivity 88; development 92, 184; distribution of industry 67; evolution of industry 24; form 105, 184, 197, 202–204; framework 136, 160; integration 191, 219; policies 111; spread of industry 44; strategies 78, 105, 161, 166

stakeholders 17, 83, 87–88, 92–93, 113, 130–131, 156–157, 160–161, 179, 182, 184; *see also* policymakers

standards 110, 194–195; and building infrastructure 116; design 198; developed 194; initiated physical

119; and policies 110, 195; updated performance 201

Stanford Industrial Park 90

state-owned enterprise 115, 144–145

state-owned incubators 93

Stockholm Innovation and Growth Organization 89

storage space 36, 41, 110, 118, 136, 198, 202, 217–219

Stormwater Management Network Plan 207

Strategic Industrial Land 220

strategic planning 117, 162, 186

strategies 60–61, 66–69, 78–79, 86–87, 91, 118–119, 130, 135, 138, 140–142, 162, 180, 183; designing industrial areas 135; designing land use policies 112

Strategies in Industrial Development *68*

Strathcona Village, Vancouver, Canada 218–219, *224, 225*

sustainability 64, 110, 112, 115, 117, 130, 162, 174, 186

sustainable development 117, 130, 169

synchronic architectural typologies 220, *223*, 230, *235, 246*; Iceland Wharf & Fish Island, East London, UK 219–220; Strathcona Village, Vancouver, Canada 218–219, 224; Westferry Studios, London, UK 220, 230; Wick Lane, East London, UK 220

synchronic typologies (concept) 73, 217–218, 221

Taiwan 78, 86, 90–92, 167

tax incentives 61, 75, 91, 179

tax policies, preferential 145, 201

tax relief 68–69

Technion-Israel Institute of Technology 66

technological developments 17, 63, 70

technology 24–25, 56–57, 66, 69, 72–73, 88–89, 91–92, 166, 168, 174, 179; agricultural 179; clean energy 183; environmental 183; industrial 91; industry 92, 114; mining 183; sector 139, 182

Tel Aviv 45

tenants 116–117, 156, 206, 219

territorial politics 175; *see also* politics

Texas 67, 71, 92

tourism 115, 179, 184, 186–187; agricultural 186; and industry 186

towns 17, 40–41, 47, 115, 182; and cities 182; company 41–42, 75; high-tech 91; new 40; rural 182

transition 136, 157, 184, 187, 212–213, 241; districts 119, 130; infrastructure 212; of inner-city neighborhoods 157; to mass production in factories 136; neighborhood 142

transportation 47, 63–65, 78, 89, 91, 117, 138, 160, 182, 194; infrastructure 46, 84, 140, 143, 182; nodes 140; systems 242

triple helix model 83, 86–87, 184–185, 190–191, 241

Trucco, Giacomo Mattè 26

TSMC *see* The Semiconductor Manufacturing Corporation

typologies 18, 73, 79, 138, 175, 198–199, 201, 217–218, 221, 242, 244; architectural 145, 198, 201, 218, 244; of buildings 79, 136, 175, 199; entwined 220; for factories and workshops 18, 24, 73, 138, 218, 242, 244; industrial 242; innovative hybrid mixed-use 218; manufacturing 201; synchronic 73, 217–218, 221, 244

underground car parks 34

universities 63, 66–67, 73, 83–84, 86–88, 90, 93, 140, 166, 168–169, 179; major 140, 179; national 91; research 63; small 87

URA *see* Urban Redevelopment Authority

urban 113, 212; areas in relation to industry 19; character of industrial areas 109; design 70, 113, 115, 135, 156, 171, 194–195, 242; design and infrastructure projects 115; environment 45, 105, 218; factories 41, 136; hybrid districts 210; industrial systems 191; land 110, 136, 195, 242; life 44, 175; manufacturing 56, 74, 175, 239; planning 93, 105, 115, 160, 166, 169, 194

Urban Redevelopment Authority 114

urbanism 18, 162, 237

urbanization 40, 65

Van Hall-Larenstein Polytechnic 87

Vancouver 69, 75, 218, 224

vision 18, 90–91, 112, 140, 142, 175, 184, 186, 206, 220; for industry 91; regional 184, 186–187; region's production 184

Wageningen 78, 82, 86–88, 102–103; Food Valley, Gelderland, Netherlands *94*; region 88; University and Research 86–87

warehouse space 110, 194

water 40, 42, 94, 96, 98, 100, 115, 120, 122, 124, 126, 128, 146, 150, 152; management projects 182; production 64; source 25; wheels 40

waterfronts 115–116

Weber, Max 25

Western Hafen City and Speicherstadt, Hamburg, Germany **60**

Westferry Studios, London, UK 220, *223*, *230*, **231**

Wick Lane, Fish Island, East London, UK 220, *228*, **229**

work environments 24–25, 27, 34

work spaces 18, 24, 27, 34–36, 136, 212–213, 217, 241; design of 24, 34; location of 35; varied 34; and work management models 36

Working Models: Academia, Government and Industry *185*

WUR *see* Wageningen University and Research